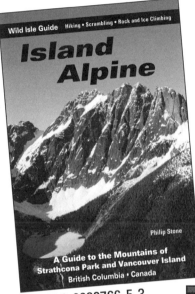

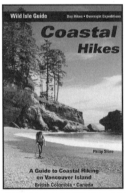

Island
Turns & Tours

Corrie Wright on the Victoria Glacier.

Island
Turns & Tours

Backcountry Skiing and Snowboarding
Strathcona Park and Vancouver Island

British Columbia • Canada

by
Philip Stone

First Edition

Wild Isle Publications
2005

Island Turns & Tours

A Guide to Backcountry Skiing and Snowboarding - Strathcona Park and Vancouver Island

2005 First Edition

© Wild Isle Publications, All Rights Reserved

Published by   Wild Isle Publications
PO Box 280 Quathiaski Cove, BC Canada V0P 1N0
www.wildisle.ca

Library and Archives Canada Cataloguing in Publication

Stone, Philip, 1965-

Island turns and tours: a guide to backcountry skiing and snowboarding Strathcona Park and Vancouver Island / Philip Stone.

Includes index.

ISBN 0-9680766-6-1

1. Backcountry skiing--British Columbia--Strathcona Park--Guidebooks.
2. Backcountry skiing--British Columbia--Vancouver Island--Guidebooks.
3. Snowboarding--British Columbia--Strathcona Park--Guidebooks.
4. Snowboarding--British Columbia--Vancouver Island--Guidebooks.
5. Strathcona Park (B.C.)--Guidebooks.
6. Vancouver Island (B.C.)--Guidebooks. I. Title.

GV854.8.C3S76 2005   796.93'09711'2   C2004-907420-2

Cover Photo: Fred Michaud on the McBride Glacier, Mt. McBride, Strathcona Park.
Back Cover: clockwise from top: Rugged Mountain and the Rugged Glacier, the author (photo: Jan Neuspiel), Morning alpenglow in Marble Meadows, Corrie Wright skiing off the Victoria Glacier photos: Philip Stone

Note of Caution

Travel in the backcountry, especially in winter can expose people to hazards that are not normally encountered in controlled alpine areas such as ski resorts. This book is written with the experienced backcountry mountaineer in mind and includes terminology and and other information that pertains to situations where a real possibility of injury or death exists.

In no way should this book be read as a definitive text on any of the subjects included herein including but not limited to any coverage whatsoever of: winter sports, mountain hazards, skills and equipment. Under no circumstances should Island Turns and Tours be used as a manual for winter recreation or interpreted to advocate that anyone should undertake any of the activities described herein other than at their own discretion. There is no substitute for experience and professional instruction to develop the self reliance and judgement required in wilderness areas. The author/publisher, distributors and retail outlets selling this book take no responsibility whatsoever for individuals using this guidebook. *You enter the backcountry at your own risk.*

For fallen friends

viii *Lyle Fast carving the sun line off Viking Dome down to Haihte Lake, Haihte Range.*

Contents

x

Canadian (or Grey) Jay, a.k.a.' Whiskey Jack' one of the few year round Island alpine residents.

Index of Maps

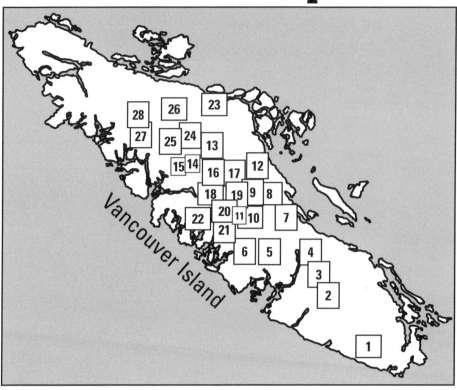

Index of Maps

The detailed topographic maps included in this guide cover the approximate areas shown in the overview map above and are found on the corresponding page references below.

Preface

Like its predecessor 'Island Alpine', Island Turns and Tours has been in the works for many years. In fact I had intended Turns and Tours to be in print long before Island Alpine mushroomed into the nearly 500 page epic it turned out to be. The interest and obvious demand for Island Alpine won the day so T&T had to take a back seat while I got on with the larger task.

When Island Alpine finally went to press, the new skills and confidence I had found with that project immediately went to work in revamping my earlier ideas for Island Turns and Tours. In particular I wanted to produce far better maps for this guide than time allowed for Island Alpine. While I'm happy to say they are now complete, readers will hopefully sympathize in the longevity of this project as they look over the maps found in here.

So the maps sucked up another winter, and quickly the summer of 2004 flew by as my other work commitments as a newspaper editor and freelance graphic designer consumed my time. As October 2004 drew to a close I still hadn't got far enough with this manuscript to have a press date in mind. Fortunately for Island skiers, at the last minute while preparing for a well earned surf vacation in Mexico, staff from two of the Valhalla stores passed on that there were increasing numbers of inquiries about when Turns and Tours might be ready. So against my original idea of escaping work on the trip I threw a laptop loaded with my work files for Turns and Tours into my pack and headed for the beach.

So perverse a pill as it might be for backcountry ski aficienados to swallow, this guide to Vancouver Island backcountry ski touring was written by a snowboarder sitting surfside in 35°C sunshine to the crashing sound of one of the sweetest point beaks in Mexico!

Finalizing the tours and areas to cover in Turns and Tours was a challenge. I realized as the page count began to climb higher and higher that I was in danger of re-writing Island Alpine with a skier on the cover. So what I have tried to include here are really only the destinations that stand out as the obvious, accessible locations for backcountry turns and tours. As the history of backcountry skiing and snowboarding is far sketchier than that of climbing and hiking, some of the material in Turns and Tours is supposition. Many tours have to my knowledge only been done a handful of times on skis and I'll admit that a few of the suggested tours in here are just an educated guess that the summer terrain we are more familiar with will translate into a good ski tour, a good example of this is the Bedwell-Moyeha Divide traverse. And there are some obvious areas still to be fully explored on skis, for example I'm pretty confident that when a party finally executes a complete ski traverse of the main Tlupana Range ridgeline they will find probably *the* classic Island ski tour.

In using this book I'd like to stress that I shyed away from repeating information already found in Island Alpine. Turns and Tours is going to be best employed in conjunction with this larger work. So if you don't have a copy I'd strongly suggest getting one or borrowing one and reading on the additional background information for your choice of tour. As a bonus for Island Alpine readers however I also avoided repeating photographs that have already appeared in I.A. so even if you are a dedicated summertime hiker Turns and Tours offers some new perspectives on many of the peaks covered in both books and will hopefully give you the confidence to stretch your hiking season into the spring a bit.

Lastly I'd like to qualify my use of the expressions 'ski tour', 'skiing', 'ski touring' etc... in this book. While there's no doubt that touring skis are one of the most versatile modes of travel in the mountains during winter, Island Turns and Tours is equally applicable to snowboarders, snowshoers, Yupi-ists (sp?) and even hikers on foot during the spring with a consolidated snowpack, as it is to skiers. Personally, while I have been known to strap on two planks, my own experience of winter touring on the Island has been often with snowshoes on foot and snowboard on back. More lately I've embraced the splitboard and have tested this equipment on several of the tours listed here. So rest assured, whatever your preferred method of travel Vancouver Island offers first rate experiences and descents in a sublimely magical winter landscape. You just might be working a little harder than the skiers!

Philip Stone

Ryan Stuart in the upper Abel Creek valley under Mt. Abraham.

Foreword

The spring of 2003 saw the publication of Philip Stone's Island Alpine, the first and eagerly anticipated comprehensive locally-written mountaineering guidebook for Vancouver Island. And the waiting really paid off! One has the impression not only that a lot of eyes have been opened to the incredible nature and extent of the mountain terrain right here at home, but also that Island Alpine is serving as a catalyst for the dreams of a whole new generation of mountaineers. Now we have the second important resource in the series, Island Turns and Tours.

In his foreword to Island Alpine Rob Wood spoke of the desirability of building a stronger sense of community and comradeship among Island climbers. It seems to me that Island Alpine is contributing greatly to this process, and indeed that the process began even before publication. The way Philip drew on the knowledge and experience of many mountaineers from all over Vancouver Island gave those of us involved a sense of community from the start. Well, we still have too few pub nights, but we do have mountain clubs with overlapping membership; we have joint trips and instructional days; we have the internet, with its well-known advantages and some disadvantages; we have the Heathens with their ever-welcoming and fun summer alpine camps; we have key individuals in many Island towns and cities who organize, instruct, lobby, and inform as well as climb, ski, board and bushwhack; and we also have, alive and well in our own unique climbing 'scene', a healthy spirit of adventure.

So you're just itching to use those new skis, lay a single track around some trees, practice your self-arrests, or maybe get a close-up of those amazing dime-sized hoar crystals with your new digital camera (or, accidentally, without it)? Well, chances are there's someone you can contact near your destination to find out where the snow is and what condition it's in, someone who knows the road conditions and someone whose floor you can crash on with just a little notice. That's a great start on a mountain community, and it's up to us to make this good Island chemistry even better.

This guidebook was born of all the reasons you really should be up there in the Island alpine snows, and it is a splendid resource to help you get there. "What reasons?" you ask. Reasons like these: that January morning when you crested the ridge on Mt Albert Edward and saw distant Elkhorn painted a remarkable pre-dawn magenta; that April day in the Maitland Range when the alpine snowfields, with the wide Pacific Ocean as a backdrop, were patterned with parallel flowing ridges created by a solar magic you could not explain; that sunny spring afternoon when the corn snow on Mt Myra was just perfect for turns and still more turns; that day when your trans-Atlantic friend, the one who makes skiing look effortless, stood awestruck with her ski tips hanging out over Canton Creek while Tlupana Inlet sparkled in the sunlight far below; that day on a windy winter ridge-top where your crazy friends, with painted faces and a knitted nose-warmer, laughed all the way to the summit and back; or even that July when you carried skis to the top of Mt. Argus for a corny photo, and down the other side for a token ski on the Cliffe Glacier.

Well, I guess you'll have to create your own list. So if your heart lives in the snow, as mine does, then it's time to get out there now. Have fun! Take care of each other, and of the wilderness. And remember, the avalanche doesn't know you're an expert.

Sandy Briggs

4 *Paul Nimmon in-bounds at Mt. Cain - Pete's Trees.*

Introduction

Chris Lawrence ski touring near Morrison Spire, the Golden Hinde to the right.

Weak grey fingers of dawn weaved through the dense snow-tortured trees. The group of would-be backcountry skiers awoke from their sleep on hastily dug snow ledges and cooked a warm breakfast and (or was that of?) coffee. The drizzle of the previous day had abated but everyone's pack and outer shell was still soaked from the canoe trip across Buttle Lake and the long climb up the Marble Meadows trail in the rain. Fading daylight forced a bivouac on a gloomy, steep side-hill somewhere on the upper part of the trail.

In no time the next morning the group is back on the move. As the first warm rays of sunshine ignite the crystal snow they break through the treeline and into the alpine and the winter wonderland of Marble Meadows. Below the skiers a thick blanket of cloud still hangs over Buttle Lake while above and around are blue skies, sparkling snow slopes and endless meandering ridges awaiting exploration.

This little tale (based on a true story!) neatly summarizes the trials and rewards of Island ski touring- strenuous approaches with glorious rewards.

Island Turns and Tours aims to describe some of the places on Vancouver Island, like Marble Meadows, where suitable terrain for backcountry descents and touring on skis, snowboard or snowshoes may be found. This book is by no means a definitive list of all the turns and tours possible on the Island. Rather Island Turns & Tours describes a selection of suggested destinations illustrating what makes up a good Island ski tour, how to plan one and in general what to expect.

This guidebook is best used in conjunction with Island Alpine (ISBN-09680766-5-3) and Hiking Trails III (ISBN-0-9697667-4-2), which both provide much more specific and comprehensive information about the history and travel routes on almost every Island mountain peak as well as the major summertime hiking routes. Additional photographs in Island Alpine portray each area in a variety of seasons and from different perspectives than most of those contained in Turns and Tours.

The huge annual snowfall that blankets the Island alpine with as much as 30 ft. for most of the year means that travel on snow is inevitable, and for many preferable, when among the Island mountains. There are places to go skiing or snowboarding on quick day trips, weekend tours and multi-day backcountry expeditions.

Travelling the Island alpine on skis or snowshoes (from here on 'skis' will serve as shorthand for: telemark skis, alpine touring skis, split snowboards, snowshoes and hybrid tools such as Yupis etc..) has certain advantages over summer time: there are no mosquitoes in winter, the deep winter snows completely bury the understory vegetation, all but eliminating the presence of the dense Island bush, the notoriously intricate and rugged micro-terrain becomes smoothed over with a full snowpack making travel fast and route finding arguably easier than in summer.

The Island has a wide variety of ski touring terrain: there are mellow areas like Forbidden Plateau with very little objective hazard, ideal for foul weather days or for novices starting out, and there are wild, remote places like the Haihte Range which only the hardy or wealthy will find possible to reach. But everywhere, once the skies clear, dramatic views of the Island's peaks in their winter regalia await. And last but not least are the big powder ski/snowboard descents waiting to be discovered and almost guaranteed solitude.

While it may have a few perks, on the whole winter in the mountains has broader challenges and requires a greater level of commitment and risk than summertime. The intensity of being amongst the winter wilderness adds an edge to the alpine experience that more and more people are seeking. This intensity can be heightened further by the thrill of a great descent and the inherent risk in that.

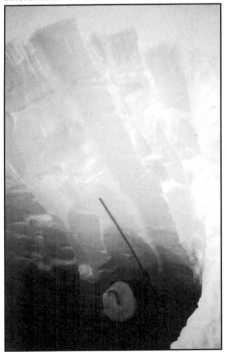

Lyle Fast taking some Island snowpack measurements at Mt. Cain photo: Corrie Wright.

To counter these risks and make the experiences less hazardous to attain, the winter backcountry enthusiast must be comparably equipped and educated. So in part that is a role of this book, to list the prevalent hazards and conditions found in the Vancouver Island Ranges. The greater one's understanding of the typical terrain, snow stability and so on the better armed one is to make decisions in the field.

Other aspects of ski touring essential to a safe and successful trip are: winter camping skills, the ability to navigate with map and compass in 'whiteout' conditions, avalanche awareness (of which one can't have too much instruction, information and experience in assessing) and appropriate fitness and skill level of all group members to undertake the trip in question.

The Island ski touring season lasts between December and mid-June depending on the year. Any later than June and the overall coverage of snow is usually too patchy and the surface becomes pocked with deep suncups making travel and descents unpleasant. Fresh snowfalls may be expected at anytime of year but generally expect that by the beginning of May percipition will fall in the alpine as rain. Snow can begin re-accumulating in the alpine anytime after mid-October.

Spring trips do have a distinct advantage in that many logging roads and trail access points become easier to reach as the snow melts at lower elevations forming a distinct, steadily rising snowline. Longer, warmer days make May a choice month for Island touring.

If there is one month of the year during which to avoid the Island alpine my vote would be for April. Spring thaw sees huge heavy, wet avalanches pouring off the mountains often running thousands of feet into the lush forested valleys below. As a result some of the trails well below treeline are subject to mountain hazards the unwary may be surprised by. If you do plan a trip during periods of thaw and avalanche activity be on your guard and choose your line of travel to minimize exposure to hazardous terrain and especially from hazards from above.

Island ski touring means frequently strenuous approaches up steep trails or routes packing skis or snowboard to reach the high snowline, skins gummed up with conifer needles and bark bits, rain storms and incredibly deep dumps of fresh snow taking brutal effort to break trail through. But the rewards are worth the toil with deep, deep snow, magical landscapes and almost guaranteed solitude among the spectacular Island mountains.

Tents, Yurts, Huts and all that

Shelter on a ski tour can be provided by one of a variety of options. Carrying a 4-season mountain tent is the sure-fire way to go on most trips. Tamping down a tent platform with skis or snowshoes and letting it sit 20 minutes before setting up the tent helps. Skis, shovels, poles and ice axes can be used to string out the guylines. Be wary of sites where trees can shed snowloads on to your tent!

There are only a few cabins on the whole Island and they play a limited role in winter travel on Vancouver Island. The Wheaton hut in Marble Meadows is a gem of a place to spend some wintertime. It sleeps four comfortably although the structure is aging. Sid's cabin in Paradise Meadows is also a sound relic worth a stay if you can find it!

The deep snowpack makes snowcaves a very viable accommodation option but less work and less weight than a tent is to dig a pit and roof it with a tarp on a rope ridgeline. This is a personal favourite of mine only surpased by a tent under the tarp, in the pit!

Travel Modes/Equipment

A wide variety of snow sliding tools are suitable for use in the Vancouver Island mountains. From October to June fresh snowfalls are to be expected and some form of skis or snowshoes are essential if you want to get around.

Snowshoeing is enjoying a resurgence of popularity and works well in the Island alpine. Snowshoes are very useful for steep winter/spring approaches such as those to Elkhorn and for valley trails like the Elk River trail up to Landslide Lake. Snowshoes are a great way to introduce children and beginners to winter mountain travel. Unless the snow is well consolidated the efforts of breaking trail with snowshoes rules them out as a viable mode of travel for longer traverses. Remember to use ski poles!

For multi-day tours and trips with specific descent objectives skis or a split-snowboard are the tools of choice. Packing a snowboard while travelling on snowshoes deserves a mention as an option but the proponents of this mode will find the additional weight gets them thinking of investing in a splitboard!

The choice of telemark versus a ski mountaineering (randoneé) setup are personal. What matters most here is that whatever the choice the equipment is solid, durable and up to the rigours of travel in remote country. Shorter day trips invite alpine trekkers

Jeni Christie touring into the East Bowl at Mt. Cain on her splitboard.   photo:Yarrow Allen.

(adapters that allow freeheel movement with downhill boots and bindings) but these gizmos are limited and are best used for quick outings involving minimal travel by ski.

Other essential equipment includes a metal shovel, avalanche transceiver, a comprehensive repair kit and a first aid kit to comprehensively repair yourself! Map and compass and the skills to use them both. Toboggans have limited use on the Island but could be handy on certain trips. Approaching up a long logging road main line or crossing a long lake chain a simple 'krazy karpet' sled might come in handy. On the whole though the distances involved and the type of terrain preclude the use of sleds. Don't forget a spare pair of sunglasses and sunscreen.

Remember winter is doubly hard on people and gear, make sure you and your stuff is up to par!

Acknowledgements

I extend my warm thanks to all the people who helped by contributing to Island Turns and Tours. First and foremost I tip my toque to all those I have been lucky enough to share the mountains with on so many great adventures and so many ripping rides! Lyle and Lorraine Fast, Corrie Wright, Robin Slieker, Tim Stanton , all the old Island Sauvage crew come at the top of that list for literally living for Island turns and tours winter after winter.

Among those in whom the aforementioned crew's maverick activities may have raised more than an eyebrow I thank Sandy Briggs for continuing to be an inspiration in his appetite for, and execution of, skiing adventures.

Sandy contributed a fitting foreword to Island Turns & Tours and helped by doing acomplete read through and corrections an early draft manuscript. Thanks to Peter Rothermel for his enthusiasm and 'back of the hand' knowledge of Arrowsmith and adjacent environs.

Some of the great photographs included were contributed by Craig 'Quagger' Wagnell and Robin Sutmoller who both provided some great Beaufort beta, Sasha Kubicek, Peter Rothermel, Jan Neuspiel, Chris Shepard and Corrie Wright. Special thanks to Lindsay Elms for digging out some great archival pictures and writing a superb snapshot on early ski history on Vancouver Island.

The author, Aureole Snowfield.   *photo: Jan Neuspiel*

Sources

A Guide To Cross-Country Ski Tours Of Central Vancouver Island.
Nanaimo Nordics Cross-Country Ski Club

Hiking Trails III - Northern Vancouver Island & Strathcona Park, ninth edition 2002, edited by Richard Blier published by Vancouver Island Trails Information Society. ISBN 0-9697667-4-2

Exploring the Coast Mountains on Skis
John Baldwin ISBN 0-9691550-1-8

Island Alpine - A Guide To The Mountains Of Strathcona Park and Vancouver Island
Philip Stone ISBN 0-9680766-5-3

Backroad Mapbook Volume II Vancouver Island and the Gulf Islands
Mussio Ventures ISBN 1-894556-10-0

www.islandhikes.com
Craig 'Quagger' Wagnell

The Top Tens

Ryan Stuart skiing on Mt. McBride.

Top Ten Ski Tour Day Trips

Top Ten Ski/Snowboard Descents

Top Ten Ski Tour Expeditions

Top Ten Moderate Destinations

10 *Jan Neuspiel skis by a huge debris pile from a spring avalanche off Mt. Rosseau, May.*

Avalanche Safety

Avalanches are a serious threat to backcountry skiers and snowboarders. Every year in British Columbia skiers, mountaineers, snowmobilers and other winter recreationalists are caught in snow slides, sometimes with fatal consquences.

Increasingly more and more people are venturing into the backcountry. Many straight from the relative safety of a ski-lift area. Safety in avalanche terrain has become a provincial issue filling our newspapers and TV screens with tragic news and lighting up the switchboards on phone-in radio shows.

The Island is no exception to anywhere else in B.C. and for example it has become the norm now on a given weekend for there to be many sets of tracks in Mt. Cain's West Bowl whereas only a dozen years ago it was the domain of very few. With increased numbers of skiers and snowboarders venturing out of bounds comes an increased risk of fatalities. It is a simple fact, if you want to avoid being caught in an avalanche STAY OUT of avalanche terrain. A golden rule of mountaineering is avoid mountain travel until at least 24 hours after a fresh snowfall.

Avalanches may happen at any time but on the Island one of the most dangerous times of the year is the spring thaw. As the thick winter snowpack warms it becomes lubricated by liquid water and comes crashing down gullies and creek beds in massive heavy wet slides. These slides may unexpectedly threaten low elevation areas below. A good example of this is the Elk River trail where avalanches from the mountain faces thousands of feet above the evergreen forest pour down long gullies in some cases right to the floor of the valley. Paying attention to what is going on high above you is another good rule of mountain travel.

Reading the Terrain

Understanding the characteristics of avalanche terrain so you can avoid travelling through hazardous areas is the most important facet of safe winter, mountain travel. By identifying terrain features prone to avalanches the careful backcountry skier can select safe routes for both the approach and descent. I'll stress it: avoiding avalanche terrain is the key to safe backcountry skiing and snowboarding.

Some points to observe when reading the terrain are:

1- Ridges offer safer lines of travel than gullies and bowls.

2 - Valley bottoms and heavily forested areas are often protected from avalanches. Cross obvious slide paths that reach the valley floor or cut through timbered areas quickly.

3 - Windward slopes are prone to windslab buildup and lee slopes collect heavy snow deposits, avoid these areas. Ridges are often the safe boundary between wind affected slopes.

4 - Slopes that face south or west may be warmed by afternoon sun making them prone to heavy wet snow avalanches.

5 - Consequences are part of the risk equation. If a small avalanche has the potential to sweep you and your party into a raging creek or glacial crevasse it *may* have more serious consequences than a large slide on more benign terrain.

6 - Always be aware of hazards from above. For example: A slope many thousands of feet above may be warming in the morning sun as you travel obliviously in the cold shaded forest below. A subsequent avalanche may drop far below its source hitting unsuspecting skiers.

An early season snowpack shearing off in a shovel shear test.

Snowpack Evaluation

On the whole the deep Vancouver Island snowpack is considered fairly stable when compared with say the Rocky Mountains. But snow stability is a complex and inexact science and jumping to generalizations is one ingredient for a serious accident. The fact is unstable snow layers do occur frequently in the Island snowpack and learning to identyify suspicious layers is an invaluable skill in the process of evaluating snowpack stability.

Potentially many avalanches may happen during and immediately after a snowfall. New snow may avalanche in powdery sluffs. More dangerously though, the additional snow load may meet old snow on a weak layer and avalanche on it or trigger an even deeper weak layer. The quandary here is that fresh snow is what most of us venture out into the backcountry to ski. It is nevertheless a lot safer to avoid the backcountry until at least 24 hours after a snowfall.

There are additional concerns with travelling in the backcountry during storm cycles. In the event of an avalanche (which as we have already noted is more likely at this time) the difficulty of a rescue is going to be compounded. Reduced visibility during a storm may make locating buried victims exceedingly difficult. In the event of requiring an outside rescue, it will be more time consuming to break trail out to a trailhead during a storm and once rescuers arrive they will in turn be slowed by the fresh

snow. Air support may be impossible with low cloud. With just minutes to survive being buried in an avalanche the additional risks associated with being in the backcountry in bad weather are high. Storm days are camp or cabin days or days for staying in-bounds behind the ropes!

When the clouds lift, the wind subsides and we venture back out into the alpine taking the time to dig a snow pit and/or conduct Rutsch block tests may provide information about suspicious layers and may identify hitherto unnoticed instabilities. Icy rain crusts with a snow load on top are an example of a suspect layer. Feathery hoar frosts and light snowflakes may also form a weak layer when new snow is loaded on top of it. Spring thaw is a time of great avalanche activity in the Island mountains but as we have noted slides and snow instability can happen at anytime.

Learning which snow crystals can form weak layers, how the snowpack stabilizes and evolves through the winter and many other aspects of snowpack evaluation may be best learned with professional instruction. Weekend avalanche awareness courses are a good place to begin. With some further experience, and/or a professional interest, courses endorsed by the Canadian Avalanche Association offer an 'industry standard' instruction and certification process.

Avalanche debris in the bottom of the West Bowl, Mt. Cain.

Safety Equipment & Procedures

If you or any members of your group are buried by an avalanche there may only be minutes to act in order to save lives. With so little time to spare the only people likely to conduct a successful rescue are those in your group who were not buried in the slide. So it is vital to familiarize yourself and everyone in your group with safe backcountry travel techniques and carry and practice self rescue with avalanche transceivers, shovels and probes.

Some of the basic precautions to take in avalanche terrain are:

1 - Keep your group spread out when crossing exposed terrain like avalanche chutes. In very exposed situations and when descending use a buddy system to watch one another from safe point to safe point. Knowing the last point seen is a crucial clue if someone is buried and must be located and dug out.

2- Move quickly and efficiently and watch constantly for possible escape routes to ski toward in the event of an avalanche.

3 - Loosen pack straps and take your hands out of the ski pole wrist loops so you can jetison them if a slide happens. Zip up outer wear so you would be as warm as possible if buried.

4 - Remain suspicious of a slope even as members of your group successfully cross it. A slope may fail as the first person or the tenth person crosses it. You never know!

5 - Ensure everyone in your group is wearing an avalanche beacon, that they know how to use it and that it is functioning correctly. Everyone travelling in the backcountry should also carry a sturdy metal snowshovel and avalanche probes.

Avalanche Rescue

Time is critical if someone in your party is buried by an avalanche. Statistically few victims survive after 20 minutes so acting quickly and efficently is the only way to save lives. An avalanche beacon or transceiver is a mandatory piece of equipment for winter backcountry travel. Without the assistance of an electronic beacon the odds of locating a buried victim drop dramatically. Wear one and insist everyone in your group is wearing a working beacon and knows how to use it.

If an avalanche buries anyone in your group the procedure for conducting a rescue might be outlined in this order:

Test everyone's transceiver before heading out.

1 - Survey the surroundings looking for signs of further avalanche activity. Post a lookout person, if the number of survivors permit, in a safe loaction where they can watch the rescue scene. Send for help if that is a viable option.

2 - Scan the debris for signs of clothing, skis etc..

3 - Identify a list of last seen points for each buried victim.

4 - Conduct a systematic beacon/transceiver search adapting an accepted and practiced technique you've learned to the accident scene.

5 - If buried victims do not transmit a locatable beacon signal or if other circumstances render a transceiver search ineffective the rescue party should begin probing the debris with avalanche probes in a systematic manner.

6 - If a buried victim is located assign a rescuer to dig the victim out with a shovel while the remaining rescuers continue to search for additional victims. Take care not to further injure the victim while digging and probing. Dig each located victim out as rapidly as possible.

7 - Additional help and/or first aid may be required as a rescue progresses.

Remember: Practicing avalanche beacon search drills from time to time in safe settings can save precious minutes if you are ever required to conduct a real rescue to save someone's life. Think about the peace of mind you will have on a trip if you spent half an hour at the trailhead testing each other's tranceivers and practicing finding them buried in a glove or toque. If you are a trip leader bring fresh batteries as a precaution.

Cornices

Cornices are familiar mountain features formed when wind blows snow over a ridge crest and deposits a wind-packed, overhanging lip above the leeward slope. They warrant a special mention as a winter hazard as on Vancouver Island cornices can reach gargantuan sizes. Not only that but they are probably the most ignored and flouted mountain hazard of all. Sadly, collapsing cornices claim the lives of hikers, climbers and skiers every year, even experienced ones.

The hazard cornices pose is compounded as they are often prominently featured in magazines and videos as playground features to be hucked at will. This is far from reality. A cornice can weigh hundreds of tonnes and is composed of complicated snow layers that have been greatly wind affected. Their shape is inherently unstable. Would you take an 8 foot length of 2x6 plank, hang 4 feet of it out a 6 storey window, tack a 3 inch nail to a tabletop and then walk out on it? Essentially that demonstrates the relative stability of cornices.

Another aspect of cornices is that the snow disguises where the hard rock terrain of the mountain ends and the overhanging snow starts. A lot of accidents with cornices occur because someone unknowingly walked too far out on one.

Familiarity with the terrain in summer can help figure out where the safe line is along a cornice but basically it's a good idea to stay as far away from the edge as possible.

Cornices also pose a threat while travelling below them. They often cap gullies or slopes and can trigger bigger avalanches if they collapse. The sun can affect the back side of a cornice weakening it while a party travels hundreds or thousands of feet below in the cold shade unaware of the growing danger above.

Spring is a time of frequent cornice activity as the thaw weakens them and they collapse along with the rest of the melting snowpack.

Experience in observing cornices and practice avoiding them is essential to stay safe around these common features. Be aware of these hazards above and below. And don't start your great ski line by hucking the cornice, it's one thing to trigger an avalanche yourself even after a big breakfast but to trigger one with 400 tonnes of hard-packed cornice snow could be a whole other story.

Avalanche Bulletins

Always check current avalanche forecasts from the Canadian Avalanche Association (C.A.A.) (www.avalanche.ca) or their certified members before embarking on any backcountry trip during avalanche season. Ensure that the forecast is up-to-date and the region covered by the forecast you obtain is the correct one for your intended destination.

Avalanche Training

When it comes to better understanding snow stability and learning safe procedures for travel in avalanche terrain there is no substitute for professional instruction and in-the-field experience.

For an introduction to the subject of avalanche awareness a weekend course taught by a C.A.A. certified instructor is a good way to start. Watch for courses at local ski hills or contact the C.A.A. for a list of qualified instructors in your area.

Those with a professional, or even a greater amateur interest the C.A.A. offers several levels of industry standard certification Level I - Avalanche Technician and Level II - Avalanche Forecaster are established industry-standard certificates. The C.A.A. now also offers courses specifically for industry and snowmobilers among other specialized fields. Contact the C.A.A. for course details province-wide.

Snowmobiles

Snowmobiles are one form of winter recreation you probably love or hate. Chances are if you prefer the peace and solitude of the mountains and the anthem 'earn your turns' you despise the noisy things and the selfish intrusion they inflict on the otherwise pristine alpine environment.

Snowmobiles have their own particular considerations when in avalanche terrain. The heavy weight of the machines and their ability to move quickly from one terrain feature to another require alert driving and specialized training. Contact local clubs or the Canadian Council of Snowmobile Organizations www.ccso-ccom.ca/for more info

Snowmobiles are not permitted in Strathcona and other wilderness parks. BC Parks does attempt to enforce these regulations but this is a difficult job. Parks relies on help from the public to report infractions. If you do witness and decide to report illegal snowmobile activity in a park it is best if a snowmobiler can be linked with an automobile licence plate or a plate on their machine.

Island Geography

Terrain

The Vancouver Island mountains run along an interior spine forming a complex topography of craggy peaks, pocket glaciers, deep forested valleys, long winding alpine ridges and wild ocean shoreline. In its 300+km length the Vancouver Island Ranges are dissected by countless gorgelike valleys. As a result while there may be long sections of ridgeline paralleling these valleys there are few high plateaus and no significant icecaps or linked glaciers.

Winter wonderland in Marble Meadows.

This rugged terrain lends itself very well to day trips and weekend trips where a quick ascent is followed by a long sweet descent (or a hideous bushwhack you never know!). These destinations would include King's Peak and Mt. Myra for example.

A selection of the classic long distance hiking routes through Strathcona Park along with several other North Island gems make for a number of good multi-day ski expeditions. The Elk River to Phillips Ridge traverse might take 5-10 days. A route has even been skied from Elk River to Port Alberni!

Island Glaciers

Like most of British Columbia's mountains the island peaks have been shaped by successive ice ages. On Vancouver Island only remnants of these once vast ice sheets remain. They cling to only the shadiest of slopes and the bottoms of north facing cirques. There are a few exceptions where glaciers retain something of their former majesty. The largest icefields on the island are only a few square kilometres in area and are found, in descending order of size, on Mariner Mountain, Rugged Mountain and the Haihte

Range, Comox Glacier, Cliffe Glacier, Mt. Tom Taylor, Big Interior Mountain and Mt. Septimus/ Rosseau. Each of these peaks has great ski terrain for both touring and cutting a few lines.

The location of the larger icefields is a result of their proximity to the west coast inlets which cleave their way inland from the open Pacific. In some cases the inlets almost cut right across Vancouver Island allowing moisture laden weather systems to reach the high peaks that then bar their way. The Comox Glacier is fed by Alberni Inlet, Mariner Mountain by Bedwell Sound and the Rugged Glacier by Tahsis Inlet.

Regardless of their small size the island glaciers still hold all the potential hazards of glaciers the world over so don't treat crossing one lightly. Crevasses, serac fall, bergschrunds and moats are just some of the obstacles that may be encountered albeit at a smaller scale than elsewhere in B.C..

Generally the immense winter snowpack, some years as deep as 30 ft (8 m), keeps crevasses well covered throughout the ski touring season until late June or even July. As summer progresses the seasonal winter snow melts away exposing the glacial ice underneath. At any time of year be prepared for glacier travel if your objective includes one. A familiarity with route finding on glaciers and crevasse rescue techniques are essential tools of the ski-mountaineer's trade.

Snow Conditions

Vancouver Island snow conditions vary but one thing can be counted on... there'll be lots of it. The snow may be heavy, heck it may even rain some days! Daily snowfalls of 40 cm are a norm in the Island alpine and extreme storm cycles can deposit a metre of snow or more. Ideal mid-winter conditions bring temperatures around -2° to -7°C cool enough to keep the snow light sometimes but mostly it's a stiff powder!.

Wind slab, strustugi and other common snow conditions can be expected after storm cycles especially those that bring strong winds.

Without new snowfall the Island snowpack often consolidates quickly as temperatures are often only a few degrees below freezing and periods of colder temperatures rarely last more than a few days. This is when travel is fast and corn snow may form in spring.

About the Island Weather

Situated between the open Pacific Ocean and the vast BC Coast Range mountains, Vancouver Island's weather is influenced by moist air off the ocean and drier continental air from the mainland Interior.

Winters are mild and wet with occasional periods of outflow conditions when cold dry air from the B.C. Interior surges down the mainland inlets bringing clear skies and freezing temperatures. Most of the annual precipitation that falls on the alpine falls as snow. The immense winter snowpack is the single biggest variable to be encountered in the Vancouver Island mountains. Snowpacks of 5-6m. / 16-20 ft are normal and produce a mini ice age every six months. Winter temperatures in the alpine vary between 5°C and -10°C. In the alpine the best ice climbing conditions usually occur between December and February. Good low elevation ice climbing conditions are very rare.

May can be great for ski touring with long days and warming temperatures. It isn't usually until late-May that the snow coverage begins to noticeably reced above treeline.

Lightning is rare on the west coast as a whole but when electrical storms do form they can be particularly violent lasting many hours, often at night.

Island creeks swell quickly after heavy rain.

The west coast of Vancouver Island receives over twice the annual precipitation of the eastern part. If a forecast predicts precipitation you would like to avoid then destinations in the Beaufort Range or Eastern Strathcona may help your chances of staying a bit drier.

Online check in at: **weatheroffice.ec.gc.ca**

Clear outflow weather in the Haihte Range.

Island Ice Climbing

Vancouver Island isn't known as a great water ice climbing destination. It is a rare winter indeed when freezing temperatures last long enough for any significant low-elevation ice to form. When a deep freeze does arrive however, the quality of the ice produced is second to none.

It is the mild West Coast temperatures that help high quality ice to form. Repeating cycles of freeze and thaw along with heavy wet snowfalls can mature Island ice into a sublime plastic nevé.

Some of the areas to look for good low elevation ice include: Comox Lake, Upper Campbell Lake, Buttle Lake, the White Ridge and Highway 28 right to the head of Muchalet Inlet. There are plenty of other places but these areas have good access.

In a more typical winter you will have to look at least as high as 1,200 m. / 3,000 ft. to find ice in any sort of decent climbing condition. The best locations for sub-alpine ice climbing are at: Mt. Arrowsmith along Pass Main, Boston Lake below Mt. Becher, Mt. Washington, and at Tennent Lake. While these areas offer waterfall climbing the very best of Vancouver Island ice is found high on the northernmost aspects of the mountains.

Mt. Colonel Foster is home, by far and away, to the most challenging winter climbing on the Island. The 1,000 m. / 3,500 ft. north-east face of 'the Colonel' is scored by several huge couloirs and numerous other more complex lines. Only a few routes have been established on this incredible peak with many new ones waiting to be done.

If you are looking for winter climbing of a less commiting nature try Mt. Arrowsmith, Big Den Mountain, the Haihte Range and King's Peak. Each of these peaks have classic gully climbs of just a few hundred metres giving a great taste of Vancouver Island's winter alpine climbing.

There are a lot of great routes all over the Island waiting for discovery in the right conditions at all elevations. For more information and details of technical climbing routes in the Vancouver Island mountains see Island Alpine.

Curtis Lyon on Boston Falls, Mt Becher.

Emergency Numbers

(no charge for these telephone numbers)

Rescue Coordination Centre: cellular *311

or 1-800-567-5111

Other Emergencies: 911

Using This Guide

Like its predecessor Island Alpine, Island Turns and Tours divides Vancouver Island into 4 distinct regions. In this book **Southern and Central Vancouver Island** are combined into one section, with **Strathcona Park** and **Northern Vancouver Island** warranting their own sections.

Each section begins with a map and an introduction giving an overview of the region covered.

The Strathcona Park section is further divided into four chapters **Eastern, Northern, Central and Southern Strathcona Park.** Each of these chapters also begin with a map and an introduction describing the area covered.

Within each section or chapter the indivdual destinations are then detailed. The type of destination varies between those that are specific locations e.g. **Mt. Cain** and those that are specific tours e.g. **Comox Glacier to Flower Ridge**.

Each destination whether location or tour has a detailed topographical map showing access, highlighted terrain and/or tour routes. The destination is then described in detail with an introduction, list of facts, access details, descriptions of the turns and tours and a list of additional information sources.

Note on nomenclature: *It is worth pointing out that some of the names used for peaks, passes and creeks etc... are unofficial. Some of these are in use to varying degrees by locals and others are just my own suggestion to help develop and clarify the descriptions.*

Map Legend

Contour Interval 200m or 500ft based on corresponding 1:50,000 NTS map sheet

Park Boundary (blue)	Paved Highway	Trail
(19) Highway (1) Trail	Logging Road	Route
▲ Backcountry Camp	🏃 Trailhead	P Parking
△ Designated Campsite	🧗 Climbing	⛗ Picnicking
🚻 Tent/Vehicle Camping	⛷ Downhill Skiing	🚹🚺 Toilet
▲▲ Group Camping	🏠 Backcountry Hut	Boat Launch

Trip Length

The number of days required for each trip or destination is given as a rough estimate. There will be those that may, under favourable conditions, travel across terrain in a day that might take others several days. By all means use this suggested trip length to assist with planning but learn to gauge with experience how long any given trip may take you and your party.

Trip and Ski Rating

Trips are rated by consensus employing a combination letter and number grading system to define the overall difficulty of a given trip. Such a rating may be used for trip leaders to select appropriate destinations and for general trip planning.

The letter grade refers to the trip difficulty. Literally how hard the trip is going to be. How an individual perceives each grade from A to D is in part a measure of fitness, stamina and also terrain and prevailing weather and snow conditions. The letter - difficulty grades may be defined as follows:

A - an easy trip with short distances covered each day, might be camp or hut based. Not strenuous.

B - a moderately strenuous outing with most of the day spent travelling. May involve complete alpine to valley elevation gains/losses (1500m+/ 4,000ft+).

C - long traveling days. May involve multiple days of strenuous travel with large elevation gains/losses carrying an overnight pack.

D - very strenuous multi-week expeditions to remote locations. Large heavy packs a given.

The numerical - skiing/snowboarding difficulty grades may be defined as follows:

1 - ideal beginner terrain, gentle slopes and/or mainly trail travel.

2 - intermediate terrain with moderate slopes, travel involving off trail travel.

3 - Off-trail skiing in rugged mountain terrain suitable for expert skiers/riders. Steep forest and/or glacier travel probable. Long runs!

4 - Difficult mountain journey with skiing in rugged terrain. For those with advanced backcountry experience.

5 - Extreme skiing!

Photographs In This Guide

The photographs used throughout this guidebook are chosen to illustrate the character of each area described as clearly as possible. In some cases photographs are selected just for inspiration because they show a peak or area from an interesting perspective.

I have tried to use only photographs taken during the typical ski touring season (December to June) but in a few instances only a later summer photo was available. The huge variation in seasonal snow cover creates widely varying conditions in the alpine throughout the year. This should be taken into consideration when looking at the photographs.

The month each picture was taken is mentioned in most captions to help put the photos into seasonal perspective.

All photos are by the author unless otherwise noted.

Maps In This Guide

Readers of Island Alpine will immediately notice a marked improvement in the maps included in Turns and Tours. These topographically accurate maps are based on the 1:50,000 Government National Topographical Series. They are simplified by including only the 500ft or 200m contours (depending on the source sheet) along with water features such as rivers, lakes and glaciers, relevant place names and spot heights as well as being set up for just a two colour printing process.

To facilitate suitable coverage and page placement, the scale of each map must be assumed to differ from any other map in this book. To compensate, every map has its own scale which should be used only for the map on which it appears . Some of the maps were rotated off grid north, again to make a better fit on the page, so check the 'north' symbol on each map.

Another limitation to be aware of is that where adjacent map sheets are in different units ie: metric or imperial (metres vs. feet) the contours simply continue across the join to the closest significant contour. So a 600m contour on one sheet will meet the 2,000ft contour of the adjacent metric sheet. This complication may have resulted in some errors and a subtle difference in accuracy but the intent of the maps to give a general topographical overview shouldn't be found to have been impeded.

Grid References

Extensive use of grid references appears throughout this guidebook. Grid references relate to the blue grid overlaying the 1:50,000 government topo map sheets. Most references are simple four figure coordinates that appear in the text as: GR 8941

The grid reference is split into two parts. So in our example 89 and 41. Grid references are read with eastings first and northings last. Reading across the top row of numbers look east to 89. Then cross reference that column with row 41 from the northings down the left edge of the map to find the square contained at 8941. The reference indicates Eena Lake.

In a six figure reference such as; GR 879378 the numbers are still split in half 879 and 378. The first two figures in each trio work as explained above. The third digit (9 and 8) refer to a further factor of ten division of the square at those coordinates. 879378 is the six figure grid reference for the summit of Horseshoe Mountain.

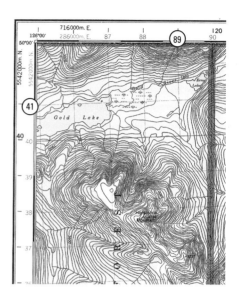

Parks Canada Avalanche Terrain Exposure Scale (A.T.E.S.)

In response to several tragic avalanches in recent years, particularly those in Roger's Pass, Park's Canada has initiated an extensive public awareness campaign highlighting the hazards of travelling in avalanche terrain.

One component of this effort is the employment of a rating scale for mountain terrain as it pertains to avalanches. The scale and Park's Canada's definitions are presented to the right.

This information is included to increase awareness of the scale for those planning trips to National Parks and as a basis for possible future implementation by other land managers such as B.C. Parks.

At the time of publication the A.T.E.S. is very new and applies only to Banff and Jasper Park where a long list of mountain areas have been rated. The A.T.E.S. has not been included in this book and no reference is made to it in the following text.

The longevity of the A.T.E.S. should not be assumed and the scale definitions may change, check online for up-to-date information.

Avalanche Terrain Exposure Scale (A.T.E.S.) v.1/04

Simple: Class 1 -Exposure to low angle or primarily forested terrain. Some forest openings may involve the runout zones of infrequent avalanches. Many options to reduce or eliminate exposure. No glacier travel.

Challenging: Class 2 -Exposure to well defined avalanche paths, starting zones or terrain traps; options exist to reduce or eliminate exposure with careful routefinding. Glacier travel is straightforward but crevasse hazards may exist.

Complex: Class 3 Exposure to multiple overlapping avalanche paths or large expanses of steep, open terrain; multiple avalanche starting zones and terrain traps below; minimal options to reduce exposure. Complicated glacier travel with extensive crevasse bands or icefalls.

For more information online visit Parks Canada's web site:

www.pc.gc.ca/pn-np/ab/banff/visit/visit7a1_E.asp

www.pc.gc.ca

Hints & Cautions

Trails versus Routes

One of the most important distinctions to understand for backcountry travel on Vancouver Island is the colloquial difference between a 'trail' and a 'route'.

It is generally accepted that a 'trail' is a purpose-built hiking thoroughfare which is regularly cleared, maintained and well signposted and marked. Examples are the loop trails at Cathedral Grove and the Elk River Trail in Strathcona Park.

An 'un-improved trail' is one that is only maintained and cleared by users. Good examples are Jack's Augerpoint trail and the Elkhorn north-west approach. Such trails are often clearly marked by ribbons of survey flagging tape or cairns.

An 'established route' is a backcountry path that may show clear signs of regular travel on the ground but sees no improvements beyond the impact of travelling hikers and wildlife. The Elk River-Phillips Ridge traverse is a great example of an established route. Flagging and cairns are sporadic but often prominent at route finding difficulties. In winter of course most of these markers are hidden by the snow.

A 'route' is on the wilderness end of the hiking spectrum and is nothing more than a suggested or accepted line of travel. Flagging and cairns are unlikely or sparse and route finding is a constant act. For experienced backcountry travellers. Preserving the experience of these routes is important and can be acheived by limiting flagging and building of cairns.

Wildlife

Vancouver Island has a unique blend of flora and fauna due to its size, isolation from and proximity to, mainland North America. The towering evergreen forests and swirling tidal oceans are home to a wide variety of fish, birds, reptiles, amphibians and mammals. The British Columbia coast is one of the richest ecosystems in the world.

When travelling in the Vancouver Island backcountry encounters with some wildlife is certain. Eagles, jays and osprey are familiar sights. In the ocean salmon, dolphins, sea lions and orca whales are all visitors to the coast. Living in the forest and on the mountains are grouse, ptarmigan, deer, Roosevelt elk, cougar, black bear, pine marten, wolf, river otters and of course marmots. Many of these larger land mammals are distinct sub-species unique to Vancouver Island. Some of these animals such as the Vancouver Island Marmot are present in dwindling numbers and are listed endangered or at risk.

There are some notable absences among the animal life of the Island. There are no grizzly bears or moose on the Island and racoons were introduced and so far have a limited range.

For the most part the larger mammals are elusive and encounters with them while hiking are rare and to be treasured when they do occur. There is of course a possibility of an aggressive brush with cougar, bear or wolf. If you find yourself confronted by a predator remain calm and maintain a confident air. Retreat from the area with deliberate steps keeping a close watch of the animal(s). If you are surprised or attacked, scream aggressively and fight back with every ounce of strength. In my humble opinion (and experience) playing dead could get you dead.

Wildlife encounters may be reported to:
1-800-663-9453

Water

A huge annual precipitation delivers an abundance of fresh water to the mountains of Vancouver Island. The numerous rivers and torrents that tumble seaward shape the land and are the lifeblood of the rich island ecosystem. Island rivers must be both respected and cared for.

Crossing rivers should be undertaken with great caution. Slick rocks and cold, fast moving water can be a deadly combination. Always undo pack waist belts and loosen straps before wading a river. This way you can shed the pack if you stumble. Use a staff or ski poles for stability. In deeper water use a roped belay, pfd and keep boots on. Avoid crossing rivers close, upstream of large rapids or waterfalls. Read and practice roped technical river crossing techniques.

The Island water supply is generally pure and untainted in the alpine. In high use areas such as Paradise Meadows and Bedwell Lake however filtration or sterilization should be practiced to avoid water borne illness. There is a duty to preserve the purity of fresh water. Read the section on 'Wilderness Travel' on page 31 and practice techniques to minimize contamination to bodies of water. Always camp in designated sites in high use areas and use the outhouses provided. If in doubt boil water to destroy any pathogens that may be present.

The Vegetation

If seasonal snow cover is the widest spanning variable for travel conditions in the alpine then the vegetation is the biggest variable encountered below treeline. The natural processes of forest growth and succession are greatly complicated on Vancouver Island by the removal of forest cover by logging activity. It is important to understand the types of natural vegetation zones and the cycles of logging activity to make off-trail travel as smooth as possible.

The ideal scenario for off-trail travel is mature old-growth forest of Douglas Fir, Western Hemlock and Red Cedar between sea level and around 1,200 m. / 3,000 ft. Very often within this zone undergrowth is limited because of the the shade cast by the tree canopy. Travel is fast and only hindered by some fallen branches and rotting logs.

On the other end of the spectrum are scenarios like avalanche paths and recent (5-20 year old) clearcuts. Here avalanches or logging remove the old-growth trees which are replaced by thick bushes like slide alder, salmonberry, devil's club and salal. Travel in this terrain can be extremely difficult, even dangerous and should be avoided if possible.

Between these two scenarios are many stages and types of forest growth. Regenerating forest may have piles of charred, rotting logs from slash fires lit after logging. An area where a forest fire burned may now be choked by two metre high tree (often fir) saplings covered in dew like carwash rollers. Logging roads which were used by heavy machinery are now deactivated and covered in a porcupine's coat of alder trees.

The best general advice is to stick to the old-growth as much as you can and look for signs of animal travel to follow. Often bear, deer, elk and other large animals wear good paths through the forest, although they don't clip the branches! Avoid recent and regenerating clearcuts by looking for points where old-growth reaches any road. Stick to the ridges and keep out of the gullies. Anticipate creeks by reading the topo map carefully. Use creeks and gullies as references in the forest when wider views are restricted.

Lastly remember when bushwhacking in dense undergrowth stay in visual contact with everyone in your group but travel far enough apart to avoid getting bushwhipped. In winter/spring the snow level and depth of snowpack will reduce the exposed bush by varying amounts. Travel at this time of year can often be much faster as a result.

Ticks

The most loathsome of creatures, ticks, are arachnids which latch on to the skin, inflict a nasty bite causing a painful swelling while they fill their abdomens with your blood. Ticks may carry Lyme's disease which can cause fever, facial paralysis and eventually severe arthritis and heart problems. If a tick attaches itself to you use tweezers or proprietary tick pliers to gently and steadily tug the tick until it releases its grip.

Don't pull so hard as to leave mouth parts embedded in your skin and don't try to burn it or pull too hard. If you suspect infection keep the tick in a Ziploc™ and take it when you seek medical attention for testing. Tick season on the Island lasts from late March to late May.

Private Property

Some of the more accessible mountain areas on Vancouver Island such as the Beaufort Range and Alexandra Peak-Mt. Adrian are on private land. The larger land owners are most often private forestry companies whose prime interest is the harvesting of timber and the safety of their employees and the public. Access restrictions therefore usually centre around safety concerns to prevent the public encountering heavy machinery and trucks on the logging roads during working hours.

Our duty is to respect posted closures and seek permission before entering private lands. Keeping good relationships by demonstrating respect for the land owner is the best way to ensure continued public access.

Ecological Reserves

Ecological reserves protect sensitive ecosystems for scientific research and conservation. Reserves differ from Provincial Parks in that public access and recreation is discouraged or even prohibited and a permit is required for a legitimate visit.

There are a few Ecological Reserves that include alpine terrain, Haley Lake near Nanaimo Lakes and the San Juan Ridge Ecological Reserves come to mind. Please respect the sensitivity and value of Ecological Reserves by avoiding travelling through them.

Cream Lake completely frozen in June.

Lake and Creek Crossings

Lakes and creeks are common parts of the mountain landscape and can offer a great benefit to the winter backcountry traveller. A frozen lake can turn a taxing summertime bushwhack along a lake shore into a speedy hassle-free beeline. And a creek criss-crossed by thick snow bridges can offer easy crossings when at other times of the year it can be challenging searching for a log jam. But before heading out on to a apparently frozen lake or hopping the next creek here's a few tips.

Unlike a lot of lakes and rivers at lower elevation and those familair as neighbourhood hockey rinks back east, the Island alpine lakes and waterways are not just frozen but are capped by variable layers of slush, ice, snow and even water. Eventually as a typical winter progresses a very deep layer of snow accumulates. Observing the lake cover during spring thaw as holes open in it, shows a thick mass of heavy snow up to several metres, suspended on the water's surface.

Creeks are often easier to assess as even in deep winter the moving water and air keeps many holes open between bridges at all but the highest elevations.

Experience shows that the snow layer on lakes is often quite uniform in thickness except around the lake edges where trees, creek outlets and inlets, active avalanche paths, and other localized effects influence the thickness to different degrees. Generally speaking the edges of open holes should be avoided and every effort should be made to assess that the cover thickness is adequate before attempting to cross.

Just how thick should the ice and snow be to safely cross? That is very difficult to predict as the variations in temperatures and snowfall can produce widely varying coverage and consistency. Experience shows that any open water is reason to be suspicious. Creeks should be assessed on a case by case basis. Often the consequences of a snow bridge collapsing on a creek crossing in winter is fairly minor. But in spring and early summer as yawning tunnels form below the snow surface and the volume of water at high thaw reaches a torrent the consequences may be far more severe.

A major warning sign that a lake is past thaw are the appearance of numerous dishes or sun cups often filled with water seeping up through the weakening snow layer. This can happen as fast as in just a couple of days during warm spring days. Long cracks are often a false alarm as they can form regardless of the thickness of snow.

By mid-May, on average, covered alpine lakes should be treated with suspicion but of course this is dependent on elevation and seasonal fluctuations in snowpack depth. Lake Helen Mackenzie has been thawed to an uncrossable point during a recent February while Big Jim Lake has been seen frozen and crossable in mid-July!

A few common sense tips are: if in doubt avoid the crossing. On lakes keep close enough to shore that in the event of a dunking as little as possible distance needs to be covered to return to land yet stay just far enough out to avoid the weakened edges. Keep pack straps, ski safety straps and pole straps undone while crossing water and if you go in and things get dangerous, save yourself and forget about your pack and gear!

Hints and Cautions **23**

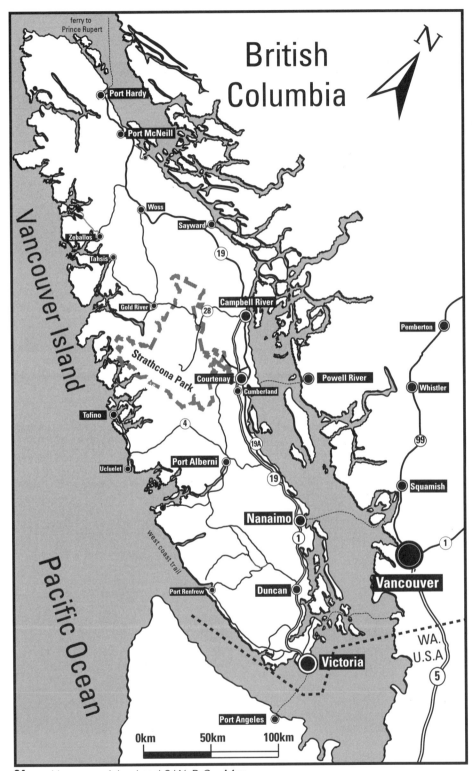

British Columbia

N

ferry to
Prince Rupert

Port Hardy

Port McNeill

Woss

Sayward

Zeballos

Tahsis

19

Gold River

Campbell River

28

Pemberton

Strathcona Park

Courtenay

Powell River

Whistler

Cumberland

Tofino

Vancouver Island

4

19A

99

Ucluelet

Port Alberni

Squamish

19

Nanaimo

1

West coast trail

1

Port Renfrew

Duncan

Vancouver

Pacific Ocean

Victoria

WA.
U.S.A

5

Port Angeles

0km   50km   100km

Island Trip Logistics

How To Get Here

Vancouver Island is a large island, some 500km long and 150km wide, lying just off the southwest coast of British Columbia, Canada. The population centres and major highway routes are concentrated along the south and east coasts of the Island and can be reached on a variety of scheduled ferry routes.

Horseshoe Bay BC—Departure Bay (Nanaimo)

Tsawwassen BC—Duke Point (Nanaimo)

Tsawwassen BC—Schwartz Bay (Victoria)

Seattle WA—Victoria

Port Angeles WA—Victoria

The major highways linking the north and south ends of the island are: the Trans Canada Highway Route 1 between Victoria and Nanaimo and the Inland Island Highway 19 which links all communities between Nanaimo and Port Hardy. An alternative scenic route along the east coast of Vancouver Island is the Oceanside Highway 19A between Parksville and Campbell River.

Some suggested driving times are; Victoria to Campbell River 3.5 hours, Nanaimo to Campbell River 1.75 hours, Campbell River to Sayward 1 hour. Campbell River to Gold River 1 hour Campbell River to Port Hardy 2.5 hours.

Visitors should note that locally the various regions of Vancouver Island are referred to as 'South Island' 'North Island' etc. This may be confusing to some as it sounds as if there may be several islands. Vancouver Island is a single island and these designations just refer to regions on the island.

Camping and Accommodation

Vancouver Island is a very popular vacation destination and accommodation facilities abound for every budget in every town. The best way to find roofed accommodation and private RV and tenting campgrounds is to consult local visitor guides or get a copy of the annual British Columbia Accommodation Guide which is all available at local Visitor Info Centres.

There are many Forest Service and Provincial campsites across the island. Some useful campsites are: Provincial campsites at Elk Falls just outside Campbell River on Highway 28, Buttle Narrows also on 28 and, Ralph River on the Buttle Lake Parkway.

Reservation systems are in place for some Park campgrounds during peak summer season and you'd be well advised to check for site availability at these campsites before showing up in the dark! Check online at www.discoverbc.com

Along the roadways in Strathcona Park and other Provincial parks, camping is not permitted within 1 km of the road. Camping is permitted only at designated sites along many of the higher use trails. Check at each trailhead for the locations of the designated sites in the area you are headed. Once in the backcountry simply use discretion in choosing low impact sites and follow our Wilderness Travel guidelines.

Planes, trains, automobiles and of course ferry boats all part of getting around on the Island.

Logging Road Travel

Many of the alpine areas of Vancouver Island can only be reached by driving on gravel roads. Some gravel roads are major Forest Service roads open at all times and well maintained under contract from the B.C. Forest Service. These roads are 2 wheel drivable and plowed during the winter. However across Vancouver Island there are thousands of kilometres of logging roads.

Logging roads whether on Crown Land or not are not required to be accessible by the public. Some roads are on private forest lands and often closed by locked gates. Current forestry practices require the regular deactivation or 'debuilding' of logging roads that have fallen out of use for current timber harvesting plans. In addition roads into areas of active logging are often closed during working hours while work commences. Great care must be taken while driving any logging roads. Road conditions may vary widely and great caution must be had around heavy machinery and the huge double wide logging trucks that may appear around any corner!

In all nothing should be taken for granted when planning an approach that includes logging road travel. Any given logging road may be closed or otherwise impassable at any time. Consider throwing a chainsaw or, at the least, an axe in the back of your vehicle, one fallen tree could ruin your day! Check with local logging companies or other climbers familiar with current conditions. A backup plan doesn't hurt.

Logging Roads in Winter

Because winter snowfall presents additional expense and logistical considerations for logging activity, the condition of any logging road should be assumed to be compromised between November and June depending on the elevation of the road, current harvesting, and seasonal snowpack conditions. Some prior research could save disappointment or an unexpectedly long trek on a snow covered road.

But there can also be pleasant surprises. Winter harvesting does occur and seems progressively more likely with the generally increasing rates of harvesting the Island forests are enduring. Active roads are plowed and occasionally a bulldozer may head up a high elevation road system in April or May in an effort to accelerate the thaw and clear a road for spring logging.

Logging Road Safety Tips

The British Columbia Forest Service recommends these safety tips when travelling on Forest Service Roads:

• Drive with your lights on at all times - day and night.

• Drive at a safe speed. You should always use caution and expect the unexpected. You must be able to stop safely in any emergency or in encountering unforeseen obstructions.

• Use seat belts while travelling on Forest Service Roads

• Please give logging trucks and other industrial traffic the right-of-way. Loaded logging trucks definitely have the right-of-weight! When you see a logging truck coming - or any other heavy equipment - get to a turn-out or a ditch and let it go by.

• Obey all road signs but do not expect the same level of signing as on public highways

CAUTION
LOGGING EQUIPMENT
USING ROADS WEEKDAYS
7 AM TO 5:30 PM
EXPECT THE UNEXPECTED

• Taking large travel trailers on steep, rough, isolated and infrequently used roads can be dangerous. Loaded logging rigs can not back up steep grades so it is best to avoid the use of trailers on these roads.

• Logging trucks take up a lot of room and Forest Service Roads are built for their use. It is essential that logging trucks and fire-fighting equipment be able to proceed without delay. Don't stop on the road surface for any reason. If you do stop, park well off the road

• In addition remember in winter conditions extra caution should be exercised on icy, snow covered roads. Heavily loaded trucks have no chance of braking and won't even try to stop in poor conditions.

Government of British Columbia
online directory: www.dir.gov.bc.ca

Ministry of Parks
http://wlapwww.gov.bc.ca/bcparks/

Discover Camping
www.discovercamping.ca
1-800-689-9025

Ministry of Forests
www.gov.bc.ca/for

South Island Forest District
3819 Trans Canada Hwy,Cobble Hill, B.C., V0R 1L0 Ph: (250) 743-8933

Alberni Forest District
4885 Cherry Creek Road, Port Alberni, B.C., V9Y 8E9 Ph: (250) 731-3000

Campbell River Forest District -
370 South Dogwood Street, Campbell River, B.C. V9W 6Y7 Ph: (250) 286-9300

Port McNeill Forest District -
P.O. Box 7000, 2217 Mine Road Port McNeill, BC V0N 2R0 Ph: 250 956-5000 eMail: Forests.PortMcN eillDistricOffice@gems3.gov.bc.ca

Logging Companies

Timberwest
www.timberwest.com

Beaver Cove Operation
-P.O. Box 2500, 5705 North Island Highway, Campbell River, BC V9W 5C5 Ph: (250) 287-9181

Cowichan Woodlands
-P.O. Box 375, 9370 South Shore Road, Mesachie Lake, BC V0R 2N0 Ph: (250) 749-7700

Nanaimo Lakes
-5055 Nanaimo River Rd. Nanaimo, BC V9X 1H3 Ph: (250) 729-3770

Johnstone Strait Operation
-P.O. Box 2500, 5705 North Island Highway Campbell River, BC V9W 5C5 Ph: (250) 287-9181

Western Forest Products Limited
-#118 – 1334 Island Hwy. Campbell River, BC V9W 8C9 Ph: 250 286-3767
-1594 Beach, Port McNeill BC V0N 2R0 Ph: 250 956-4446

Weyerhaeuser - Brascan
South Island Timberlands
-1825 Timberlands Rd, P.O. Box 75, Cassidy, BC V0R 1H0 Ph: 250-245-6300

West Island Timberlands - Franklin Operations
-Bag 2001, Port Alberni, BC V9Y 7N3 Ph: 250-720-4200

West Island Timberlands - Sproat Lake Operations
-Port Alberni, BC V9Y 7N4 Ph: 250-720-4100

North Island Timberlands
-P.O. Box 6000, 8010 Island Highway, Campbell River, BC V9W 5E1 Ph: 250-287-5000

Port McNeill Timberlands -
-400 South-west Main, P.O. Box 5000 Port McNeill, BC V0N 2R0 Ph: 250 956-5200

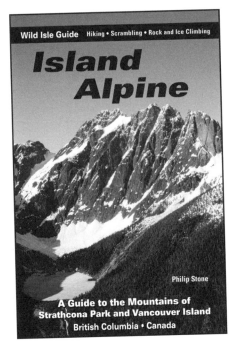

Wild Isle Guide   Hiking • Scrambling • Rock and Ice Climbing

Island Alpine

Philip Stone

A Guide to the Mountains of Strathcona Park and Vancouver Island
British Columbia • Canada

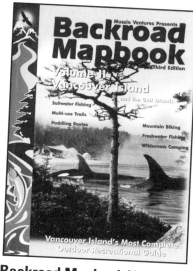

Mussio Ventures Presents

Backroad Mapbook

Third Edition

Volume II
Vancouver Island
and the Gulf Islands

Saltwater Fishing
Multi-use Trails
Paddling Routes
Mountain Biking
Freshwater Fishing
Wilderness Camping

Vancouver Island's Most Complete Outdoor Recreational Guide

Backroad Mapbook Volume II
ISBN 1-894556-10-0

Island Alpine
A guide to the mountains of Strathcona Park & Vancouver Island.
ISBN 0-9680766-5-3

HIKING TRAILS II

South-Central Vancouver Island and the Gulf Islands

includes TOPOGRAPHICAL MAPS

EIGHTH EDITION

HIKING TRAILS III

Northern Vancouver Island including Strathcona Park

and for the first time
Malcolm Island
Nootka Island and the Beaufort Range

includes topographical maps

Vancouver Island Hiking Trails Volume 2
ISBN 0-9697667-3-4

Vancouver Island Hiking Trails Volume 3
ISBN 0-9697667-1-9

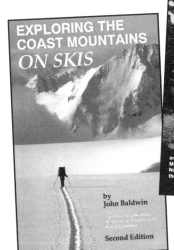

EXPLORING THE COAST MOUNTAINS
ON SKIS

by
John Baldwin

Second Edition

Exploring the Coast Mountains on Skis.
ISBN 0-9691550-1-8

Additional Resources

Maps

The following National Topographic Series (NTS) maps cover the regions included in this guide. They can be bought locally or ordered from the Geological Survey of Canada: 604 666-0271. All maps are in the 92 series.

South Island: C/16 Cowichan Lake, F/1 Nanaimo Lakes, F/2 Alberni Inlet • F/3 Effingham River • F/6 Great Central Lake • F/7 Horne Lake

Strathcona Park: F/11 Forbidden Plateau • F/12 Buttle Lake • F/13 Upper Campbell Lake • F/5 Bedwell River • F/6 Great Central Lake

North Island: L/1 Schoen Lake • E/16 Gold River • L/1 Schoen Lake • L/8 Adam River • K/5 Sayward • L/7 Nimpkish • L/6 Alice Lake • L/3 Kyuquot

Publications

• **Island Alpine** - A guide to the mountains of Strathcona Park & Vancouver Island. First Edition 2003 by Philip Stone. ISBN 0-9680766-5-3

• **Vancouver Island Hiking Trails Volume 1** - Twelfth Edition 1997 by Susan Lawrence
ISBN 0-9697667-2-6
Covers the Capital Regional District, Saltspring Island, Saanich Peninsula, the Juan de Fuca Marine trail. There is no overlap with this guide but volume 1 does offer some great island hiking ideas.

• **Vancouver Island Hiking Trails Volume 2** - Eighth Edition 2000 by Richard Blier
ISBN 0-9697667-3-4
Covers Duncan, Cowichan Valley, Gulf Islands including Gabriola, Nanaimo, Parksville, Port Alberni Caramanah Walbran Provincial Park and the West Coast Trail.

• **Vancouver Island Hiking Trails Volume 3** - Ninth Edition 2002 by Richard Blier
ISBN 0-9697667-1-9
Covers Strathcona Park, Schoen Lake Park, Cape Scott Park and Quadra Island among others. An essential compliment to Turns and Tours.

• **Backroad Mapbook Volume II Vancouver Island,** Mussio Ventures
ISBN 1-894556-10-0
If you're looking for a comprehensive overview of all the logging roads on Vancouver Island and some basic info on trails and other recreation opportunities this is a good bet. Beware though, the book has a few inaccuracies. Any logging road information shouldn't be relied on as conditions and openings may change at any time.

• **Beyond Nootka** - A Historical Perspective of Vancouver Island Mountains by Lindsay Elms
ISBN 0-9680159-0-5
A thouroughly researched book detailing the early history of European exploration on Vancouver Island. Profiles six of the more prominent peaks on the island. Excellent read.

• **Exploring the Coast Mountains on Skis**- by John Baldwin
ISBN 0-9691550-1-8
Comprehensive guidebook to backcountry skiing in one of the world's greatest wilderness mountain ranges. A must have book for the BC backcountry enthusiast.

• **Island Bushwhacker** - journal of the Vancouver Island Section of the Alpine Club of Canada

• **Alpine Club of Canada Journal** - annual publication

Online Resources

BC Government Map Place: www.em.gov.bc.ca/Mining/Geolsurv/MapPlace
Online database of Bristish Columbia topographical maps

Canadian Avalanche Association: www.avalanche.ca
The home page for the Canadian Avalanche Association. Lots of links to weather and avalanche resources including current avalanche conditions posted at: **www.avalanche.ca/weather/bulletins**

Canadian Mountain Encyclopedia: www.bivouac.com
The Canadian climber's yellow pages! A paid membership is required to access the whole site.

Centre for Topographical Information: www.maps.nrcan.gc.ca
A complete database of Canadian topographical maps. Search for map sheets using terrain name searches, retreive coordinates for thousands of Canadian places.

Climbers Access Society of BC (CASBC): www.casbc.bivouac.com
Box 72013, 4479 West 10th, Vancouver, B.C. V6R 4P2

CoastalBC.com: www.coastalbc.com
Another excellent comprhensive overview of adventure activities on Vancouver Island. Also see its associated site surfingVancouverIsland.com

Mt. Cain Alpine Park Society: www.mountcain.com
Snow reports, event information, accommodation links.

Mt. Washington Alpine Resort: www.mountwashington.ca
Current ski conditions, web cam, snowpack statistics and event information.

Online Hiking Guide: www.islandhikes.com
Features trip reports, peak route info and a bulletin board messaging system for research and online chats.

Vancouver Island Trails Information Society: www.hikingtrailsbooks.com
The Vancouver Island Trails Information Society is a non-profit society dedicated to providing accurate information to the public about parks and trails on Vancouver Island. VITIS achieves this goal by self-publishing hiking trail guides covering Vancouver Island.

Weather Office: weatheroffice.ec.gc.ca

Wild Isle: www.wildisle.ca
A vast online resource of information, back issues, links and stories of adventure sports on Vancouver Island. Covers the whole gamut from sea kayaking to mountain biking but there is a bias with plenty about hiking, climbing and mountaineering all over the island.

Clubs

Alpine Club of Canada: www.alpineclubofcanada.ca
Home page of the Alpine Club of Canada.

Alpine Club of Canada Vancouver Island section: www.alpineclubofcanada.ca/vi
direct/local url: www.horizon.bc.ca/~acc/

Federation of Mountain Clubs of BC: www.mountainclubs.bc.ca
Umbrella organization for mountain clubs in British Columbia.

The Heathens: www.heathens.ca
Web site of Heathens Outdoor Club, based in Campbell River members interest span the full range of outdoor activities. Mountains a specialty! eMail: the_heathens@hotmail.com

Wilderness Travel

Skiers and other backcountry travellers have a special duty to familiarize themselves with, and practice strict no trace camping techniques. By leaving the wilderness untouched by our passage we ensure that the environment endures in as pristine a state as possible. By minimizing our impact on the wildlife, vegetation and terrain we preserve the wilderness integrity of wild places and ensure that others who follow will have an experience comparable to our own. Winter travellers have a unique opportunity to leave a minimum of impact in their wake.

Please do not light fires, the presence of firepits is unsightly and the collection of firewood at higher elevations places undue pressure on the fragile alpine ecology. The continuing cycles of growth and decomposition are disrupted by burning wood that is otherwise destined to die and rot creating new soil for future generations of trees and other vegetation.

Fires are discouraged within Provincial Parks year round. If you do encounter firepits left by those unfamiliar with no-trace ethics, take the time to dismantle them. We must not only ensure our own passage leaves no trace but also take positive action in caring for our diminishing wilderness.

Buy a lightweight campstove and use it for cooking. Extreme care must be exercised when lighting stoves and smoking. A forest fire can be devastating, and many fires start each year through carelessness.

Pack out what you pack in and please take the time to remove any garbage left by others. Dispose of all personal waste with due care to the water supply and do not leave toilet paper or other paper products lying around on the ground. Most trails and other high use areas within the Provincial Parks have outhouses and designated campsites that should be used.

Around camp pay attention to your belongings and keep a tidy camp as even a light dusting of snow overnight can hide small items and a big dump can bury all sorts of things that either you may need or regardless shouldn't be left behind.

Vancouver Island is one of the wettest places on Earth and water is rarely far away. The mountains of Strathcona are the headwaters of watersheds supplying drinking water for several island communities. The purity of the water supply can be preserved by following some simple measures.

Never wash dishes or yourself with soap, even with socalled biodegradable soap, don't drop food scraps in fragile alpine lakes. Pack out food waste and learn to cook only what you need to eat.

Toilet waste should be buried in cat holes far from any bodies of water. Human coliform bacteria in water is an increasing global problem. Please help stop the spread of water borne bacteria and disease by defecating responsibly. In the backcountry pack all soiled toilet paper out, or carry a small tin can which can be used to burn it in a safe manner.

Last but not least, please be sparing with flagging tape and cairns especially in the alpine. Many wilderness routes by nature do not require marking and if you found your way, then you can trust that others who follow will figure it out too. You may feel you are helping out those who come after you but remember that they may be seeking the pioneering experience too. Marking routes has its place but please note it is a form of impact and not everyone appreciates the sign of human presence it implies.

White-tailed Ptarmigan in the Island alpine.

Island Ski History

Skiers outside the old Forbidden Forestry Lookout circa 1939.　　　　　　photo: Ruth Masters

By Lindsay Elms

In the 21st century winter sports enthusiast have a multitude of choices to make about what they are going to do and where they are going to do it. Skiers have to decide if they are downhill, back-country, telemark or X-country skiing (which is also divided into classic and skating) and then there is snowboarding. There are numerous types of snowshoes depending on whether you are going into the backcountry with a large pack for snowshoe running and then there are all the different types of toboggans and don't forget the tubing! There are all the different makes and models of skis, boots, bindings and poles to chose from and the type and colour of clothing to be worn. Obviously it is dependent on current trends and attitude. Then there is where to go to undertake the chosen winter sport. Airline companies expediate the decisions by flying to popular destinations where shuttle services whisk you up to the resort and then there are a full range of style and comfort when choosing which hotel to stay in.

Eighty years ago all these choices weren't there or at least very few of them. On Vancouver Island winter sports activities really only began in 1928 although there are accounts of tobogganing on Mt. Arrowsmith back in the 1890's. In 1928 the Courtenay-Comox Mountaineering Club (now the Comox District Mountaineering Club) began when a core of outdoor enthusiasts who had

been hiking and climbing together decided to build a hut on the slopes of Mt. Becher. A trail had been built from the town of Bevan on the Puntledge River to the summit as it was the most accessible mountain. A little later Clinton Wood built the Forbidden Plateau Lodge as a base for guided trips into the back country and the logging road was pushed through to the lodge to shorten access time.

Gertie Wepsala Western Canada Ski Champion on Mt Albert Edward 1939 - Bob Gibson photo Courtesy of the Courtenay and District Museum and Archives

Ruth Masters   Sid Williams - 1941

Courtesy of the Courtenay and District
Museum and Archives

In the fall of 1935 at a meeting of the Tourist Development Bureau of the Courtenay-Comox Board of Trade discussed what this end of the island needed most in the way of development. After a long discussion about winter sports on Mt. Becher, the local mountaineering club was asked to promote them that season. That winter Clinton Wood kept the road open to his lodge all winter and he laid out a ski run from the edge of the timber to the lodge with plans for a longer and more ambitious run. The next year saw an increase in the number of visitors coming up island to ski on Forbidden Plateau with the Vancouver Island Coach line busing people from Victoria up to the lodge.

In March 1938, the first ski meet was held on Vancouver Island at Forbidden Plateau/Mt. Becher. While the majority of the of the skiers came from clubs in Vancouver (Grouse and Hollyburn), there was a keen interest from Victoria, Port Alberni and Courtenay enthusiasts. There were two different style of races: Saturday morning was devoted to the slalom races. The slalom was staged on the slopes of Mt. Becher near the Mountaineering Club's cabin and the racers were timed over two runs. The officials of the Vancouver Ski Zone had selected as the course the cliffs of the creek, which flows just west of the cabin to Boston Lake. The snow was fifteen feet deep and the skiers had to burrow to the cabin to brew some tea between runs. On Sunday the downhill events took place. Although not as spectacular as the slalom, the races were more accessible to the general public to view. The men's downhill course covered two and a half miles and finished in front of the Forbidden Plateau Lodge. Clinton Wood had cleared a course through the trees cutting brush and trees, however, there was still plenty of obstacles to make the course thrilling for the "most hardened skier." The women's course was shorter at one and a half miles while the Vancouver Island Downhill for local women was half a mile. As was expected, Vancouver skiers swept the board in both the

We have brought in a special stock of

Ski Boots at $5

Also our stock of RUBBERS and RUBBER BOOTS for the snow and slushy weather is complete.

The best way to avoid cold or 'flu is to keep your feet dry.

Searle's Shoes

downhill and slalom events but this event set the course for races at Forbidden Plateau for many years to come. Lindsay Loutet, the chairman of the Vancouver Ski Zone Committee, and one of the judges of the meet, said the plateau was ideal for langlauf or cross-country events but the present downhill course was a bit dangerous and

Forbidden Plateau day lodge still standing in 1996.

Sun rises over Mt. Abel lighting up the Mt. Cain day lodge.

should be widened. He also suggested that Mt. Becher was the only place on the British Columbia coast where ski jumps over two hundred could be obtained.

1938 also saw the visit of Don and Phyllis Munday, B.C. mountaineering pioneers. They skied the plateau and then with Captain Rex Gibson, Miss Ethne Gale and local guides Len Rossiter and Dick Idiens, they made a winter ski ascent of Mt. Albert Edward. Although not the first winter ascent on skis their write up drew the attention of back-country skiers from further afield to the potential on Vancouver Island.

With skiing at Forbidden Plateau taking off, the Port Alberni skiers began looking for somewhere close to home for them. In January 1939 a party of ten from the Comox District Mountaineering Club met up with a group from Port Alberni and decided to check out the slopes of Mt. Cokely. From Cameron Lake they hiked up the easy grades of the old CPR trail to the top of the mountain. By the end of the day the skiers were satisfied with the days skiing but found that packing skis for four hours to get two hours of skiing was a little out of proportion. Eventually a logging road was built and the locals built a ski-hill on the slopes of Mt. Cokely which for many years served their purpose. Thus skiing on the Island was conceived.

North-east cirque of Mt. Arrowsmith. *photo: Peter Rothermel*

Southern & Central

Vancouver Island

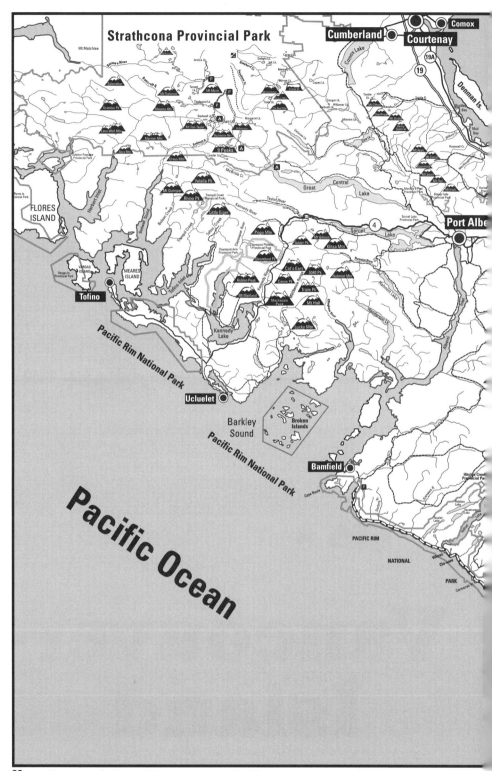

Strathcona Provincial Park

Mt Matchlee

Cumberland
Courtenay
Comox
19A
19

Denman Is.

FLORES ISLAND

9 Peaks

Port Albe

Tofino

MEARES ISLAND

VARGAS ISLAND

Pacific Rim National Park

Ucluelet

Kennedy Lake

Barkley Sound

Broken Islands

Pacific Rim National Park

Bamfield

PACIFIC RIM

NATIONAL

PARK

Pacific Ocean

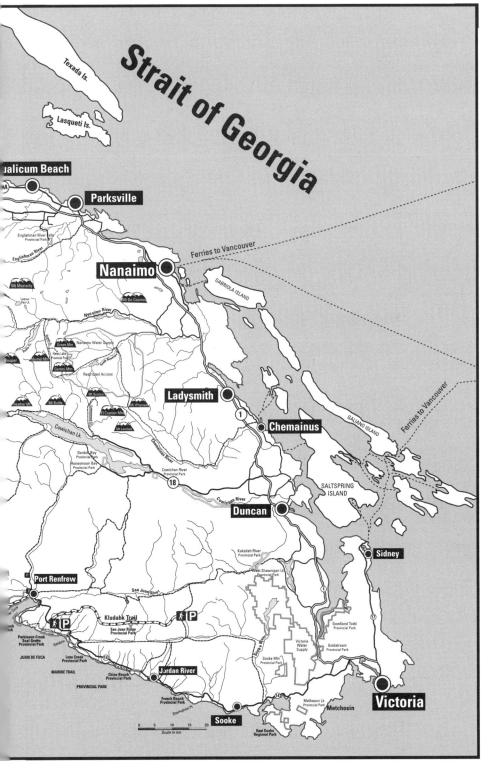

Strait of Georgia

Texada Is.

Lasqueti Is.

alicum Beach

Parksville

Englishman River Falls
Provincial Park

Englishman River

Mt Moriarty

Labour
Day Lk.

Nanaimo

Ferries to Vancouver

GABRIOLA ISLAND

Mt De Cosmos

Nanaimo River

Hooper

Green Mtn

Nanaimo Water Supply

Haley Lake
Provincial Park

Marmot Mtn

Gemini Mtn

Restricted Access

Heather Mtn

Mt Buttle

Mt Service

El Capitan Mtn

Mt Whymper

Ladysmith

Mt Landale

1

Chemainus

GALIANO ISLAND

Ferries to Vancouver

Cowichan Lk.

Humpback River

Gordon Bay
Provincial Park

Honeymoon Bay
Provincial Park

Cowichan River
Provincial Park

18

Cowichan River

Duncan

SALTSPRING
ISLAND

Kokailah River
Provincial Park

Port Renfrew

San Juan River

West Shawnigan Lk
Provincial Park

Sidney

Kludahk Trail

San Juan Ridge
Provincial Park

P

Gowlland Todd
Provincial Park

Parkinson Creek
Seal Grotto
Provincial Park

JUAN DE FUCA

Loss Creek
Provincial Park

Victoria
Water
Supply

Goldstream
Provincial Park

MARINE TRAIL

China Beach
Provincial Park

PROVINCIAL PARK

Jordan River

French Beach
Provincial Park

14

Sooke Mtn
Provincial Park

Matheson Lk
Provincial Park

Metchosin

Victoria

Sooke

East Sooke
Regional Park

0   5   10   15   20
Scale in km

Snowshoeing up Heather Mountain looking south-west.   *photo: Chris Shepard*

Southern & Central Island

Southern and Central Vancouver Island

Southern and Central Vancouver Island for the purposes of this guidebook consists of that part of Vancouver Island that falls to the south of a line extending from Tofino eastward along the southern boundary of Strathcona Park to the Valley Connector Road and from there to Courtenay. There are many mountains in this region of Vancouver Island as detailed in Island Alpine but only a few are singled out as recommended backcountry ski destinations.

Those destinations that have 'made-the-mark' together offer some fine backcountry ski terrain including great descent terrain on Mt. Arrowsmith and without question one of the Island's best moderate long distance tours down the Beaufort Range.

Highest Point: Summit of Mt. Arrowsmith 5,962 ft. / 1,817 m

Most Vertical Descent Possible: ~600m

Map Sheets: 92 C/16 Cowichan Lake, 92 F/1 Nanaimo Lakes, 92 F/2 Alberni Inlet, 92 F/3 Effingham River, 92 F/6 Great Central Lake, 92 F/7 Horne Lake, 92 F/11 Forbidden Plateau.

Access: Access is becoming increasingly difficult to many of the mountain areas in this region of the Island. Particularly those areas to the east side of the southern and central Island where most if not all the alpine terrain is privately owned by large forestry companies. Before planning a trip into any of these areas make some inquiries to ensure access may be granted to avoid disappointment on departure day.

The peaks to the west of Port Alberni are located on Crown Land with fewer of the locked gates prevalent on the private holdings. As with all mountain areas in winter access is ultimately determined by snow levels and logging activity both of which may limit the proximity to which you may be able to drive. Access into the southern and central Island mountains is from logging road mainlines branching off the two major highways serving this part of Vancouver Island along with the Valley Connector.

Highway 4: Highway 4 crosses Vancouver Island east to west from a junction on the Inland Island Highway 19 near Qualicum Beach through Port Alberni and from there out to Tofino and Pacific Rim National Park. This is a very busy highway which varies widely from a 4-lane freeway to a twisting, winding mountain road. In winter expect snow at Alberni Summit and Sutton Pass and be prepared for snow to cover the road anywhere.

Highway 19: The main highway from Nanaimo all the way up the east side of Vancouver Island to Port Hardy. Through the southern and central Island Highway 19 takes too routes the old Island Highway now the Oceanside route 19A follows the scenic coastal route and the Inland Island Highway 19 takes a faster more direct line and is more useful for reaching alpine areas in the Beaufort Range with spurs into the Cowichan Valley, Nanaimo Lakes and Englishman River.

Valley Connector: The Valley Connector is a useful gravel road linking Port Alberni to the Comox Valley accessing the Beaufort Range and eastern Strathcona Park but high levels of logging acitivity often result in restrictions on the road and some advance planning is best before heading out.

Cabins: As with most of Vancouver Island there are few backcountry cabins in the southern and central Island. Those that are out there are operated by clubs for members and their closure should be respected.

Additional Info: Island Alpine, Hiking Trails II www.islandhikes.com

San Juan Ridge

San Juan Ridge - Kludahk Trail

The San Juan Ridge is the divide between the San Juan River which runs westward to its outlet at Port Renfrew, and the west coast. The Kludahk Trail runs approximately 37 km on the height of land of the ridge and is something of a South Island enigma, rumours of its existence circulate in internet bulletin boards and coveted maps are passed around discreetly. The lure of a significant semi-wilderness hiking and skiing route so close to Victoria certainly warrants discretion if it is to avoid being overrun by Gore-Tex™ clad hordes.

There are no less than five cabins along the route which adds to the intrigue but access to the huts is restricted to members of the Kludahk Club. Judging by some of the online discussions I read researching this route sentiments run high surrounding the Kludahk Trail and to maintain goodwill the integrity of both cabins and trail should be treated with the greatest of respect to avoid any conflict. The cabins are mapped below purely for reference. Consider joining the club and pitching in on trail maintenance days, that seems to be the main beef: lack of help.

The terrain is sub-alpine forest dotted with lakes and meadows and there are some excellent views through the trees of the west coast. In winter San Juan Ridge may have sufficient snow cover for an enjoyable snowshoe or ski tour but coverage can be sporadic and the possibility of rain if it precipitates, is very real. The gentle terrain makes this an ideal destination for novices with little if any objective hazard.

Highest Point: 1065m

Difficulty/Duration: Day trips A1-B2 / 1-4 days

Map Sheets: 92 C/9 Port Renfrew

Access: Access is difficult apparently due to the ever prevalent locked logging road gates and this could be compounded in a heavy snow winter as many of the roads that reach the trailheads will be unplowed. There are a few descriptions to reach the trailheads available but careful scrutiny of logging road maps yield the following suggestions.

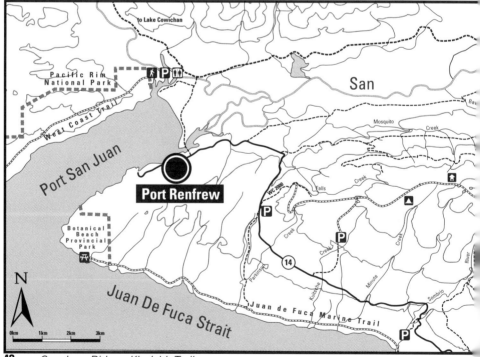

Walker Lake Trailhead: To reach the east end trailhead at Walker Lake you may want to try Jordan River Main which leaves Highway 14 2.5 km west of Jordan River. JR Main heads north-east to Diversion Reservoir and at the lake makes a sharp turn westward. The road is gated at the outlet of Wye Creek and through the gate the road crosses the creek and JR 100 winds up toward Wye Lake and comes within a 100m of the Kludakh trail at the north end of Wye Lake.

It's a much longer drive but an alternative is to head west on the Old Port Renfrew Road from Shawnigan Lake as far as the South San Juan Main which is on the left (south). Wind through two sharp curves in the road to a junction with Jordan Main and Williams Main. Go right on Williams Main and follow it to the trailhead.

Parkinson Creek Trailhead: The west end of the Kludahk Trail is easier to locate off WC2000 which leaves Highway 14 to the right (north) at Parkinson Creek Provincial Park. With Highway 14 paralleling the ridge a two vehicle shuttle or hitch back to the car makes for straightforward logistics coming in and out on the highway (south) side of the route.

Other options: As the map below illustrates their are a number of other logging roads in the many valleys dropping off the ridge and some have established trails/routes that join the Kludahk Trail.

Route Description: Given that you are able to reach the trail in winter and snow coverage is adequate for travel on skis or snowshoes etc... expect a 37 km ski (or hike) through sub-alpine forest and meadows along the meandering ridge top. Some care may be needed with route finding in poor visibility as the gentle indistinct terrain and wandering line of the ridge crest makes it easy to take a wrong turn especially with the beaten path hidden by the snow. Possible camp sites and water sources would be expected to be numerous in such terrain but particular care should be exercised to keep water sources clean and free from contamination. In spite of the misgivings from some quarters this area has the potential to become well used and careful management could help mitigate negative impacts of any increase in visitors.

Additional Info: www.clubtread.org/kludahk.htm

Kludahk Outdoors Club by snail mail: 2037 Kaltasin Road, Sooke, B.C. V0S 1N0

Adjacent Areas of Interest: Juan de Fuca Marine Trail, West Coast Trail

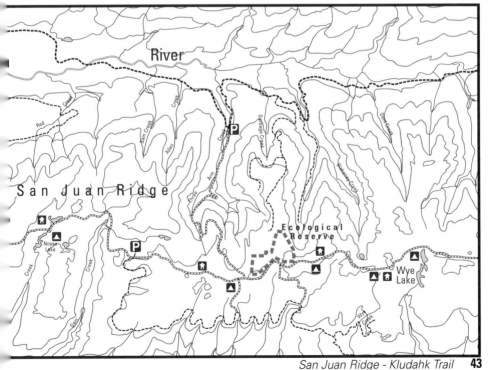

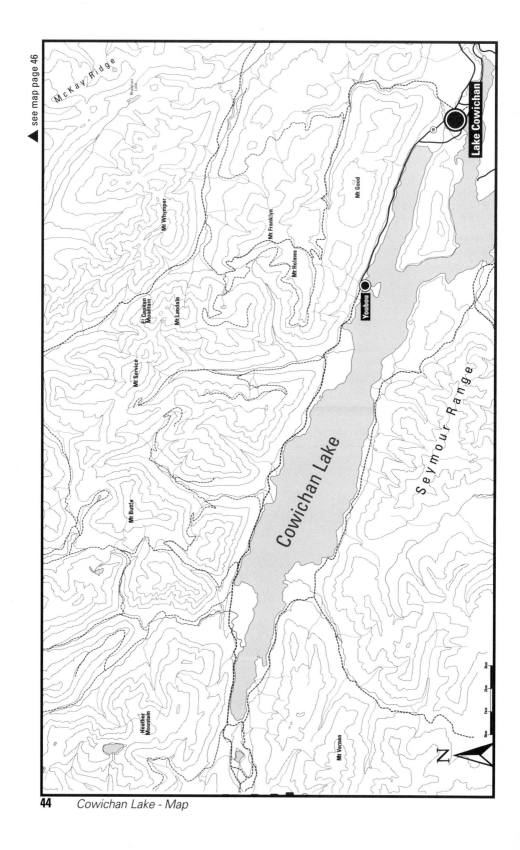

McKay Ridge

Rinehart Lake

Mt Whymper

El Capitan Mountain

Mt Landale

Mt Franklyn

Mt Holmes

Mt Good

Lake Cowichan

Youbou

Mt Service

Mt Buttle

Seymour Range

Cowichan Lake

Heather Mountain

Mt Vernon

N

0km   1km   25m   30m

Cowichan Lake

Snowshoeing on to the summit of Heather Mountain.   photo: Chris Shepard

Cowichan Lake

The mountain group above the north shore of Cowichan Lake is the southernmost area of significant alpine on Vancouver Island and it has long been a favorite destination for south islanders' day trips and weekend overnighters. In recent years access has become increasingly difficult with locked gates barring the otherwise easy access from the network of logging roads that weave and wind all over this terrain.

The peaks of interest in the Cowichan Lake area include; Mt. Whymper, Mt. Landale, El Capitan Mountain, Mt. Service Mt. Buttle and Heather Mountain. All make good destinations on snowshoe and depending on snow coverage some good ski touring and descents may be found in the meadows and off the ridges.

Highest Point: Summit of Mt. Whymper 5,055 ft. / 1,541 m

Most Vertical Descent Possible: ~600m

Difficulty/Duration: B2 B3 / 1-2 days

Map Sheet: 92 C/16 Cowichan Lake

Access: The Cowichan Lake peaks can be reached from spur logging roads off North Shore Road which continues along the lake from Youbou. Cottonwood Main and Shaw Main are the main roads off North Shore with Chemainus River Road offering an alternative to the north-east side of the peaks.

Turns

Don't get too excited but look at terrain on either side of the El Capitan-Landale ridge and the clearcut on the south-west side of Mt. Service can be good if the snow is deep. The south east ridge of Mt. Whymper has some possible descent lines too.

Tours

The traverse from El Capitan to Mt. Landale is one recommended tour with some limited exposure that can be avoided off the ridge crest. Heather Mountain is one of the best southern Island touring destinations. Heather Mountain is a gentle alpine knoll at the west end of Cowichan Lake above the north shore. The approach is long if the gate is locked but the meadows and summit make it worth the extra 2-3 hour trek. Rolling meadows for skiing touring or snowshoeing with good views.

Additional Info: Island Alpine 1st Edition p. 51-56, www.islandhikes.com

Adjacent Areas of Interest: McKay Ridge (north of Reinhart Lake), Mt. Brenton

▲ see map page 50

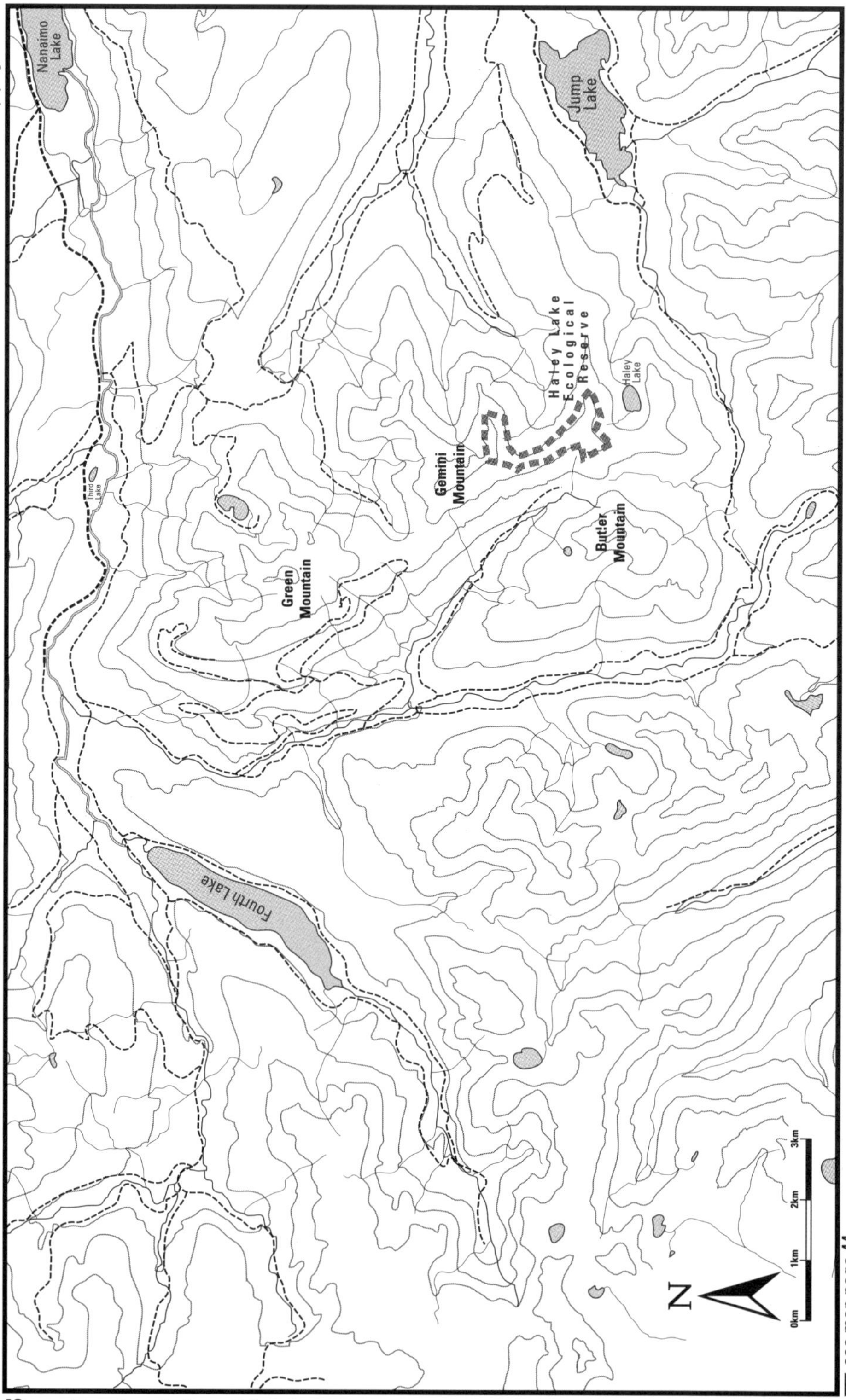

Nanaimo Lake
Jump Lake
Haley Lake Ecological Reserve
Haley Lake
Gemini Mountain
Butler Mountain
Third Lake
Green Mountain
Fourth Lake
N
0km
1km
2km
3km

▼ see map page 44

Nanaimo Lakes

Mt. Moriarty west aspect from Mt. McQuillan.   photo: Craig Wagnell

Nanaimo Lakes

At the headwaters of the Nanaimo River, Green Mountain used to be home to one of the Island's lift serviced ski hills serving the Greater Nanaimo community now, along with neighbouring Gemini Mountain, it still holds attractions for the skier and snowboarder. Access restrictions to the Nanaimo Lakes area and progressively lower snowfalls eventually forced the lifts to close down and now only a remnant of the facility remains including the original 4-storey A-frame which can still offer some shelter despite its state of decay. The mountain, surrounding meadows and old runs are still worth a visit for the views and the homage to Island ski history but access on the gated logging roads is difficult to negotiate and you may be better off spending at least one night out just to deal with the gate.

Green Mountain and the nearby Haley Lake Ecological Reserve are home to a small population of the celebrated and endangered Vancouver Island Marmot. This charming, diminutive mammal is the subject of elaborate recovery efforts with captive breeding programs at several locations across Canada operating with a vision of re-establishing a viable wild population. As the marmots hibernate through the winter the visiting skier is unlikely to disturb them. However, responsible backcountry travellers will become educated with protocol in this area to minimize any impact on the sensitive ecology of the area and the times of the year when disruption may have more impact than others. For more info log on to www.marmot.org

Highest Point: Summit of Green Mountain 4,806 ft. / 1,465 m

Most Vertical Descent Possible: ~300m

Difficulty/Duration: B1- B2 / 1-2 days

Map Sheet: 92 F/1 Nanaimo Lakes

Access: Like other areas along the east side of the Island the mountains found in the Nanaimo River valley are frought with access hassles from locked gates. To reach Green and Gemini mountains drive west from Nanaimo on the Nanaimo Lakes Road, take spur K-15 from Nanaimo Lakes Road which eventually splits into K-30 and another unnamed road. Take K-30 and follow it as close to the old ski area facility as snow levels determine.

Turns and Tours: It is about an hour hike from the old day lodge to the summit of Green Mountain. The old ski runs still offer some good terrain if snow cover is sufficient. Be sure to descend with enough time to make the 2:30 pm gate closure or be prepared to spend the night.

Additional Info: Island Alpine 1st Edition p. 60, www.islandhikes.com

Adjacent Areas of Interest: Tangle Mountain Meadows, Mt. Benson, Blackjack Ridge.

Skiers approaching Mt.Cokely up Rosseau Chute. *photo: Sasha Kubicek*

Arrowsmith-Moriarty

the Bumps

Looking across from Mt. Cokely along the Saddle Route to Mt. Arrowsmith.

Arrowsmith - Moriarty

The Arrowsmith-Moriarty divide runs in a straight line over 25 km from Mt. Arrowsmith south to Mt. Moriarty. The ridge divides the Cameron River valley on its west side from the Englishman and Nanaimo river valleys. Mt. Arrowsmith has had a torrid relationship with skiing and the history of the lift operation that occupied the flanks of Mt. Cokely is now part of Vancouver Island skiing lore. Within easy reach of Port Alberni, early development on Arrowsmith saw cross country trails and cabins established at the head of McBey Creek. A chairlift was eventually installed but the elevation of the chair proved to be too low and it never opened. The Arrowsmith Ski Club later installed two T-bars higher up on the north ridge of Mt. Cokely. A bustling little ski hill operated when the snow was good for a number of years. Eventually though fickle snow conditions and a string of warm rainy winters spelt the death knell for the Arrowsmith Ski Club's small but warm ski area. Vandalism and a fire in the day lodge sealed its fate and the hill subsequently ceased operations.

The legacy that remains is that along with all the attractions of the greater Arrowsmith massif are a maze of ski runs and trails that from time to time are in great condition and easy to reach.

Highest Point: Summit of Mt. Arrowsmith 5,962 ft. / 1,817 m

Most Vertical Descent Possible: ~400m

Difficulty/Duration: B2-C3 / 1-3 days

Map Sheets: 92 F./2 Alberni Inlet, 92 F/1 Nanaimo Lakes

Mt Cokely north-east aspect from CPR (Cameron Lake) trail.   *photo: Jeni Christie*

see map page 62-63

see map page 54

Cameron Lake

0km   1km   2km   3km

N

McBey Creek

Lockwood Creek

Arrowsmith Regional Park

Whisky C.

Mt. Cokely

Mt. Arrowsmith

Fishtail Lake

Habb Lake

Arrowsmith Lake

McLaughlin Ridge

Cameron River

Englishman River

Rumbot Lake

Peak Lake

McKinley Peak

Minnas Ridge

Sunny's Spring

Mt. Moriarty

Labour Day Lake

Knight Lake

Moriarty Lake

• 1369

Tangle Mountain

see map page 46

Looking south from Mt. Cokely over Stegosaurus Ridge & the Dome to Mt. Moriarty (L), January.

Access: As with access to all the mountain areas along Vancouver Island's east coast that fall within the Esquimalt-Nanaimo Railway Grant and then subsequently fell into private forestry company hands, access to the Arrowsmith-Moiarty divide is at the whim of the landowners. Negotiating locked gates on logging roads is par for the course in reaching this area. The one notable exception is the historic CPR trail from Highway 4 at Cameron Lake up to Mt. Cokely. Luckily the terrain on the massif is of sufficient interest to warrant the access hassles and spending at least a weekend exploring the ridges and lakes.

To reach Mt. Cokely and Mt. Arrowsmith by the original CPR Trail start at the trailhead at the east end of Cameron Lake on Highway. 4. The well graded trail gently switch backs up the north slopes of Mt. Cokely. About a third of the way up the trail divides with the left fork (Lookout Trail) and the right fork (CPR Trail) and join together again in the Regional Ski Park providing about a five hour loop hike or an all day round trip to Mt. Cokely.

Most skiers now prefer to utilize the high logging roads in the Cameron River valley but access to these roads is restricted from time to time. From the well sign posted junction on the south side of Highway 4 just west of the Alberni Summit turn south onto a gravel road and continue to a prominent junction on the far side of a bridge. Turn left and drive up the valley, cross back over the Cameron River and then take the left fork, up a steep road, under the west side of Arrowsmith on to Pass Main. From here the Judge's Route and other routes on the west side can be reached or continue higher, through switch backs, to a hair pin turn where a second access point leads up a narrow valley to the col between Mt. Cokely and Arrowsmith on the "Saddle Route". Further up the road, if the gate is open, continue to the ski area and ascend Mt. Cokely from the runs which run right up its ridge.

Access to Mt. Moriarty at the south end of the divide is also dependent on logging road openings and negotiating access through the gated roads in the Nanaimo and Englishman Rivers. From the Nanaimo Lakes Road spurs in both the Rush and Rockyrun creek valleys offer routes on to the south-east side of Moriarty. Out of the Englishman River Main take the spur in to Moriarty Creek or Marshall Creek and gain the ridge north of Mt. Moriarty via Scotty's Pond. For the purposes of a winter visit it may be more productive to approach the west flanks of Mt. Moriarty from the Cameron River valley via Labour Day Lake which can be a good tour destination itself.

Mt. Arrowsmith and Mt. Cokely east aspect from Georgia Strait.

Rudy Brugger and Brook George about to descend Cokely. photo: Doug Hurrell

Turns

The Arrowsmith massif has some of the best and most easily accessed backcountry ski touring and descent terrain on Vancouver Island (the vagaries of getting through the gates notwithstanding!). The old ski runs on Mt. Cokely are an obvious attraction and in particular the 'out-of-bounds' terrain on the north side of the ridge down toward the ski hill road and the Lockwood Creek bowl on the north-east aspect of Cokely.

Higher up on Mt. Arrowsmith there is more commiting terrain off both sides of the mountain down to the Cameron River side and down to the lake country on the east side of the peak.

Tours

The most popular tour options on the Arrowsmith-Moriarty massif are from the old ski area at Mt. Cokely. Cokely itself is a good day tour with the additional attractions of good descents and climbing higher onto Mt. Arrowsmith. The lakes on the north-east side of Arrowsmith at the head of the Englishman River hold some of the more dramatic touring terrain although access from Englishman River is a hassle.

The terrain between Arrowsmith and Moriarty including Judy's Meadows is worth a look. Judy's Meadows can be reached from the Cameron side is off Pass Main and up the first spur (P10). Near it's end is a patch of first growth (deer winter range) that has a flagged route up through the steep forest.

Additional Info: Island Alpine 1st Edition p.71-78, www.islandhikes.com

Adjacent Areas of Interest: Scotty's Pond, Minna's Ridge, Labour Day Lake, St. Mary's Lakes and Tangle Mountain.

Mt. Moriarty east aspect from Highway 19.

Mt. Klitsa - Mt. Gibson

Mt. Klitsa Grand Gully.   photo: Peter Rothermel

Mt. Klitsa - Mt. Gibson

Klitsa and Gibson are part of a steep sided alpine plateau located on the south side of the west end of Sproat Lake along the Highway 4 route between Port Alberni and Tofino. The proximity to the highway and the breadth of the lake-covered plateau are highlights of the Klitsa-Gibson massif.

Highest Point: Summit of Mt. Klitsa 5,387 ft. / 1,642 m

Most Vertical Descent Possible: ~450m

Difficulty/Duration: B2 / 1-3 days

Map Sheets: 92 F/6 Great Central Lake (see also 92 F/3 Effingham River)

Access: Follow Highway 4 from Port Alberni west along the north shore of Sproat Lake. Just west of the Taylor River rest area take a left off the highway onto the South Taylor Main logging road. Take spur road 552E right to the Gibson-Klitsa trailhead.

Mt. Klitsa can also be reached from the Brigade Lake Trail which starts from an upper logging road above a major logging road intersection just off Highway 4 near South Sutton Creek. From Brigade Lake make your way to the north end of Richards Lake (lake furthest south), and then up the west ridge of Klitsa. There is also a route flagged from the Nahmint valley off Br 600 near the water survey tower.

Turns

The Grand Gully which drops off the summit ridge of Klitsa taking a direct line through the north bowl to join the trail up from Sproat Lake makes a good choice for a day trip descent objective. The top of the gully is pretty steep though and regular slides sweep down this gully, skiers have been caught in avalanches in here. The west face of Klitsa has some possible lines down to the Klitsa-Gibson plateau and easy routes to rejoin either the Brigade Lake Trail or the Mt. Klitsa Trail on the north-west ridge.

Tours

The Gibson-Klitsa plateau has great touring in open meadows and a maze of lakes and sub-alpine forest to explore. The area is worth at least a weekend trip. A fine circuit climbs up the gully to Mt. Gibson and down the Brigade Lake Trail route to the highway. For a more challenging tour check out the ridge that connects Klitsa to Adder Peak which might take 2-3 days to complete, see Mackenzie Range page 55 for more details.

Additional Info: Island Alpine 1st Edition p. 87-90, www.islandhikes.com

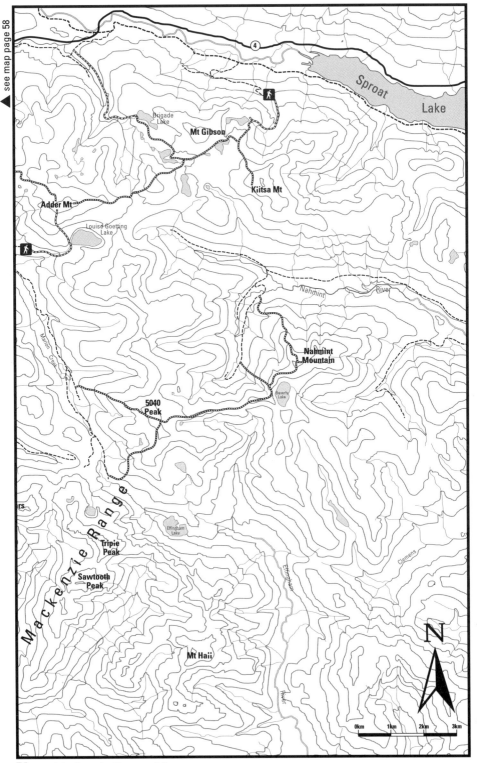

see map page 58

Sproat Lake

Brigade Lake

Mt Gibson

Kiitsa Mt

Adder Mt

Louise Goetting Lake

Marion Creek

Nahmint River

Nahmint Mountain

Beverly Lake

5040 Peak

Effingham Lake

Mackenzie Range

Tripie Peak

Sawtooth Peak

Effingham River

Clemens

Mt Haii

N

0km   1km   2km   3km

Mackenzie Range

Looking up Adder Peak's north ridge.   *photo: Craig Wagnell*

Mackenzie Range

The greater Mackenzie Range includes all the peaks east of the Kennedy River from Draw Mountain above Kennedy Lake to Mt. Klitsa at the west end of Sproat Lake. Many of the mountains are craggy peaks known for their superb alpine climbing routes but amongst them are several gentler summits with some sweet turns and tours. The good ski peaks include Mt. Klitsa-Gibson (detailed preceeding page), Adder Peak, 5040 Peak and Nahmint Mountain. This area is noted for its close highway access and the stunning views of Kennedy Lake and the Pacific Rim.

Highest Point: Summit of Nahmint Mountain 5,144 ft / 1,568 m

Most Vertical Descent Possible: ~300m

Difficulty/Duration: B2-C3 / 1-3 days

Map Sheets: 92 F/3 Effingham River

Access: Adder Peak can be reached from logging roads in Marion Creek which leaves Highway 4 8km west of Sutton Pass. Hike up branch MC 30 which switchbacks up the west flank of the mountain. Take a long snow gully (the Adder's Tongue) to the ridge north of the summit. An alternative approach may be made from the south-east in the Nahmint valley by following spur road N-800 to the very end, or directly from logging roads above Sutton Pass.

The Louise Geotting Lake Trail is another good way to access Adder Peak. Follow Marion Creek Main to MC40. Follow MC40 to upper left clearcut near a creek. Head up cut looking for flagging tape marking trail. Trail follows south side of creek to lake. Cut down to west side of lake crossing start of creek and then up slopes, staying left of rock bluffs to the east. Ski directly to the summit.

5040 Peak can also be reached from Marion Creek. From ~10 km along Marion Creek Main park at the foot of the broad north-west ridge of the mountain between the two bridges. Walk up the deactivated road, Marion 80, for about 50m before heading up into the timber. Follow a rough flagged route through a band of cliffs just below treeline. Continue on easy terrain along the ridge directly to the summit.

Mt. Hall (far L) and 5040 Peak north aspect.   *photo: Craig Wagnell*

Triple Peak   Cat's Ears Peak

Looking down north-west face of 5040 Peak, Cat's Ears behind, March.   photo: Jeni Christie

A fast route to 5040 takes the south ridge from Effingham Creek. Follow the road up to the very end. Hike into the timber up the steep bushy south ridge to the alpine. Head around the rock buttress on the south side and head up to the col. Left takes you to the summit of 5040 , and straight takes you down towards the high alpine ridge that leads towards Nahmint Mountain and Beverly Lake.

Turns

It is the gentler topography of Adder Peak and 5040 Peak that offer the best of the descent terrain in the Mackenzie Range. The north and east ridges of Adder give 400 m of descent on open mellow terrain. More committing lines may be found dropping deep into the cirque on Adder's north-east aspect. Adder Peak's proximity to Highway 4 makes it a particularly good day trip destination.

5040 Peak takes some extra luck to get the full 10 km or so back along the Marion Creek logging road but if the cards fall right you'll be rewarded with some of the better descent terrain in the range. Look in particular for lines off the summit down the north-west cirque and also the south-west aspect of the mountain too.

Tours

There are a couple of suggested ski tour routes through the Mackenzie Range, One of the logistically least complicated is a 2-3 day through-trip from Mt. Klitsa to Adder Peak. The trip could be done in either direction and a vehicle shuttle or hitchiking back along Highway 4 required at the end. At the Mt. Klitsa end either the Brigade Lake trail or the Mt. Klitsa trail up the north-west ridge may be used to gain the sub-alpine plateau and lakes between Klitsa and Mt. Gibson. Both these peaks can be ascended on skis from the plateau with Mt. Klitsa offering a 500m descent back down its west flank. Head due west from the Klitsa-Gibson Plateau over a small knoll then ascend Adder Mountain up the east ridge. Descend either the Lousie Goetting Trail or the route up the west ridge.

The terrain between 5040 Peak and Nahmint Mountain is great touring country but as is often the case access logistics dictate the possible trip options. One possibility from the Nahmint River valley would be to ascend 5040 up the ridge to its north-east, or even from the Marion-Nahmint Pass just east of Louise Goetting Lake and over the two unnamed knolls between Adder Mountain and 5040. From 5040 descend the east ridge and continue east to Beverly Lake. Descend to the Nahmint valley either from Beverly Lake or from the route off the north side of Nahmint Mountain near the summit.

From Marion Creek consider a route up the Lousie Goetting Trail (side tripping up to Adder Mountain) and then from the Marion-Nahmint Pass head south over the unnamed knolls and on to the long winding north ridge of 5040 Peak. Ski up the north ridge to the summit of 5040 descending back to Marion Creek and hoof out the logging road to your vehicle at the Lousie Goetting trailhead.

Additional Info: Island Alpine 1st Edition p. 90-93, www.islandhikes.com

Maitland Range

Pogo Mountain east aspect from Adder Peak, May.   *photo: Craig Wagnell*

Maitland Range

The Maitland Range are the mountains on the west side of the Kenndey River valley including Mt. Maitland, Hidden Peak, Steamboat Peak and Pogo Mountain. The latter two are the most appealling for backcountry touring and riding.

Steamboat Peak lies in the middle of the Maitland Range in Clayoquot Plateau Provincial Park. It overlooks Kennedy River and Highway 4, which run along its east side, while to the west is the open sub-alpine terrain of the Clayoquot Plateau and the Clayoquot River valley beyond. Steamboat Peak and the surrounding alpine across the plateau offer some of the more expansive and readily accessible areas of alpine in the central Island. There is enough terrain to soak up a few days exploring on snowshoes or on skis. There are numerous sink holes and grikes in the limestone that makes up this area so caution should be exercised travelling around Steamboat Peak when snow disguises these hazards.

Pogo Mountain is a familiar landmark from Highway 4 clearly visible overlooking the Kennedy River valley from just west of Sutton Pass. It was previously, unelegantly known as 'Tit Mountain'. The best of the Maitland Range ski terrain is found on Pogo.

Highest Point: Summit Pogo Mountain 4,888 ft / 1,490 m

Most Vertical Descent Possible: ~400m

Difficulty/Duration: B2-C3 / 1-3 days

Map Sheets: 92 F/3 Effingham River

Access: To approach Steamboat Peak leave Highway 4, 1.5 km west of Sutton Pass on the logging road that breaks off the highway westward just before Kennedy River joins the highway corridor. This road follows the upper Kennedy River. Leave it after only .8 km, turning left on BR 560. Drive south on BR 560 cross the bridge over Kennedy River to just before a bridge over an unnamed creek draining the north side of Steamboat Peak. Turn right onto this road to locate Quagger's 'Cavers' Trail at the end.

To reach Pogo Mountain, park at the bridge over Kennedy River and continue on foot for a total of 2 km. Locate a spur road, which may help gaining some elevation on Pogo Mountain's east flank. Hike up the forested hillside east of the summit to the top. Great on the snow.

Alternatively, Pogo Mountain can be climbed by its elegant north ridge. Follow Upper Kennedy River logging road (513) across the bridge over Kennedy River. Park about 100m farther in small pullout on right. Head south through short clearcut and then old-growth to alpine. Follow the open north ridge to reach the summit.

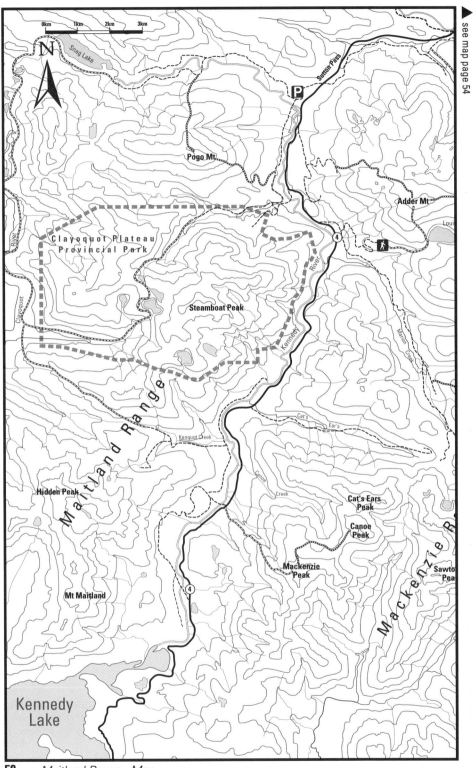

N

0km 1km 2km 3km

Snag Lake

P

Sutton Pass

Pogo Mt.

Adder Mt

Loui

4

Clayoquot Plateau
Provincial Park

River

Clayoquot

Kennedy River

Steamboat Peak

Maitland Range

Kenquot Creek

Cat's

Ear's

Canoe Creek

Hidden Peak

Cat's Ears Peak

Canoe Peak

Mackenzie Peak

Sawto Pea

Marion Creek

Mackenzie R

Mt Maitland

4

Kennedy
Lake

Looking east from summit of Steamboat Peak.   photo: Craig Wagnell

Turns

The Maitland Range has some good descent terrain. A few short lines might be found on Steamboat Peak but there are cliffs to watch for and the ubiquitous sink holes to avoid. Best of all is the elegant north ridge of Pogo Peak with at least a 400m run and more if snow conditions are good. Look for the long gully off the east side of the North Ridge (see right side of photo on page 57). The large basin on the north aspect of Hidden Peak offers some great terrain and is reached fairly easily off the Kenquot Main.

Tours

Any travel around Steamboat Peak and the Maitland Range as a whole comes with the caveat that care should be exercised regarding the sink holes, caves and grikes that cleave the surface of the terrain in this area. Beyond that warning however there is some incredible country to explore particularly in the meadows and knolls around Steamboat Peak and the Clayouquot Plateau Provincial Park.

Steamboat Peak is an obvious touring destination and from a camp at the lakes below its north-west face the peak and the surrounding plateau is readily explored on skis. To reach Steamboat Peak start up Quagger's Cavers' trail onto the high open summits north-west of Steamboat Peak. Head south-east to a col ("the lake district") below Steamboat then take the open ridge above the north side of the lakes over Peak 1113 and on to the ridge just north of the summit. From the col the unnamed peaks to the north-west are easily reached through open meadows and sub-alpine forest.

A traverse over Steamboat Peak may also be completed using the access from the south off the Kenquot Main logging road. Ski up the south ridge to the summit to connect the route from the north.

With good snow cover the Clayoquot Witness Trail from the upper Kennedy River through to Kenquot Creek might make a good snowshoe trip but the rugged forested terrain is unlikely to be a good experience on skis.

Pogo Mountain is a good winter destination but mostly as a day trip for the descent possibilities as there is little surrounding high terrain. Either of routes up the north or east ridge are suitable for snowshoes and skis for the vertically inclined. A traverse up and over the peak using both routes might work well if you can handle the link on the roads below. The north ridge is by far the better descent line.

Additional Info: Island Alpine 1st Edition p. 102-105, www.islandhikes.com

Mt. Maitland (L) & Hidden Peak (R) north-east aspect, June   photo: Craig Wagnell

Backcountry skiing is for all ages!!!   *photo: Bob Schroeder*

Beaufort Range

Caroline Bradfield with 'Suzi' and 'Frank' skiing off Mt Apps.   photo: Robin Sutmoller

Beaufort Range

The Beauforts are a 25km long ridgeline of sub-alpine and alpine terrain running parallel to the east coast of Vancouver Island between Port Alberni and Cumberland. From the ridge-tops there are stunning views of the Georgia Strait, Coast Mountains, Denman & Hornby Islands and the peaks of Strathcona Park. The mountains have a gentle character and travel along the Beaufort Range is generally straightforward with little objective hazard.

A complete traverse of the Beauforts may be undertaken in either direction and there are several shorter day trip options taking in some good touring terrain. There are a few notable descents on the Beauforts but none greater than about 200m (600ft.). The low elevation of the Beaufort Range makes it a place to avoid if warm temperatures and precipitation is forecast.

The whole range is essentially private land held by forestry companies who regulate access with locked gates. Negotiating these gates is a notorious hassle but once through the extensive network of logging roads provides excellent access to points all along the range.

The Beaufort Range is named for Sir Francis Beaufort a hydrographer with the British Royal Navy in the mid-1800s. The Beaufort Range is separated to the west by a fault line. This fault shifted more than 2 metres during the 1946 earthquake.

Highest Point: Summit of Mt. Joan 5,108 ft / 1,557 m

Most Vertical Descent Possible: ~200m

Difficulty/Duration: Day trips B1, Beaufort Traverse B2 / 3-5 days

Map Sheets: 92 F/11 Forbidden Plateau, 92 F/6 Great Central Lake, 92 F/7 Horne Lake

Access: Roads surround the Beaufort Range: the Inland Island Highway 19 parallels the range on its east side between Horne Lake and Cumberland while the Comox Lake Main a.k.a. 'the Valley Connector' and associated spurs offer access along its west flank between Comox Lake and Port Alberni although access to these private logging roads are often restricted and negotiating an opening should be factored in if planning to enter the range from the west.

Mt. Chief Frank: To reach Mt. Chief Frank: take Buckley Bay Main logging road which heads west from the Buckley Bay (Denman-Hornby Island ferry) junction on the Inland Island Highway 19. Access

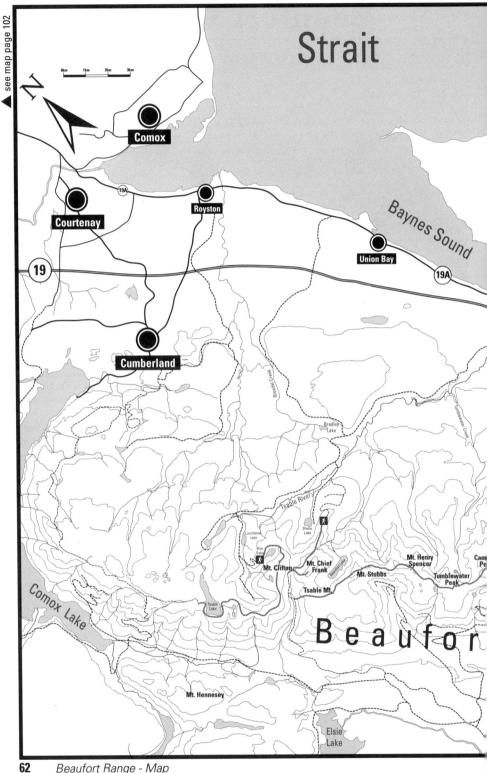

Strait

0km   1km   2km   3km

N

Comox

19A

Royston

Baynes Sound

Courtenay

19

Union Bay

19A

Cumberland

Blondel Creek

Tumblewater Creek

Bradley
Lake

Tsable River

Shela
Lake

Lunchtime
Lake

Kim
Lake

Barclay Lake

Mt. Clifton

Mt. Chief
Frank

Mt. Henry
Spencer

Cam
Pe

Mt. Stubbs

Tumblewater
Peak

Tsable Mt.

Comox Lake

Tsable
Lake

B e a u f o r

Mt. Hennesey

Elsie
Lake

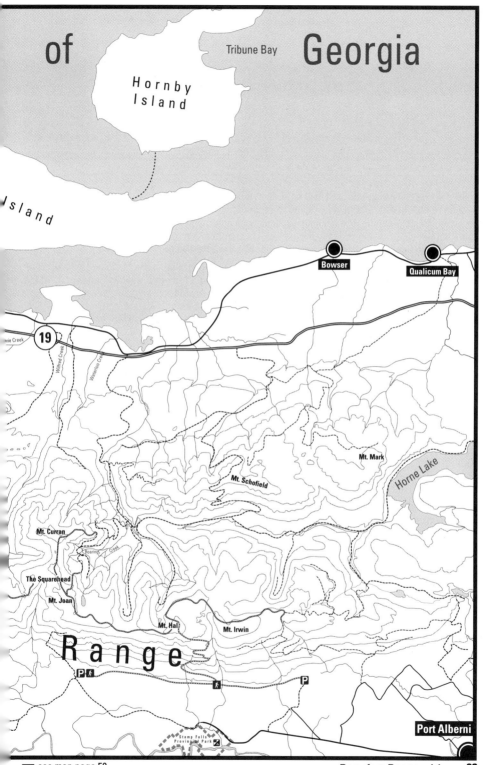

of

Tribune Bay

Georgia

Hornby
Island

Island

Bowser

Qualicum Bay

Dowie Creek

19

Wilfred Creek

Waterloo Creek

Mt. Mark

Mt. Schofield

Horne Lake

Mt. Curran

Roaring Creek

The Squarehead

Mt. Joan

Mt. Hal

Mt. Irwin

Range

Stamp Falls
Provincial Park

Port Alberni

▼ see map page 50

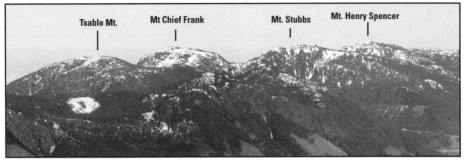

Beaufort Range, north-west aspect from Aureloe Snowfield, Strathcona, May.

to Buckley Bay Main is restricted by a gate. On weekends the key for the gate is available from Ken Keenan 250-335-2328. Special permission is required for overnight use. Only one party is allowed the key at a time, so planning and booking ahead is recommended. On weekdays the gate is generally open, but the public is theoretically prohibited. Use caution and respect as always when travelling on private land and be careful of logging traffic who always have the right of way.

With the gate as km 0 follow these directions: at 0.7 km keep straight, pass BB25 on L and BB33 on the right. At 3.1km the Buckley Bay Main diverges to the right from the 'Holiday Connector' which is the fork to the left. 12.25 km from the gate take Sheila Lake Main to your left and drive over the bridge across Tsable River. Take 2nd spur on left from Tsable River bridge and drive a further 3km to to the trailhead, a 4-wheel drive vehicle is highly recommended to get all the way up.

Mt. Apps: Like Mt. Chief Frank and the peaks around Beaufort Lake Mt. Apps may also be reached off the Inland Island Highway 19 at the Buckley Bay (Denman-Hornby Island ferry) junction. From the gate on the Buckley Bay Main (km 0) drive east to the junction at 3.1 km only here take the left fork onto the 'Holiday Connector'. At 3.5 km the Holiday Connector crosses the Tsable River, head straight through the 4-way intersection on the other side of the bridge. Pass spur HR28 keeping left at 6.2 km on the 'connector to Jacob Main Line'. Watch for and avoid these spurs HR33 on the right, HR40 on the right, HR49 on the left, and at 10.2 km avoid the spur to the right. At 10.9 km pass a major spur which drops to the left keeping right on the 'Holiday Hookup'. Take the middle fork at 11.3 km curving rightward uphill through a recent cutblock. Park at the trailhead at 16.5 km which is about 45 min. from the Buckley Bay Main gate. Park at the pullout on the left side of the road.

Mt Apps may also be reached from Port Alberni via logging roads in Wolf Creek on the west side of the Beaufort Range. From Port Alberni head north on Beaver Creek Road. This road parallels the Beauforts along the valley floor eventually becoming Toma Main which continues northward to Comox Lake and forms a major portion of the 'Valley Connector' a.k.a. 'the Valley Link Highway. Leave the Valley Connector before the bridge over Laternman Creek turning right through a gate onto BR112. Just 1 km past the gate turn left onto BR113 and follow this road way up the hillside to the Mt. Apps trailhead. It is a short haul up to the summit of Mt. Apps.

Looking up Mt. Stubbs' north ridge from Tsable Mountain. photo: Craig Wagnell

Turns

Flanking the sides of the main Beaufort Range ridge system are several bowls on the higher points that offer some short but decent descent terrain making it well worth a day trip or stripping off the skins once in a while while undertaking a tour on the Beauforts for an afternoon of spring corn snow. Look in particular for lines at the north end of the range between Mt. Chief Frank and Mt. Stubbs and in the centre of the range around Mt. Apps.

Mt. Apps' wide open north bowl is an attractive ski feature overlooking Denman Island. There's 200m of vertical from a number of points along the ridge north of the summit.

From the rounded summit of Mt. Chief Frank there is easy access to Tsable Mt. and Mt. Stubbs, with a fair amount of ski terrain dropping off the ridge system in a variety of aspects. Look for some commiting lines down to Beaufort Lake up to 260m.

Nice looking lines in the north bowl. Mt Joan appears to have a nice run down its north face for about 250 m. Elsewhere along the ridge there are numerous short descents either on the ridge crest or in small bowls to either side.

At the south end of the range on Mt. Hal there are some short but worthwhile descent lines down the east ridge and into the bowls on the east aspect of the peak. Reach this side of Hal from logging road spurs off the Cook Creek/Horne Lake Forest Service Road.

Beaufort Range, north-west aspect from Aureloe Snowfield, Strathcona, May.

Caroline Bradfield - all smiles after a run down Mt. Apps   *photo: Robin Sutmoller*

Mt. Apps north bowl   *photo: Craig Wagnell*

Tours

The touring terrain on the Beauforts is the great attraction of the range. Little objective hazard, rolling alpine and sub-alpine terrain, easy camping and good road access (if you can get through the gates) are all reasons to visit the Beaufort Range. There are several good horseshoe day tours from a single vehicle approach and longer overnight trips are possible taking in different sections or all the main Beaufort Range ridgeline.

Of the good day tours count in: Mt. Chief Frank from the Comox District Mountaineering Club (C.D.M.C.) trail, a circuit on the height of land around Beaufort Lake ascending Mt. Chief Frank to its summit and then following the main Beaufort ridge south over Tsable Mt. and then east to Mt. Stubbs, descending the north-east ridge off Mt. Stubbs to the Mt. Chief Frank trailhead (see photo below).

The C.D.M.C. trailhead is at on the north-east spur of Mt. Chief Frank on the north side of Beaufort Creek. The flagged route heads up through old growth timber along the ridge crest to a point just below a band of cliffs from here two options are possible to gain the higher terrain on the mountain:

Looking over Beaufort Lake from Mt. Stubbs to Tsable Mt. (L)   *photo: Craig Wagnell*

Looking south from Mt. Apps across Apps south basin and on to Mt. Joan   photo: Craig Wagnell

A) Traverse right along a system of benches, contouring through two north facing bowls which are separated by the north spur and gain the north north-west ridge (which connects Mt. Chief Frank to Mt. Clifton on the main Beaufort ridge). Follow this ridge south-eastward trending east near the top to the summit.

B) Traverse leftwards (south) around the head of the north fork of Beaufort Creek with some exposure and gain the easy slopes on the south-west side of Mt. Chief Frank and head north-westward to the summit.

Mt. Apps is another of the good day tour destinations. From the parking spot mentioned in the access details for Mt. Apps hike or ski up rough spur on the right to as high as you can. A flagged route goes up the bushy south-east aspect of ridge. The best winter/spring route heads up the north-east snow-covered aspect. Gain northern spur of north-east ridge of Mt Apps through open old-growth following flagged route on ramps on the south-east aspect. From GR 589804 the route along the ridge is obvious.

Looking north from Mt. Apps   photo: Craig Wagnell

Mt. Joan summit and north bowl   *photo: Craig Wagnell*

For an overnight tour there are two main areas to consider along with the third option of traversing the entire range. At the north (Cumberland) end the area between Mt. Clifton and Mt. Henry Spencer is worth 1-2 nights, while at the south end closer to Port Alberni short traverses from Mt. Apps to Mt. Joan from Wolf Creek logging roads and a horseshoe route around the Roaring Creek headwaters taking in Mt. Curran, Squarehead and Mt. Joan are among the better possibilities.

Both these areas can also be linked in a complete traverse down the length of the Beaufort Range. The best of this ridgeline is from Mt. Chief Frank to Mt. Apps but the whole range can also be crossed from Mt. Clifton to Mt. Hal. Theoretically in some winters it would be possible to ski right out of Cumberland following the road system up to Tsable Lake and from there along the height of land to descend the Mt. Hal trail down to Port Alberni. An estimated time for such a traverse would be 3-5 nights depending on prevailing conditions and the party.

Additional Info: Island Alpine 1st Edition p.114-123, Hiking Trails III 9th Edition, www.islandhikes.com

Looking south from Elk Pass toward toward the Golden Hinde and Mt. De Voe.

Strathcona Park

72 *Robin Sutmoller freeheeling off Rees Ridge down to Milla Lake.*

Strathcona Park

The Strathcona Park Elk Portal on Highway 28.

Strathcona Provincial Park

Established: 1911

Size: 245,807 hectares

The spectacular landscape and sense of wilderness of Strathcona Park becomes transformed and enhanced during the winter months when a deep cloak of snow envelopes the land. The character of the mountains becomes more akin to peaks of much greater height and the remoteness of the park's backcountry is amplified by the increased challenges of access and travel. Quiet and solitude descend on the park and winter visitors to Strathcona are almost certainly guaranteed the place to themselves wherever they venture.

Those that are a match for the greater physical and mental challenges of winter backcountry travel are rewarded by a winter wonderland and the magical experiences it provides. The high, interconnecting ridge systems familiar to summertime hikers lend themselves well to travel by ski, splitboard or snowshoe. In fact apart from the heavier pack loads and rigors of living at sub-zero temperatures some might claim they prefer the fast travel over frozen lakes and the complete absence of any bush. And amongst all this are to be found sweeping ridgelines, deep-cut couliors and wide-open glaciers beckoning the skier and snowboader to float down their bottomless powder or carve across the firm spring corn snow.

The best time to plan a backcountry tour in Strathcona Park is between the months of December and early-June with seasonal variations in snowpack to be accounted for from year to year. May is a particularly good month to plan a longer tour as usually by mid-month the initial rush of spring thaw avalanches are over, many of the more hazardous cornices have dropped and the snowpack is consolidated yet still at or near complete coverage, and most lakes are still frozen. The days are longer and warmer by May, lightening packs and offering fast travel and allowing longer distances to be covered each day.

Highest Point: Summit of the Golden Hinde 7,218ft. / 2,200m

Most Vertical Descent Possible: 3,300ft / ~1,000m

Map Sheets: 92 F/11 Forbidden Plateau, 92 F/12 Buttle Lake, 92 F/13 Upper Campbell Lake, 92 F/6 Great Central Lake, 92 F/5 Bedwell River.

Cabins: Divers or Rossiter, Moat Lake, Sid's Cabin, Beadnell Lake

Major Access Routes: Strathcona Park is well serviced by paved highway access while retaining a great deal of wilderness land in its core. Along the east coast of the Island the Oceanside Island Highway 19A and the Inland Island Highway 19 provide the main links between the communities of Cumberland, Courtenay and Campbell River on the east side of the park. The following highways and logging road mainlines branch off to the west giving access into the mountains.

Highway 4: To the south of the park Highway 4 runs west from Parksville on the Island Highway 19 through Port Alberni on to the Pacific Rim National Park and the communities of Ucluelet and Tofino. Highway 4 by way of gravel logging roads which branch off it gives access to Great Central Lake, Oshinow Lake and the south boundary of Strathcona. From Tofino much of the south-west corner of Strathcona Park may be reached by boat or air.

Comox Lake Main: Is one of the main access roads from the Comox Valley into the east side of the Park. Comox Lake Main runs down the west shore of Comox Lake eventually linking up with logging roads from Port Alberni to make the 'Valley Connector'. The Glacier trail, Kookjai Mountain and routes out of the Cruickshank valley can all be reached from spurs off this main road. The road is private, has heavy logging traffic and is often timeconsuming to gain entry to.

Plateau Road: Provides access to the far east end of Forbidden Plateau near Mt. Becher. The road used to service the long running skihill at Wood Mountain, known as Forbidden Plateau Ski Area. The lifts no longer operate but the backcountry access is excellent. From Piercy Road north of Courtenay just east of the Piercy Road junction on Highway 19 head west up Plateau Road, follow the paved road to the base of the hill where gravel continues up to the parking lot and trailhead.

Strathcona Parkway: The Strathcona Parkway is a paved highway reached off junction 130 of the Inland Island Highway 19. The Parkway services the ski resort and growing village at Mt. Washington and provides unquestionably the best winter alpine access on the island: into Paradise Meadows, Mt. Albert Edward and a large part of eastern Strathcona Park.

Highway 28: The only paved road system to actually run through the park is Highway 28 which runs 90 km east to west between Campbell River and Gold River. This road provides access to the Elk River and Crest Mountain trails and other areas in northern and central Strathcona.

Buttle Lake Parkway: The Buttle Lake Parkway a.k.a. Western Mines Road is a long spur road that leaves Highway 28 45 km west of Campbell River and runs due south down the east shore of Buttle Lake. The Buttle Lake Parkway provides access to many trails and access routes into the park's centre and southern regions.

Menzies & Gold Mains: To reach the north boundary of Strathcona two unlinked logging road systems can be used. On the north-east corner the Menzies Main and Salmon Main branch off Highway 19 north of Campbell River at Menzies Bay. In the north-west corner of Strathcona Park, the East and West Main roads (which can be reached off Nimpkish Road which links Gold River and Woss) give access to Gold Lake and the mountains in the remote north-west part of the park.

Camping: Buttle Lake campground has vehicle accessible campsites. Campsite reservations are accepted and there are first-come, first-served sites. Driftwood Bay group site on Buttle Lake is serviced by disabled access toilets and covered picnic shelter. This site is available by reservation only. Ralph River also offers vehicle accessible campsites on a first-come, first-served basis - campsite no reservations accepted.

Backcountry users are permitted to camp 1 km from main roads or, at designated sites where established, such as: Bedwell Lake trail, Elk River trail, Della Falls trail and Forbidden Plateau area. Check notices at trailheads for site locations and any special cautions.

Strathcona Park Trails

Strathcona Park Trails

The trails of Strathcona Park are one of the greatest recreational assets in British Columbia and are enjoyed by thousands of day hikers, backpackers and mountaineers every summer. Most of the trails are the result of hard work by members of the Comox District Mountaineering Club, the Island Ramblers and other volunteer groups. In winter the trails provide a vital link from roadside to alpine that is in short supply when the snow covers the logging roads in other areas. Many of the best Island ski destinations and tours start using one of Strathcona's trails although it is important to note that none of the trails are marked for winter travel. The individual trails descriptions listed here are referred to in the detailed destination descriptions that follow throughout the chapter.

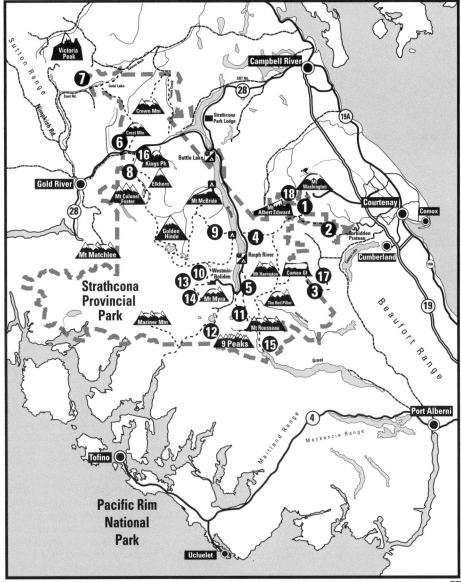

Philip Stone enjoying some spring hiking above Volcano Lake.

1- Paradise Meadows Trail: The Paradise Meadows Trail starts at Mt. Washington's Raven Lodge and winds through the forest and lakes of Paradise Meadows to gently climb onto Forbidden Plateau. The trail offers access to Forbidden Plateau, Mt. Albert Edward and points beyond including traverses to Augerpoint, Comox Glacier and Flower Ridge.

From the Raven Lodge follow the cross country trail route to Lake Helen Mackenzie. The trail follows the north and west shores around the lake and then makes a few short switchbacks into a forested sub-alpine pass between Mt. Brooks and Mt. Elma. Beyond the pass the forest thins into a maze of meadows, creeks, lakes and stands of hardy trees. There is a Park's Ranger cabin en route and a couple of other open cabins on the Plateau. There are designated campsites at Kwai and Circlet Lakes. Beyond Circlet Lake the terrain becomes more mountainous and the trail gives way to backcountry routes.

2- Becher Trail: The Becher Trail crosses Forbidden Plateau from the old Wood Mountain ski area to Paradise Meadows and Mt Washington. To reach the trailhead exit the Inland Island Highway at Piercy Road and turn west onto Plateau Road. Drive up to the parking lot at the old ski facility. Hike up the overgrown ski runs past the T-Bar line and to a point just north and below the top of the old Orange Chair. Locate the trail heading across the plateau to Mt. Becher, Mackenzie Meadows, Paradise Meadows and linking with trails from Mt. Washington. The terrain is very gentle and pretty with some great views off the high points. Mt. Becher is an easy day trip and a traverse across to Mt. Washington a steady weekend tour. Leads to Mt. Albert Edward and points beyond too.

3- Glacier Trail: The Comox Glacier Trail is a popular mountain trail offering an excellent hike to one of the west coast's most famous mountain landmarks. Drive west from Courtenay on Laketrail Rd. to Comox Lake and cross the causeway over the Puntledge River by the BC Hydro dam. Continue south on the Comox Main a.k.a. the Valley Connector around the west shore of the lake. Access to this road is often restricted by logging activity. 15 km south of the causeway cross a high bridge over the Cruickshank River and immediately turn right and down a steep grade on the Cruickshank Main. Follow the newly reopened road 3 km to a T junction. Turn left (south) and drive for 5.5 km to another junction where you make a righthand turn and drive a further 5 km to the trailhead.

From the trailhead the trail switchbacks up a steep forested hillside to a campsite at the 'Frog Ponds'. The trail continues along a narrow ridge that is exposed in a few places over Black Cat Mountain and on to Lone Tree Pass immediately below the Comox Glacier. From the pass a straightforward hike leads up to the glacier. In winter a preferable alternative is the route from Comox Gap over Kookjai Mountain to Lone Tree Pass.

4- Jack's (Augerpoint) Trail:
Jack's Trail is an unimproved trail that rises from the Buttle Lake Parkway, 19 km south of Buttle Narrows and 1km north of the Augerpoint Day use area. No signs mark the trailhead but for many years a large blue arrow has remained spraypainted on the asphalt on the Buttle Lake Parkway showing the start. The trail climbs up a steep forested hillside on gorgeous moss covered bluffs and open scree to the alpine north-west of Augerpoint Mountain. There are several superb viewpoints overlooking Buttle Lake and a small lake at 800m. Toward the treeline the route winds through several talus slopes, routefinding through these under snow cover needs a sharp eye. Jack's Trail is not a Park's sanctioned trail and takes a steeper line than would be normally expected on a Park's trail. The steep grade notwithstanding Jack's is an excellent trail providing access to some of the finest ski touring terrain in Strathcona Park.

5- Flower Ridge:
Flower Ridge is one of Strathcona's most popular trails. This trail is a Park's trail and rises up gentle switchbacks from Buttle Lake to the alpine on the Price Creek - Henshaw Creek divide. Park at the signposted trailhead 30 km south of Buttle Narrows on the Buttle Lake Parkway. Hike up the well maintained trail passing a good campsite halfway to the treeline right up the snout of the ridge. Continue on the unimproved route beyond along the height of land to the top of Central Crags. From here longer traverses may be made via Tzela Lake east to the Comox Glacier and north via Rees Ridge to Mt. Albert Edward, Paradise Meadows and Mt. Washington.

Flower Ridge is also part of one of the very best horseshoe routes on the Island around the Henshaw Creek valley and Shepherd Ridge.

6- Crest Mountain Trail:
The Crest Mountain Trail is a popular trail and an excellent dirtect route into the alpine. From the trailhead on Highway 28, 60 km west of Campbell River head down to the bridge across Drum Lakes and then up a long series of switchbacks past a creek crossing in the lower third and two openings in the forest, where trees were cut for snowpack measurements. In the upper third the trail routes takes a steep gully which is exited to hiker's left to more open ground. A steep direct route leads into the alpine at a small lake at the south end of the summit plateau. The Crest Mountain trail can be used to reach Idsardi Mountain and to begin a traverse around Idsardi Creek to Big Den Mountain.

7- Gold Lake Trail:
The Gold Lake Trail is a through route linking the Salmon and Gold rivers. The trail leads through the park in a forest of huge cedar trees past Eena Lake, open bogs and around the south shore of Gold Lake. It can be found at the east side along Menzies Main to Grisle Creek and from the west up East Main from Gold River.

8- Elk River Trail:
The Elk River Trail is the single most important route for alpine climbing access on Vancouver Island and is the start for the classic traverse from Elk River to Phillips Ridge. From Highway 28, 60 km west of Campbell River the Elk River Trail leads south up the Elk River valley providing access to Elkhorn, Mt. Colonel Foster, Rambler Peak, Elk Pass and from there on to the Golden Hinde and Phillips Ridge. The trail goes as far as Landslide Lake where in 1946 an earthquake triggered a huge landslide off the North Tower of Mt. Colonel Foster. The resulting wave as the debris swept down into the lake flushed old growth trees and scoured soil down to bedrock for several kilometres down the valley. The lake is backdropped by the imposing East Face of Mt. Colonel Foster forming one of the most impressive vistas on Vancouver Island.

Usual times from the trailhead, 10 km to Landslide Lake, are 2-6 hours. With winter snow cover expect the time to at least double. This is a high use area and overnight stays must be at the designated campsites at Butterwort Creek and the Gravel Flats. No camping is permitted at Landslide Lake and skiers should respect the rationale behind this regulation and avoid camping at Foster Lake too. To continue onto Elk Pass, locate the unimproved trail which branches off just 200m up the open rock slab from the bridge over Landslide Creek and follow it into the upper Elk valley.

9- Marble Meadows Trail: Reaching Marble Meadows from Buttle Lake Parkway requires a boat to cross Buttle Lake, from either the Augerpoint Day Area parking lot or the Karst Creek boat ramp to the north side of the outlet of Phillips Creek on the west shore of Buttle Lake. After securing your boat (keeping in mind that the level of Buttle Lake can vary widely even over just a few days) hike the well maintained trail up past a small swampy pond and steepening switchbacks above. As it passes through the treeline the trail takes an open rock slab alongside a creek that is best avoided in winter. Instead, keep to hiker's left (south) as ascending, finding a safe less exposed line between the thinning trees.

10- Phillips Ridge Trail: The Phillips Ridge trail leads up from the mine site in the Myra Creek valley to the alpine at Arnica Lake. To reach the trailhead leave Highway 28 at Buttle Narrows and drive down the Buttle Lake Parkway to the Myra Falls mine site. Continue right through the mine site to the signposted parking lot on the far (west) side. The trail begins a short way past the gate on the righthand side of a gravel road to the mine's hydro-electric powerhouse. Easy sweeping switchbacks wind up the hillside above the mine. The route passes a stunning waterfall near the bottom. Near Arnica Lake the terrain levels out and the trail winds up gently the last few hundred metres to the lake. From Arnica Lake routes continue out to the Golden Hinde, Elk River, Marble Meadows, and Mt. Phillips and the Phillips Ridge traverse.

11- Price Creek Trail: The Price Creek Trail is part of the historic route between Buttle Lake and Port Alberni. From the east side of the Thelwood Creek bridge, on the Buttle Lake Parkway, an old gravel logging and prospecting road heads south-east across the wide open lower Thelwood valley until narrowing into a trail and heading into the Price Creek valley. The trail continues along the east bank of the creek, often up on the slope ~50 m or so above the creek but occasionally dropping to follow the creek side. After 8 km the trail reaches a popular campsite and then crosses the creek. From here the trail continues up a steep hillside to eventually crosses Cream Creek and an open avalanche path under Mt. Septimus to the final pull up to Cream Lake. From the Price Creek crossing, a route leaves the trail and heads up in to the upper part of Price Creek, Green Lake and Price Pass below the dramatic north-east face of Mt. Rosseau. This trail is no longer maintained.

12- Bedwell Trail: The piece-de-resistance of Strathcona's trails. The Bedwell Trail is a highly engineered route from the Jim Mitchell Lake Road to Bedwell Lake. Suspension bridges, boardwalks and even steel stairs combine to provide some of the fastest alpine access in the park. From the west side of the Thelwood Creek bridge on Buttle Lake Parkway turn south onto the Jim Mitchell Lake Road. Drive for ~7 km to the clearly signposted trailhead and park. Follow the incredible trail up to Bedwell-Thelwood Pass and then on to the first campsite at Baby Bedwell Lake. In winter simply cross Baby Bedwell Lake to its outlet and follow the short creek down to Bedwell Lake.

One of the approaches to Mt. Tom Taylor leaves the trail route at the outlet of Baby Bedwell. The trail takes the south shore of Bedwell Lake to a second designated campsite. From here the route to Cream Lake, Big Interior Mountain and Mt. Septimus branches off, as well as the Friends of Strathcona's Oinimitis trail down the Bedwell valley to the west coast at Bedwell Sound. The Oinimitis trail is an essential return leg of a superb traverse over Mt. Tom Taylor and Mariner Mountain from Bedwell Lake as well as offering a route between Buttle Lake and Tofino.

13- Upper Myra Falls Trail: Provides access to both forks of the Myra Creek valley as well as to Mt. Thelwood, Bancroft Peak, Mt. Myra and even Phillips Ridge. Follow the Buttle Lake Parkway to its very end at the mine. Park at the lot at the west end of the mine site. Walk down the gravel powerhouse road past the Phillips Ridge trailhead and to the start of the Upper Myra Falls trail just before the bridge over Myra Creek to the powerhouse. A short 40 minute hike through huge old growth forest leads to a lookout above the spectacular waterfall on the north fork of Myra Creek. The route up the Myra Creek valley to Mt. Thelwood breaks off before the viewing platform. Drop through the forest to the creek and cross the north fork below the falls above its confluence with the main south fork. Gain the forested ridge crest between the creek forks and follow it into the alpine near Mt. Thelwood.

14- Mt. Myra Trail: Park at the lot at the west end of the mine. Walk down the gravel powerhouse road past the Phillips Ridge and Upper Myra Falls trailheads. Cross the bridge over Myra Creek to the powerhouse and locate the trailhead immediately on the other side of the bridge. The trail follows a steep cat road that Westmin used to construct the dam and penstock at Tennent Lake. The road is prone to erosion but recent work on the trail and alder clearing has improved it significantly.

Hike the trail up to the dam at Tennent Lake taking care when crossing East Tennent Creek by the little penstock valvehouse. The trail is basically a road and is hard to lose! From the dam, to reach Mt. Myra follow the route south-east to cross open meadows then climb up a steep gully to Sandbag Lake and onto the south-west ridge of Mt. Myra. Alternatively, to head toward Mt. Thelwood, head west straight across Tennent Lake or around the north shore to gain a short bushy gully which leads up to more open meadows and lakes near McNish Lake. This ridge continues westward to Mt. Thelwood.

15- Della Falls Trail:
The Della Falls trail is one of the few access routes into Strathcona Park along the southern park boundary. From Port Alberni continue on Highway 4 west toward Tofino. Just a few kilometres out of 'Port' head north on Great Central Lake Road to the Ark Resort. Parking and a launch for your boat are available at the resort. Boat transport may also be arranged at the resort up Great Central Lake to the trailhead. The trail starts at the west end of Great Central Lake and follows the course of Drinkwater Creek up the valley to the base of Della Falls, Canada's highest waterfall at over 450 metres. There are several good campsites along the trail and the combination of the falls, lake travel, rainforest and Island alpine all add to the atmosphere of this great hike.Routes depart off the Della Falls trail to Nine Peaks-Big Interior, straight up the valley to Cream Lake and up to Love Lake and Mt. Rosseau.

16- King's Peak Trail:
Leave Highway 28, 3 km west of Lady Falls, turning left (south) on to the Elk River Timber Co. Rd. Look for the signposted trail next to a bridge over the Elk River,1 km off the highway, and follow it up under the powerlines and into the forest where immediately it crosses a torrent of a creek on a Heathenic bridge. The trail winds up a steep forested slope to enter a flat bottomed hanging valley just below the treeline. The trail continues along the left side of the creek entering a steep walled creek canyon just past a fork in the creek. Take care on the trail as it makes an exposed traverse along the canyon's left wall and into the lower meadow.

In winter and spring, exposure to avalanches in the canyon may be avoided by taking a steep

gully up the right side of the hanging valley before the fork in the creek. From the top of the gully hike across a forested bench and into the meadow. From the lower meadow three route options lead up higher on the mountain.

17- Century Sam Lake Trail:
Branches off the Glacier trail to the exquisite Century Sam Lake under the steep cliffs and gullies of the Comox Glacier. A fine hike in its own right and also offers access to the direct routes right up on to the glacier.

18- Gem Lake Trail:
The C.D.M.C.'s Gem Lake trail starts near Norm Lake on the Oyster River Main north of Mt. Albert Edward. Access to the Oyster River logging roads is often restricted so after arranging access drive the road system, up to Norm Lake. Park and locate the trailhead on the south side of the creek. The trail follows the valley up to Gem Lake.

Additional Info: Hiking Trails III - Northern Vancouver Island & Strathcona Park - (9th ed. 2002 Richard K. Blier, ed.) VITIS

Island Alpine - A guide to the mountains of Strathcona Park & Vancouver Island. ISBN 0-9680766-5-3

At the Bedwell Lake trailhead.

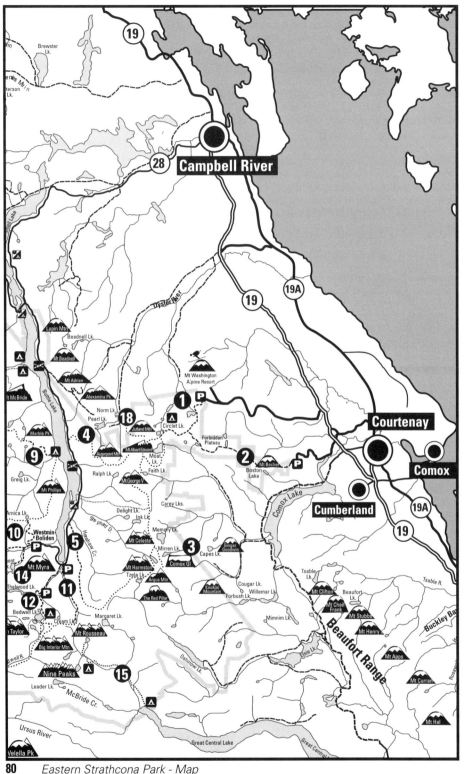

Eastern Strathcona Park

Argus Mt. (L), Red Pillar (C) and Mt. Harmston (R) from Rees Ridge, May.

Eastern Strathcona Park

The mountain range dividing Buttle Lake from the Comox Valley dominates the topography of Eastern Strathcona Park and offers some of the finest high alpine ski touring on Vancouver Island through dramatic terrain. Such Island landmarks as Forbidden Plateau, Mt. Albert Edward, the Comox Glacier, Cliffe Glacier, Red Pillar, Flower Ridge and Milla Lake are all found in this area and all are accessible on skis, splitboard or snowshoes. The lakes and meadows of Forbidden Plateau invite exploration on moderately paced day trips and short overnighters while the mountains of the main divide offer expedition-style ski tours through rugged and challenging terrain.

Sub-alpine forest covers Forbidden Plateau defining the magical character of the meadows and lakes on the plateau. Historical home of skiing on the Island, Forbidden has given countless Islanders their first experiences of alpine and x-country skiing. The ski lift area that operated on the flanks of Mt. Becher since the 1960s shut down in 1999 after the day lodge roof collapsed from the heavy snow load leaving this corner of the plateau quiet again.

At the north-east corner of Forbidden Plateau overlooking Paradise Meadows is Mt. Washington, the Island's most developed ski lift area and one of the busiest alpine resorts in British Columbia. From humble beginnings Mt. Washington's lift facilities are expanding on an almost annual basis and will certainly cover all the good descent terrain on this isolated mountain within a few years. The downhill terrain of Mt. Washington is at best described as 'modest'. Huge powder dumps, excellent cross-country ski terrain, wild views of the Georgia Strait, Coast Range and Strathcona, along with superb road access to eastern Strathcona Park and generally mild temperatures are its redeeming features.

To the west of Forbidden Plateau the mountains of the main Buttle-Comox divide form one of the longest and highest sections of alpine terrain on the Island. Good travelling is found along the tops of the interconnecting ridges weaving through this range and all the popular summer routes offer equally high-quality experiences to the winter traveller. Above the treeline these ridge tops are generally rounded while the flanks are typically steep limiting access points to spur ridgelines.

Highest Point: Summit of Mt. Albert Edward 6,868 ft / 2,093 m

Most Vertical Descent Possible: ~600m

Map Sheets: 92 F/11 Forbidden Plateau

Greg Shea ascending east ridge of Mt. Albert Edward above Moat Lake with Castlecrag behind, March.

Access: Access into eastern Strathcona Park is its great attraction during the winter months. Quick alpine access is still possible at the retired Forbidden Plateau ski area by driving up Plateau Rd from the Piercy Road junction on the Inland Island Highway 19 north of Courtenay. The high elevation (paved and plowed!) access afforded by the Strathcona Parkway to Mt. Washington Alpine Resort and Paradise Meadows puts some of the best terrain within reach of a long day trip and a weekend trip will guarantee you reach some great steeps. The main access roads by name are:

Comox Lake Main: Is one of the main access roads from the Comox Valley into the east side of this region of the Park. Comox Lake Main runs down the west shore of Comox Lake eventually linking up with logging roads from Port Alberni to make the 'Valley Connector'. The Glacier Trail, Kookjai Mountain and routes out of the Cruickshank valley can all be reached from spurs off this main road.

Plateau Road: Provides access to the far east end of Forbidden Palteau near Mt. Becher. The road used to service the long running skihill at Wood Mountain, known as Forbidden Plateau Ski Area. The lifts no longer run but the backcountry access is excellent. From Piercy Road north of Courtenay just east of the Piercy Road junction on Highway 19 head west up Plateau Road, follow the paved road to the base of the hill where gravel continues up to the parking lot and trailhead.

Strathcona Parkway: which services Mt. Washington Alpine Resort is the finest way to get to the Island alpine and reaches the Paradise Meadows trail at the Raven Lodge.

Oyster River Main: Logging roads in the Oyster River offer access to the north end of Forbidden Plateau, the Gem Lake trail, Mt. Alexandra and Mt. Adrian and even into the Augerpoint area. Oyster Main is found off Cranberry Road from the Inland Island Highway. All the land between the highway and the park boundary is private forest company land and access is often restricted by locked gates and limited openings.

Buttle Lake Parkway: The Buttle Lake Parkway offers access into the west side of the range, specifically to Jack's Augerpoint Trail, Ralph River-Shepherd Creek divide, Shepherd Ridge and the Flower Ridge trail.

Ash River: Midway between Courtenay and Port Alberni on the Valley Connector is a loop of logging road that goes along the Ash River to the end of Oshinow Lake and rejoins the Valley Connector via Ramsay Creek. Long Lake Road as it is called gives access to the south end of the eastern Strathcona area including, the Red Pillar-Cliffe Glacier and the proposed Margaret Creek trail that links up with Price Creek and the Della Falls trail.

Cabins: Divers or Rossiter lakes, Moat Lake, Sid's Cabin, Beadnell Lake

Turns

Some of the longest descents and most dramatic alpine terrain on Vancouver Island are found in eastern Strathcona Park. Look for lines off Mt. Jutland down to Circlet Lake and even Rossiter Lake, steep tree skiing off the north and east aspects of Mt. Brooks and great open treelines on the west side of Mt. Elma down to the pass with Mt. Brooks. Mt. Becher is worth a look for its easy day trip access and some nice if short drops. At the east side of the plateau check out the glades on Mt. Drabble and Indianhead Mountain. There are long easy lines off the summit of Mt. Albert Edward with steeper terrain along the trail route back down to Circlet Lake.

Further out in the backcountry long descents can be found off most of the high points along the main Buttle-Comox divide. Highlights include lines off Mt. Frink toward Castlecrag, Mt. George V, both the north and south sides of Siokum Mountain, scary but doable steeps off the north face of Mt. Celeste, elegant and long drops off Rees Ridge to Milla Lake and of course some superb big-country turns off the Comox Glacier. Along the Augerpoint Traverse look for ski descents down toward Pearl Peak off Augerpoint Mountain and commiting drops off the west side of Syd Watts Peak overlooking Buttle Lake. Along Shepherd's Ridge there look to be some choice lines on the north aspects.

Outside of the Strathcona Park boundaries good ski terrain can be found on Mt. Alexandra, Mt. Adrian's west bowl and off Mt. Beadnell (Rodger's Ridge) both to the east down to Beadnell Lake and to the west above Buttle Lake. Rodger's Ridge is a winter backcountry gem and in fact there has been much talk over the years that it would make a good choice for a ski resort. Mt. Washington's proximity to the Comox Valley and the available terrain for real estate there could be the only explaination it superceded Rodger's Ridge as the latter certainly has superior ski terrain.

Tours

The expanse of Forbidden Plateau and the maze of long uninterrupted alpine ridges and branching spurs on the high country of the Buttle-Comox divide offer numerous overnight trip options. The terrain on Forbidden Plateau is suitable for novices and day trips while the routes further out on the divide take in rugged terrain requiring experienced route finding and strong skiing skills to negotiate.

A classic introductory tour is to traverse Forbidden Plateau from the old ski area at Forbidden to Paradise Meadows and Mt. Washington. This trip may be undertaken in either direction as a long day trip in good conditions and/or by a fit party or as a weekend outing as conditions and/or the party prefers.

For the more ambitious ski mountaineer there are a number of Vancouver Island's highest and most alluring summits in eastern Strathcona, some summited right along the main lines of travel. The central ridge of the Buttle-Comox divide runs from Jutland Mountain due south, 22 km as the crow flies, to the Red Pillar and terminates at the foot of the Pillar's south ridge. On both sides of this divide, spur ridges branch off toward Buttle Lake to the west and into the Cruickshank River valley to the east. A number of trip options are possible starting or finishing along either of these spurs.

The more recommended of these trip options include: **i)** the Castlecrag Circuit- a circular route around Moat Lake, **ii)** the Augerpoint Traverse between Paradise Meadows and Buttle Lake via Mt. Albert Edward, **iii)** Paradise Meadows to Comox Glacier via Mt. George V, Rees Ridge and Flower Ridge, **iv)** Comox Glacier to Buttle Lake via Cliffe Glacier and Flower Ridge, **v)** Mt. Adrain to Lupin Mountain **vi)** Carey Lakes to Comox Glacier and **vii)** the Flower Ridge - Shepherd Ridge horseshoe.

As there is a rich history of summer hiking along these routes those planning winter traverses are well advised to read journal accounts and consult Hiking Trails III and Island Alpine for background information on the many trip possibilities in this area.

One of the major considerations in planning any of the traverses through this range is the transportation logistics. Most of the through trips require a second vehicle that can be left in advance at your point of exit, or another option is to arrange a drop-off or pick-up. Often it is less complicated to enter and exit on the same side of the range or even to do an 'out and back' trip retracing your route back to your vehicle .

Additional Info: Hiking Trails III 9th Edition, Island Alpine 1st Edition p.140-181, www.islandhikes.com Beyond Nootka online www.members.shaw.ca/beyondnootka

Kris Oetter dropping off Mt. Becher.

Forbidden Plateau

Chris Lawrence ski touring up to Mt. Becher, March.

Forbidden Plateau

The magic of Forbidden Plateau is hinted at in a story perpetuated by Comox Argus publisher Ben Hughes that tells of the supernatural spirits that dwell there. It is among the wizened sub-alpine trees and exquisitely be-laked terrain of Forbidden Plateau that Island skiing can claim its deepest historical roots. While the Coast Salish people regarded the high country with caution, colonialists in the early 1900s quickly saw the potential for recreation on the plateau and the mountainous interior of Strathcona Park beyond. By the 1920s a well worn horse trail led from Bevan, near Cumberland, up to Forbidden Plateau and the wonders of the mountain air were touted in local brochures. A few cabins were constructed and camps dotted the picturesque alpine during the summer months as local outdoors people and visitors came to explore its beauty.

The interest in Forbidden Plateau for winter recreation naturally evolved with the sport of skiing the world over. In the 1920s skiers trekked up to Mt. Becher and there can be little doubt that a great deal of the plateau was explored at this time by local skiers. Around 1949 a ski lift was installed at Wood Mountain Park and the facility eventually became known as Forbidden Plateau. For many Vancouver Islanders of this generation Forbidden was where they learnt to ski and it remains in fond memories since the day lodge collapsed due to excessive snowload in the epic winter of 1999. The lodge has since been torched by vandals but the site is bound to receive a new life eventually.

With the surge in growth and the improved road access to Mt. Washington Alpine Resort much of the acitivity on the plateau is now centred around the groomed nordic ski trails that wind across the Paradise Meadows region of Forbidden and the bustling village and skihill at Mt. Washington.

Highest Point: Summit of Mt. Brooks 4,921 ft / 1,500 m

Most Vertical Descent Possible: ~400m

Difficulty/Duration: Forbidden Plateau Traverse A2, Day tips A1 / 1-3 days

Map Sheets: 92 F/11 Forbidden Plateau

Access: Forbidden Plateau is served by well-maintained roads on its eastern and northern edge. Plateau Road winds up from Courtenay and the Inland Island Highway to the site of the now defunct

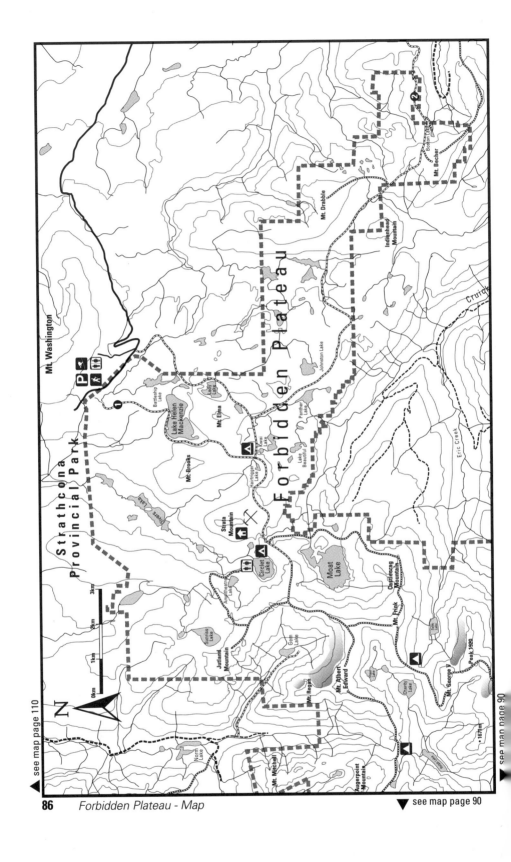

Mt. Washington

Strathcona
Provincial Park

Battleship
Lake

Lake Helen
Mackenzie

Mt. Brooks

Lady
Lake

Mt Elma

Kwai
Lake

Panther
Lake

Lake
Beautiful

Johnston Lake

Forbidden Plateau

Mt. Drabble

Indianhead
Mountain

Boston Trail

Mt. Becher

Crutch

Eric Creek

Hartrigel
Lake

Strata
Mountain

Croteau
Lake

Amphitheatre
Lake

Sunrise
Lake

Jutland
Mountain

Gem
Lake

Moat
Lake

Castlecrag
Mountain

Mt. Frink

Gem
Lake

Peak 1920

Mt. George V

Cruikshank
Lake

Mt. Regan

Mt. Albert
Edward

Norm
Lake

Mt. Mitchell

Augerpoint
Mountain

1671m

0km 1km 2km 3km

N

86 *Forbidden Plateau - Map*

▼ see map page 90

Looking from Jutland-Albert Edward col across Forbidden Plateau toward Mt. Washington, March.

Forbidden Plateau Ski Area. This road is generally open year round and there is ample parking at the old lift area lots. Hiking or skiing up the runs to the base of the old T-bar (down and to the right (north) of the main chairlift line) leads to the Becher trail trailhead just a hundred metres or two uphill from the T-bar base. The Becher Trail heads west across the plateau to the low summit of Mt. Becher. The Dove Creek Trail continues further across Mackenzie Meadows and the heart of Forbidden Plateau to Paradise Meadows and the village base-area at Mt. Washington Alpine Resort.

The groomed cross country ski trails from Mt. Washington across Paradise Meadows offer superb access into Strathcona Park weaving through the meadows to Lake Helen Mackenzie where the backcountry begins up onto the main plateau. To reach Mt. Washington village and the Paradise Meadows trailhead leave the Inland Island Highway 19 at Exit 130 on the Strathcona Parkway. The Parkway is a wide, usually well-maintained paved road servicing the growing attractions of Mt. Washington's Alpine Resort. Turn left just below the village on the clearly signposted road to Paradise Meadows and the Raven Lodge Nordic Lodge where you'll find the Paradise Meadows trailhead.

Turns

Look for lines off Mt. Jutland down to Circlet Lake and even Rossiter Lake, steep tree skiing off the north and east aspects of Mt. Brooks and great open treelines on the west side of Mt. Elma down to the pass with Mt. Brooks. Mt. Becher is worth a look for its easy day trip access and some nice if short drops.

Tours

The gentle terrain and easy access make Forbidden Plateau an ideal destination for cross-country skiing, snowshoeing and ski touring on both day trips and weekend overnight camping trips. It is perfect for novices and a good destination to keep in mind for periods of poor weather and/or snow stability. One of the best routes follows the Becher trail route from the old Forbidden Plateau ski area across the plateau to Paradise Meadows and Mt. Washington. There are a number of good side trips possible up Mt. Becher, Mt. Drabble, Indianhead Mountain, Mt. Elma and Mt. Brooks along with a maze of meadows and lakes to explore. Checkout the Cruickshank Canyon view near Johnston Lake.

Good map reading and compass skills will be handy navigating through the flat terrain. For longer trips and more experienced parties Forbidden Plateau provides access to more difficult terrain including Mt. Albert Edward and the Castlecrag Circuit.

Additional Info: Hiking Trails III 9th Edition, Island Alpine 1st Edition p.143-148, Beyond Nootka online www.members.shaw.ca/beyondnootka

Rider at Mt. Washington with Mt. Albert Edward behind.

Castlecrag Circuit

The Castlecrag Circuit and Mt Albert Edward south-east aspect from Mt Becher, March.

Castlecrag Circuit

Castlecrag is a small but jagged summit, south-east of Mt. Albert Edward, overlooking Moat Lake. The Castlecrag Circuit is a superb, easily accessed ski tour around the height of land encircling Moat Lake. It can be undertaken in either direction and takes in some of the most dramatic terrain in this region of Strathcona Park including an easy side trip to the summit of Mt Albert Edward.

Highest Point: Summit of Mt. Albert Edward 6,868 ft / 2,093 m

Most Vertical Descent Possible: ~600m

Difficulty/Duration: To summit B2 / 1-2 days

Map Sheets: 92 F/11 Forbidden Plateau

Access: The only recommended way to start the Castlecrag Circuit is from Mt. Washington Resort taking the Paradise Meadows trail, via Lake Helen Mackenzie, to the ridge between Circlet and Moat lakes.

Route Description: From the parking lot at Mt. Washington's Raven Lodge, head south-west either on the groomed cross-country track with a pass, or off-piste 'sans billet', following the Paradise Meadows trail up to Lake Helen Mackenzie. If conditions allow cross the lake directly, aiming for the low pass between Mt. Brooks and Mt. Elma, if the lake is too thawed or otherwise impassable follow the trail counterclockwise around the north and west shores of the lake and gain the Brooks-Elma Pass.

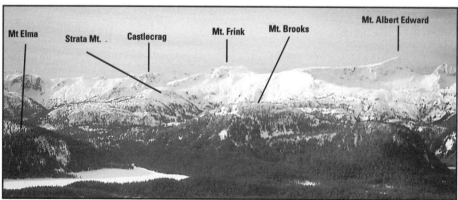

Paradise Meadows, Castlecrag and Mt Albert Edward north-east aspect from Mt Washington

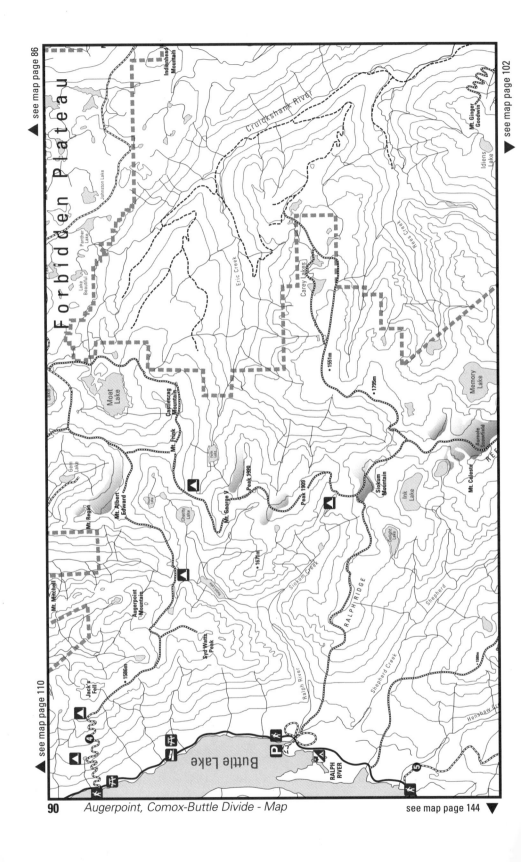

Forbidden Plateau

Indianhead Mountain

Cruickshank River

Johnston Lake

Panther Lake

Lake Beautiful

Eric Creek

Rees Creek

Carey Lakes

Mt. Ginger Goodwin

Idiens Lake

• 1551m

• 1795m

Memory Lake

Aureole Snowfield

RES

Moat Lake

Castlecrag Mountain

Mt. Frink

Gem Lake

Mt. Regan

Mt. Albert Edward

Peak 1990

Mt. George V

Peak 1909

Siokum Mountain

Ink Lake

Mt. Celeste

Mt. Mitchell

Augerpoint Mountain

• 1671m

Siokum Creek

Shepherd Creek

Shepherd

Syd Watts Peak

1586m

Jack's Fell

RALPH RIDGE

Ralph River

Shepherd Creek

Henshaw

Buttle Lake

P

RALPH RIVER

4

5

Mt. Albert Edward (L) and Castlecrag (C) south aspect from Siokum Mountain, May.

From the Brooks-Elma pass continue along the general route of the trail, past the Park's hut south-west to Hairtrigger and Kwai lakes and on to the low saddle between Moat and Circlet lakes. Here you decide which direction to complete the Castlecrag Circuit. If you plan to spend the night out Circlet Lake is the best place to plan a camp. The recommended direction to complete the Castlecrag Circuit is clockwise, so from the pass between the lakes descend due south to the outlet of Moat Lake.

Follow the shore of Moat Lake south and continue straight up onto the shoulder of the north-west ridge of Castlecrag. There is some short ski terrain from here back to Moat Lake. To continue higher up choose a safe line near the 1400m contour and make a long traverse across the east flank of Castlecrag to the open slopes on its south side. Switchback up the south face to take in the summit of Castlecrag. If time allows take advantage of some of the short but sweet ski lines on this face of the mountain down into the timbered slopes below (see photo above).

Cross the south face from below the summit to the col between Castlecrag and Mt. Frink then ascend Frink's east ridge to its top. A few short turns lead down onto the wide open terrain of Mt. Albert Edward's east ridge. If plans permit, make the long steady climb up to the summit of Mt. Albert Edward. On fast snow you'll enjoy some nice carves off Albert Edward retracing your line back down the east ridge. Swing north-east following the natural height of land toward the col with Jutland Mountain.

Fit parties or those with more time may want to continue along the ridge to Jutland Mountain and descend some of the steeper terrain down to Circlet Lake. More directly follow the summer route to Mt. Albert Edward and descend due east down the steep ridge between Circlet Lake and Moat Lake. Continue down to Circlet Lake to camp or return along the Paradise Meadows trail to the parking lot.

Additional Info: Island Alpine 1st Edition p.146-154

Castlecrag north aspect from approach to Albert Edward-Jutland col, March.

Augerpoint Traverse

Melissa De Hann & Chris Lawrence looking from Marble Meadows over Buttle Lake to Mt. Albert Edward, February.

Augerpoint Traverse

The Augerpoint traverse is one of the more popular backcountry hiking routes in Strathcona and the route lends itself well to travel on skis. Excellent road access and few route finding difficulties combine with great touring terrain and stunning views of the Georgia Strait, Buttle Lake and the surrounding Strathcona mountains to make it a highly recommended tour. Some fine descents may be had en route along with several optional side trips up to the summits of the mountains along the way. For a sample of what the longer traverses entail the Augerpoint route is an excellent introduction.

Highest Point: Summit of Mt. Albert Edward 6,868 ft / 2,093 m

Most Vertical Descent Possible: ~700m

Difficulty/Duration: B3 / 3-5 days

Map Sheets: 92 F/11 Forbidden Plateau

Access: The east end of the traverse is begun on the Paradise Meadows Trail which is reached on the Strathcona Parkway to Mt. Washington. At the west end of the route is Jack's Trail from the Buttle Lake Parkway see page 77.

Route Description: The route of the Augerpoint Traverse runs perpendicular to the main Buttle-Comox divide from the Paradise Meadows trailhead at Mt. Washington Alpine Resort over Mt. Albert Edward to Ruth Masters Lake and up onto the height of land between Augerpoint Moutain and Syd Watts Peak to join Jack's Trail down to Buttle Lake. Typically this route is travelled from east to west taking advantage of the high elevation, paved road access to the alpine at the Paradise Meadows trailhead and descending the knee-knackering descent down Jack's Trail to the Buttle Lake Parkway.

From the Paradise Meadows parking lot you have the option of purchasing a pass from Mt. Washington to ski on the groomed nordic trails up as far as Lake Helen Mackenzie or breaking trail parallel to the tracks. Follow the trail to Lake Helen Mackenzie. If the lake is frozen solid enough cross the lake, otherwise take the summer trail route counterclockwise around the right (north and west) shore. A short climb through the sub-alpine forest leads up to the Brooks-Elma pass at

Mt. Albert Edward south aspect from Siokum Mountain, May.

the edge of Forbidden Plateau. Ski past the Park Ranger's cabin and on to a first possible camp at either Kwai or Circlet lakes.

Continue up the summer route on the steep ridge between Circlet and Moat lakes to join the north arm of Mt. Albert Edward's east ridge just to the south of Jutland Mountain. Swing south then east following the elegant arc of the east ridge up to the summit of Mt. Albert Edward. After soaking up the summit views (or peering into the clag!) descend the long south-west ridge off Albert Edward down to the col at its toe. It's a 700m descent down this ridge so if you've kept the packs light and have good snow it might be a great descent.

Cross the pass between Ralph River and Norm Creek keeping westward and ascend a drainage into a small cirque and onto Ruth Masters Lake. Cross the lake or in thaw keep to the north shore and ascend up the back of the cirque to the west col of Augerpoint Mountain. Augerpoint may be climbed as a side trip and there could be some great skiing had around it and the neighbouring peaks. Worth planning a day to explore between Augerpoint, Pearl Peak and Syd Watts Peak.

The traverse continues west then north from Augerpoint toward Jack's Fell. Just below the fell the route traverses down the west side of this little peak to join the top of Jack's Trail at a bench of alpine lakes overlooking Buttle Lake. Descend the steep trail taking care with route finding through a number of small talus slopes. There is a good campsite at a small pond perched on a bench at 800m. Continue down the trail to the Buttle Lake Parkway.

Note: Although this route is fairly short and accessible it does cover some very rugged and high mountain terrain. Camping on Forbidden Plateau must be at one of the designated sites at Kwai and Circlet lakes.

Additional Info: Island Alpine 1st Edition p.146-151, p.170-177,

Syd Watts Peak and Augerpoint Mountain south aspect from Siokum Mountain, May.

John (J.D.) Waibel approaching Mt. Albert Edward.

Paradise Meadows to Comox Glacier

Looking south from Mt. Albert Edward-Frink col to Mt. Frink, March.

Paradise Meadows to Comox Glacier

The traverse from Mt. Washington / Paradise Meadows to the Comox Glacier is one of the finest, long backcountry treks in Strathcona Park. This route and its variations (notably Paradise Meadows to Flower Ridge) are relatively popular hiking trips in the summer months but only a handful of parties have followed these routes on skis in winter conditions which is more a reflection of the seriousness of the undertaking than the quality of the experience. The ridgeline this route follows is all high mountain terrain going right over the summits of some of the Island's highest peaks. Glacier crossings are made and parties should be equipped and able to deal with serious routefinding, terrain requiring mountaineering skills and the real posibility of severe weather. Views are outstanding and the terrain intense!

Highest Point: Summit of Mt. Albert Edward 6,868 ft / 2,093 m

Most Vertical Descent Possible: ~800m

Difficulty/Duration: C3 / 4-8 days

Map Sheets: 92 F/11 Forbidden Plateau

Access: The north end of the Paradise Meadows to Comox Glacier route is at the Paradise Meadows trailhead at Mt. Washington Alpine Resort. To reach this trailhead leave the Inland Island Highway 19 at the Mt. Washingtion exit (130) north of Courtenay and drive up the Strathcona Parkway following the clearly posted signs for Paradise Meadows, Strathcona Park. Leave your vehicle at the new parking lot and trailhead at Mt. Washington's Raven Lodge.

Peak 1909 south aspect from Carey Ridge, May.

Looking northwest along Ralph Ridge toward Buttle Lake from Siokum Mountain, May.

At the south end of the route the entry or exit point is on the Glacier Trail out of Comox Creek or Comox Gap from Kookjai Mountain. To reach these trailheads drive south 15 km from of the Puntledge River bridge on the Valley Connector (Comox Lake Main) and turn right (east) onto the Cruickshank River logging roads. Drive 3 km west to a prominent T junction and take the lefthand road, South Main. Drive a further 5.5 km to a second junction. Continue straight for Comox Gap and the Kookjai Mountain route or take the right for another 5 km to the Glacier trailhead. For more information see page 76. This road system may be snow covered depending on season, check before committing.

How best to travel this route is a matter of opinion, there is the obvious benefit of starting with full packs at the higher elevation of Paradise Meadows and the more impressive views heading

Mt. George V north aspect from Mt. Albert Edward, March.

southward toward the mountains' north faces. A pre-arranged (or cellphone arranged) pickup or pre-trip vehicle shuttle will then be needed in the Cruickshank, ideally at the Glacier trailhead or close to Comox Gap if descending over Kookjai Mountain. On the flip side if heading north it might be easier to arrange a drop off at the Glacier trailhead and then hitch a ride down from Mt. Washington and then you'd have the sun on your back which in the heat of spring days is a welcome relief on the snowfields.

Route Description: The route is described from north to south. Leave from the Raven Lodge parking lot following the cross-country tracks or general line of the summer trail south to Lake Helen Mackenzie. If the lake is well frozen cross the lake of during thaw, keep to the trail route along the north and west shores of the lake. Aim for the obvious pass between Mt. Brooks and Mt. Elma. From the Brooks-Elma Pass head south-west sticking still to the summer trail line to a low saddle between Circlet and Moat Lake. This makes an obvious first nights campsite.

Carey Ridge where it joins the main Comox-Buttle divide, May.

From Circlet Lake continue due west up the steep ridge spur that joins the Mt. Albert Edward - Jutland Mountain connecting ridge. Head south along Albert Edward's north-east ridge to a flat open area where the ridge arcs westerly up to Mt. Albert Edward's summit. Drop your packs and make a quick trip to the top if desired then/or continue south toward Mt. Frink. Ascend the north ridge of Frink to its summit ridge then make a right angle turn westerly and descend the exposed west ridge until a safe line can be seen into the col between Charity and Faith lakes (Eric-Ralph Pass). The next section involves a stretch of high terrain so if weather is doubtful this col makes a good place to wait it out.

From the Eric-Ralph Pass climb a sweeping traverse line rightward (south-westward) above Charity Lake across the north flank of Mt. George V until a good line pops you up onto the crest of George's west ridge. Take care here as the route is exposed to avalanche on the slope itself as well as from the cliffs high above the route (see photo middle of page 96). Turn gradually around to the east and follow the west ridge up to the wide open summit dome of Mt. George V.

From the summit of George V ski south descending a little, then ascending again onto the summit of Peak 1920. It is easy going along this high ridge, just watch out for cornices overhanging the steep cliffs at their edge otherwise just stick to height of land and hope for good visibility! A little dogleg east and then south again arrives at the summit of Peak 1909 from where one of the more significant route finding problems needs to be solved. A safe line must be worked down the south-west flank of Peak 1909 into the Siokum Creek valley. Follow the ridge south until a route down can be seen to the right (west). Watch for a narrow gully that cuts through a short cliff band from skiers left to right that works well or find your own line with care. The head of the Siokum Creek valley makes a good sheltered camp remember to locate well away from the avalanche run outs..

From Siokum Creek a wide open slope leads up to the top of Siokum Mountain. There are great descents all around this unassuming peak so plan a lunch stop or nearby camp to get some turns in. Two possible exit routes leave Siokum Mountain. To the west is the more obvious Ralph Ridge

Comox-Buttle divide east aspect from Georgia Strait, June.

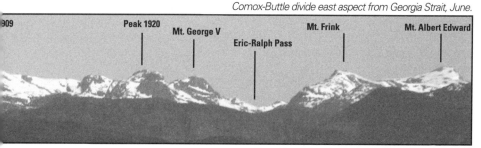

Mt Celeste

North Face of Mt. Celeste from Siokum Mountain, May.

which leads out to Buttle Lake at the Ralph River campground. And to the east is a spur between Eric and Rees creeks which gives a route down to the Cruickshank valley.

From the easternmost of the twin summit domes of Siokum Mountain head south on the wide open ridge to another high knoll at GR2697. From here a route in to the range from the north fork of the Cruickshank enters via Carey Lakes and logging road branch 75 which is currently drivable to 1100m! This route is a superb way to access Rees Ridge and the Aureole Snowfield in the spring. Some care is needed on the steep north ridge of Peak 1795 but snowmobile tracks have been seen up on this ridge so it can't be all that bad!

South of the high point at GR2697 are a series of small rocky domes most of which are easily negotiated but might require a short scramble in spring conditons as more rock becomes exposed. Most signicficantly is the southernmost and largest of these domes at GR264958. There are two ways around this feature. The first and most direct is down the steep gully which is easily found to your right (west) as you approach the knoll on the height of land. The terrain below the base of the gully is exposed but this exposure is short lived and if snow stability is good or the gully is thawed out it's the best choice. Alternatively climb up and over the knoll and scramble down a short steep rock section on the south-east side of the dome. South of this dome is the Aureole Snowfield and Rees Ridge.

Sadly the Aureole Snowfield promises a lot in terms of ski terrain but delivers very little. There are some good lines around but you'll need to work to get them. Of the easily reached and outstanding variety is the intense line off the north face of Mt. Celeste down to the lake below and possibly a second drop to Ink Lake further down. There also might be a serious line down to Memory Lake but scout it well before commiting! On the safer side are lines down to Milla Lake up to 800m!

Iceberg Peak north aspect from Rees Ridge, Comox Glacier behind, May.

The touring terrain across Rees Ridge is fantastic and both Mt. Celeste and Iceberg Peak are two of the Island's highest and more inacessible peaks so enjoy their summits and the stunning views over Milla Lake to Harmston, Argus and Red Pillar before tackling the next route finding challenge, reaching the Comox Glacier.

There are two main options each with two variations. Firstly you can choose between two gullies that offer lines up through the cliffs on the glacier's north-west face. One can be reached by following Rees Ridge south-eastward to a low col between Milla and Mirren lakes. From this col continue directly up toward the cliff band on the Comox Glacier trending to your left (east). Look for and take the shortest and lowest angled of the gullies (see photo bottom page 103 & top of page 105). Alternatively drop down to Milla Lake and ski to its far (south) end. Climb directly up the back of the cirque onto the Moving Glacier and up into a narrowing gully that leads up onto the ridge between Argus Mountain and the Comox Glacier. Each of these routes may require mountaineering skills and gear to negotiate.

The second option is to ski down to Milla Lake and use the standard gully route up from the south-west corner of the lake up to the toe of Mt. Harmston's south-east ridge and on to the Cliffe Glacier. Pass Argus either over the summit or around the exposed traverse on its south-east flank. From either option head north-east onto the Comox Glacier plateau. Follow details of Comox Glacier to Buttle Lake traverse (see overleaf) for route options down to the Cruickshank valley.

Additional Info: Hiking Trails III 9th Edition, Island Alpine 1st Edition p.146, 150-160, 162.

The Aureole Snowfield and the Comox Glacier north aspect from ridge north of Mt. Celeste, May.

Iceberg Peak   Gully onto Aureole Snowfield   Mt Celeste

100 *Shane Mawhinney Mt. Ginger Goodwin, Comox Glacier behind.*

Comox Glacier to Buttle Lake

Comox Glacier and Rees Ridge from Mt. Ginger Goodwin, March.

Comox Glacier to Buttle Lake

Crossing from the Comox Glacier to Buttle Lake via the Cliffe Glacier and Flower Ridge is a classic alpine traverse and one of the more serious expeditions on the Island. This route is perhaps a little shorter distance wise than its variation of traversing from Paradise Meadows to Comox Glacier but has comparable commitment and passes through equally impressive terrain.

Highest Point: Summit of Comox Glacier 6,430 ft / 1,960 m

Most Vertical Descent Possible: ~600m

Difficulty/Duration: C3 / 4-7 days

Map Sheets: 92 F/11 Forbidden Plateau

Access: Like all the major Island traverses access logistics are the primary trip planning factor and how each party addresses their access needs with available time and vehicle/driver resources determines the direction of travel. For this route it is suggested to travel east to west starting with a drop off at the Comox Glacier end and finishing at Flower Ridge with a pickup or hitchiking out the Buttle Lake Parkway and Highway 28 to Campbell River.

The Comox Glacier is reached from Cruickshank River logging roads off the Valley Connector (Comox Lake Main) 15 km south of the Puntledge River bridge. Drive 3 km west to the T junction and take the lefthand road, South Main. Drive a further 5.5 km to a second junction. Take the right for another 5 km to the trailhead or keep straight to Comox Gap for the Kookjai Mountain route. Active logging in the Cruickshank valley may change road conditions, locations and access may be restricted. An alternative way to reach Comox Gap is from new logging roads at the west end of Forbush Lake.

Route Description: The recommended route to the Comox Glacier in winter is from Comox Gap over Kookjai Mountain. This may add as much as a day to the trip but avoids a difficult and very exposed section of ridge between the Frog Ponds and Lone Tree Pass on the Glacier Trail approach.

Comox Glacier east aspect from Georgia Strait, June.

see map page 62-63

see map page 90

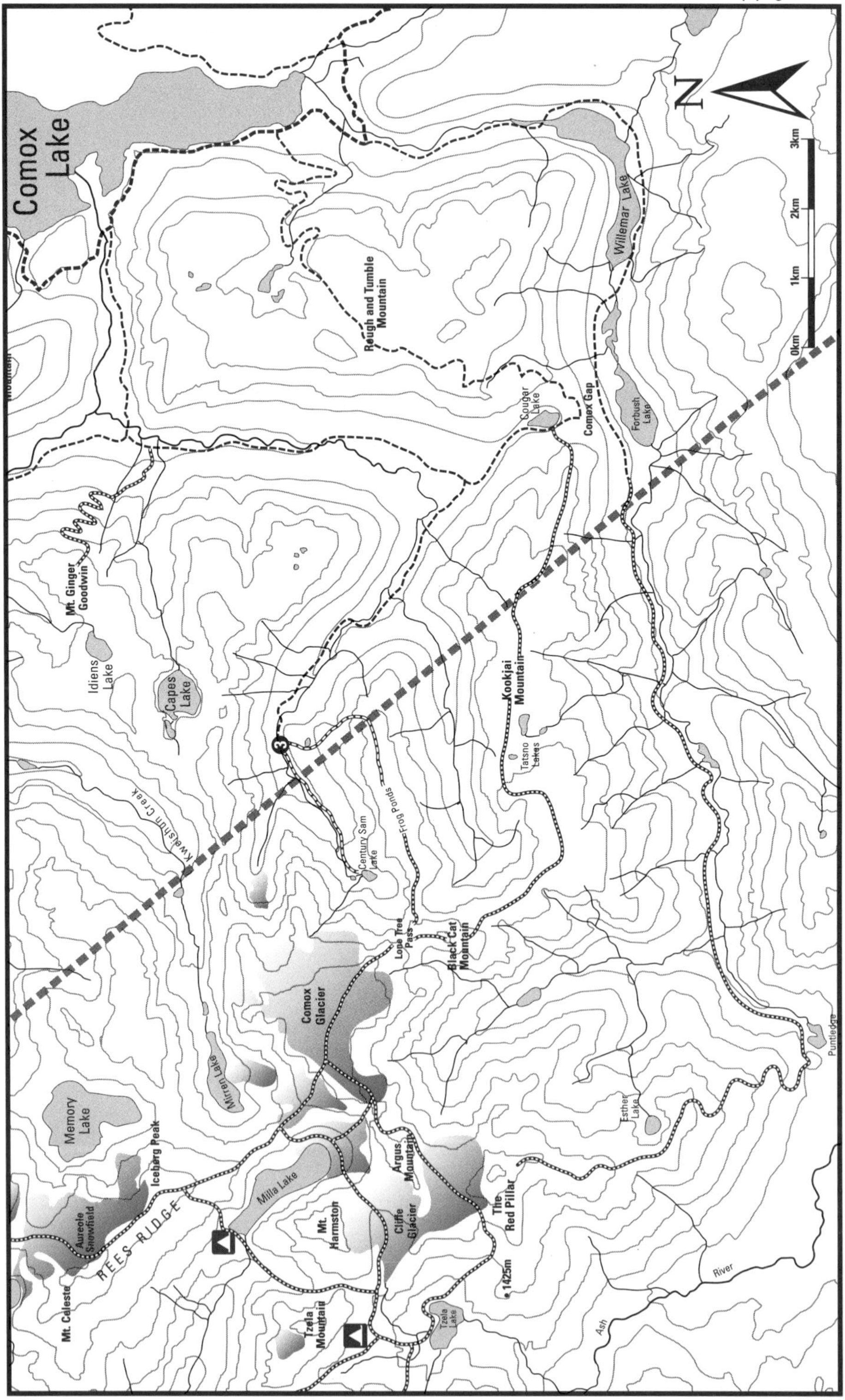

N

3km
2km
1km
0km

Comox Lake

Rough and Tumble Mountain

Willemar Lake

Cougar Lake

Comox Gap

Forbush Lake

Mt. Ginger Goodwin

Idiens Lake

Capes Lake

Kookjai Mountain

Tatsno Lakes

Kwalshun Creek

Century Sam Lake

Frog Ponds

Lone Tree Pass

Black Cat Mountain

Comox Glacier

Mirren Lake

Memory Lake

Iceberg Peak

Milla Lake

Mt. Harmston

Argus Mountain

Cliffe Glacier

The Red Pillar

Esther Lake

Puntledge

Aureole Snowfield

R E E S   R I D G E

Mt. Celeste

Izdia Mountain

Tzela Lake

1425m

Ash

River

see map page 158

see map pages 144, 152

Mt. Harmston (L) and Tzela Mountain (R) north aspect from Rees Ridge.

To take this route drive up the Cruickshank South Main, following the description for the Glacier Trail. At the second junction go left for 2.5 km into Comox Gap. Or from Forbush Lake locate an old trail up the hillside to the gap from near the west end of the lake. From Comox Gap hike west up a long forested ridge on to Kookjai Mountain. Keep to the ridge crest past Tatsno Lake and then swing north-west to Black Cat Mountain and Lone Tree Pass and up the south-east ridge onto the glacier.

Once on the Comox Glacier plateau head north-west across its flat top to take in the summit and then assess the route options on the next leg to the Cliffe Glacier. There are two main route options each with variations. The first and the standard line for travel in summer is to climb up and over Argus Mountain with one variation being an exposed traverse across Argus' south-east side an exposed traverse is also possible on the north flank of Argus (see photo page 105).

Alternatively Argus might be avoided altogether by dropping down to Milla Lake and climbing back up the well used gully on to the Cliffe Glacier at the foot of Mt. Harmston's south-east ridge. The variations are that there are two gullies which cut down the north-west side of the Comox Glacier's south-west ridge, one leads onto the ridge which connects with Rees Ridge and from there down to Milla Lake and the second leads directly down the Moving Glacier to Milla Lake. Some mountaineering skills may be needed here. Snow stability, cornices and the party's expertise are also factors to be considered. Either way you've got to make it across to the Cliffe Glacier to make the traverse.

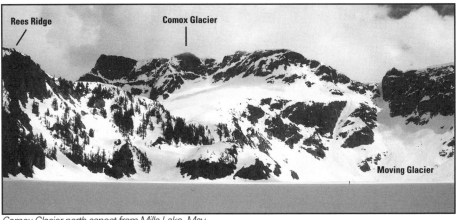

Comox Glacier north aspect from Milla Lake, May.

Red Pillar, Cliffe Glacier, Argus Mountain. and Comox Glacier south-east aspect from Mt. Cokely

Once safely on the Cliffe Glacier there are the chances of climbing Mt. Harmston, Red Pillar and Argus Mountain (if you haven't already done so on your way over). There are a few turns to be had here too, particularly off Harmston's south and west flanks and eventually all the way down to Tzela Lake which is en route. There is also a nice ski descent down the basin between Mt. Harmston and Tzela Mountain into the Shepherd Creek valley. You'll need time to kill to take this one in but it does put you at the mouth of Milla Lake which can then be crossed and the gully ascended back to the Cliffe Glacier making a sweet circumnavigation of Mt. Harmston, ideal for a long, challenging day trip from a base camp on the Cliffe Glacier.

Continuing the route from the Cliffe Glacier, drop down to Tzela Lake and your only visit below treeline on this traverse. Pick a safe line up the slope overlooking the lake's west shore, either in the bowl or more likely up the spur ridge to gain the high ridge at GR2389. Immediately the route descends slightly south-westward along the Henshaw-Ash divide. Keep to the height of land where safe route finding allows over the east summit of Central Crags and from there to Peak 1636.

From Peak 1636 the ridge top narrows and makes a tight arc around the head of Henshaw Creek to trend north-west and become Flower Ridge. This section of the route will take some care and possibly a rope to safely negotiate but the difficulties are fairly short lived and in no time the open cruising terrain of Flower Ridge leads gradually down to the treeline and the trail down to Buttle Lake.

Additional Info: Island Alpine 1st Edition, Hiking Trails III 9th Edition, IB 2001 p.30

Jan Neuspiel skiing along Flower Ridge, May.

Paradise Meadows to Flower Ridge

Argus Mountain and Milla Lake, May

Paradise Meadows to Flower Ridge

Making this expedition-like traverse from Paradise Meadows to Buttle Lake via Flower Ridge is one of the longest and most commiting of the classic ski traverses on Vancouver Island. Much of the terrain is above 6,000 ft exposing parties to severe weather if it should arrive and requiring strong mountaineering skills to negotiate some of the mountain obstacles encountered en route.

Highest Point: Summit of Mt. Celeste 6,709 ft. / 2,045 m.

Most Vertical Descent Possible: ~600

Difficulty/Duration: C3 / 5-9 days

Map Sheets: 92 F/11 Forbidden Plateau

Access: Follow the access options and route description for Paradise Meadows to Comox Glacier traverse from Mt. Washington to Rees Ridge. To start from Flower Ridge follow the Flower Ridge trail description and Comox Glacier to Flower Ridge traverse details to the Cliffe Glacier. See details page 76

Route Description: This route is fully described in the two route descriptions for the Paradise Meadows to Comox Glacier Traverse (page 95) and the Comox Glacier to Buttle Lake Traverse (page 101). The connecting point of these two routes that combine to make the longer outing is at Milla Lake/Cliffe Glacier. To make the connection travesing north to south, descend off Rees Ridge from Iceberg Peak to Milla Lake on one of three good route options.

First of the options is a fairly direct line from Iceberg Peak toward the outlet of Milla Lake. As the slope steepens find a narrow skiable gully and follow it down to the lake. Second is a longer gully that takes a plumbline down to a mid-point along the lake. Both these gullies take care to find because of the convex shape of the slope above Milla Lake, they also need at least 2m of snowpack to remain skiable. In shallower snow take the first gully and scramble down the rock bluffs along its right (north) edge, or take the ridgeline down the connecting ridge southward from Rees Ridge to the low col between Iceberg Peak and the Comox Glacier and descend easy terrain on to Milla Lake.

From Milla Lake the usual route up to the Cliffe Glacier takes an obvious gully that links the lake to the toe of Mt. Harmston's south-east ridge. Take care in assessing snow stability before heading up this exposed gully. Another option and a faster route to Flower Ridge is to descend under the toe of Mt. Harmston's north ridge from the outlet of Milla Lake and ascend the long snow chute into the pass between Harmston and Tzela Mountain (see photo page 103). Continue south down to Tzela Lake and join the route to Flower Ridge.

Additional Info: Island Alpine 1st Edition p.159-160, 164, 167

Shepherd-Flower Ridges

The Shepherd's Horn from Rees Ridge, May.

Shepherd Ridge - Flower Ridge Horseshoe

The horseshoe traverse around Henshaw Creek on Shepherd and Flower ridges is destined to become on of the most popular overnight trips in Strathcona Park in any season. The scenery along this route is breathtaking and it passes by some of the more imposing peaks like the Cliffe Glacier group and the Septimus-Rosseau massif while sticking itself to more moderate terrain. There are some good places for some ski descents and the touring terrain is high and impressive itself. The icing on the cake for this trip though is that it is one of the only such circuits on the whole Island that starts and finishes at the same point, and at a provincial campground to boot! This turns the usual Island alpine vehicle shuttle shuffle in to a snap. Park and go!

Highest Point: Shepherd Peak 6,299 ft. / 1,920 m

Most Vertical Descent Possible: ~300m

Difficulty/Duration: C3 / 3-6 days

Map Sheets: 92 F/11 Forbidden Plateau

Access: Straightforward access from the Ralph River campground or Flower Ridge trailhead parking lot. Drive west on Highway 28 from Campbell River and at the Buttle Narrows junction leave the Gold River Highway and head straight up Buttle Lake.

Shepherd's Horn   Shepherd Peak

Shepherd Ridge, Tzela Mt. and the Red Pillar south aspect from Mt. Bueby, November.   photo: Craig Wagnell

Route Description: The route is best tackled clockwise starting up Shepherd Ridge so from either the Flower Ridge trailhead parking lot of the Ralph River campground hike back up the Buttle Lake Parkway 400m north and head into the forest. Trend east to south-east across the first 2-3 kilometres of fairly flat forested terrain. Gradually the slope increases and the toe of Shepherd Ridge becomes more defined by the 800m mark. There are few creeks running through the forest up the ridge toe so pack water until you are at least among clean snow.

With short winter days and slow first day starts the first high point at Peak 1580 might be as far as you make it for a first camp. From Peak 1580 the ridge runs south-east and the route finding is straightforward keeping to the top of the ridge crest. Watch for some ski terrain down the south-west flank of the ridge into the exquisite cirque with the flock of lakes at GR2092.

As you near the higher peaks on the Shepherd Ridge watch for route options that avoid the more exposed terrain on the peaks by traversing below their north faces on the glacial shelves. There is also a lower level route off the ridge crest that makes a descending traverse down to the lake and cirque at GR2292. From this lake a good route takes a subtle ridge south-eastward below Shepherd Peak and into the col between Shepherd Peak and Tzela Mountain. Look for good ski terrain on the Shepherd Glacier and in the bowl above Tzela Lake. A good side trip is down to Tzela Lake and onto the Cliffe Glacier.

Once past Shepherd Ridge keep to the Henshaw-Ash divide. Follow the height of land where safe route finding allows over the east summit of Central Crags and from there to Peak 1636.

From Peak 1636 the ridge top narrows and makes a tight arc around the head of Henshaw Creek to trend north-west and become Flower Ridge. This section of the route will take some care and possibly a rope to safely negotiate but the difficulties are fairly short lived and in no time the open cruising terrain of Flower Ridge leads gradually down to the treeline and the trail down to Buttle Lake.

Additional Info: Island Alpine 1st Edition p.167-169, Hiking Trails III 9th Edition

Panoramic view of Shepherd Ridge from Rees Ridge, May.

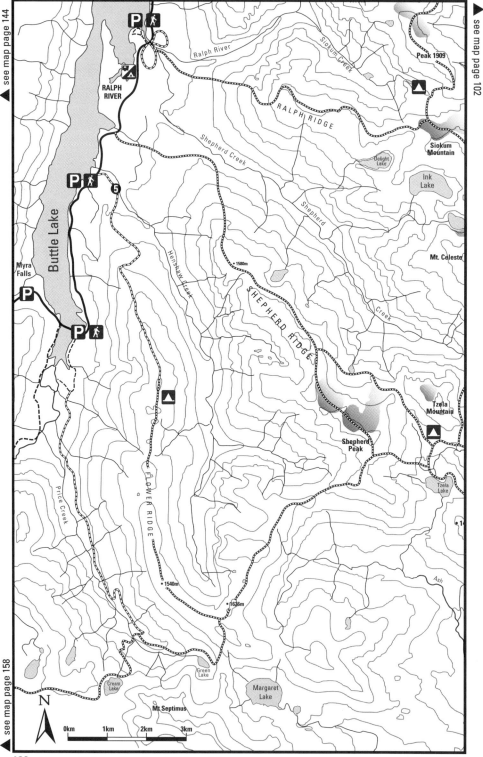

Ralph River

Siokum Creek

Peak 1909

RALPH RIVER

RALPH RIDGE

Shepherd Creek

Delight Lake

Siokum Mountain

Ink Lake

Shepherd

Myra Falls

Buttle Lake

•1580m

Henshaw Creek

SHEPHERD RIDGE

Creek

Mt. Celeste

Tzela Mountain

Shepherd Peak

Tzela Lake

•14

Price Creek

FLOWER RIDGE

•1540m

•1636m

Ash

Green Lake

Margaret Lake

Cream Lake

Mt. Septimus

N

0km   1km   2km   3km

Rodger's Ridge

Rodgers Ridge from Mt. Washington, February. Note Elkhorn and Mt. Filberg behind.

Rodgers Ridge

Before there was Mt. Washington, back when Green Mountain still had snow, the talk was of a ski hill at Rodger's Ridge. Things played out differently as it turned out and Mt. Washington won the day. But the great ski terrain that first caught skiers attention on Rodger's Ridge and the surrounding mountains is still there. Rodger's Ridge refers to the high alpine ridge on the east side of Buttle Lake at the head of Sihun Creek including Mt. Beadnell. The greater ridge system also includes Mt. Adrian and Alexandra Peak to the south and Lupin Mountain to the north. The area has long been a favourite destination of local snowmobilers.

All this mountain terrain lies outside the Strathcona Park boundary and is in fact private land, owned by forestry company TimberWest as a result of the fateful Esquimalt-Nanaimo Railway Land Grant. The questionable origins of this land grant has resulted in an obscene rate of timber harvesting all along the eastern boundary of Strathcona Park and this is apparent in the Oyster River - Rodger's Ridge area. Recent road construction has just about encircled this group of mountains and the timber is being stripped off their slopes at a fast rate.

Access is difficult at any time of year as the gates on the logging roads are staffed and often locked. However as the timber is removed and harvesting rates slow down it is conceivable that for a few years while the roads remain in decent shape that this area may continue to be a choice destination for backcountry skiing.

Highest Point: Summit of Alexandra Peak 6,506 ft. / 1,982 m.

Most Vertical Descent Possible: ~400m

Difficulty/Duration: B2 / 1-4 days

Map Sheets: 92 F/11 Forbidden Plateau

Alexandra Peak east aspect from Georgia Strait, June.

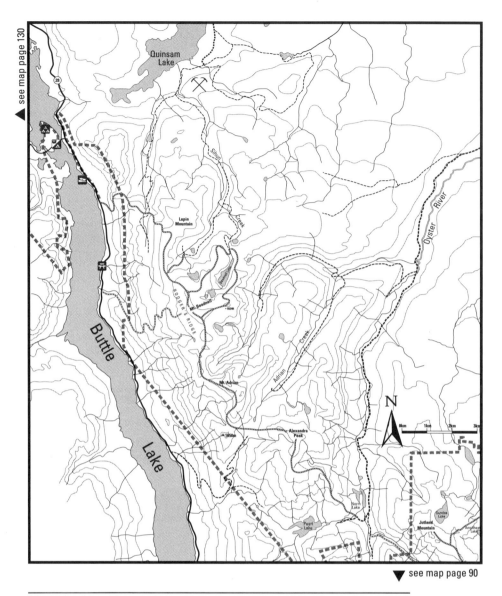

see map page 130

Quinsam
Lake

Sihun

Lupin
Mountain

Mt Beaufort

RODGER'S RIDGE

Buttle

Lake

Mt Adrian

Adrian

Oyster River

1850m

N

0km 1km 2km 3km

Alexandra
Peak

Norm
Lake

Sunrise
Lake

Pearl
Mountain

Jutland
Mountain

Amphion
Lake

see map page 90

Mt. Adrian (L) and Roger's Ridge (R) east aspect as seen from Quadra Island, April.

Mt Adrian

Mt. Adrian (C) and Alexandra Peak (far R) west aspect from Marble Meadows, February.

Access: Rodger's Ridge and the neighbouring peaks may be reached from several logging road systems. From the east new spur roads climb up from the Buttle Lake Parkway across the slope and into the pass south of Mt. Adrian toward Pearl Lake. Additional spurs lead high into the col between Mt. Adrian and Alexandra Peak offering excellent access to both these mountains. From Buttle Lake Parkway just to the south of the Lupin Falls parking lot a trail long used by Strathcona Park Lodge takes an old logging road up onto a bench overlooking Buttle Lake. A flagged route from this bench continues right up into the alpine near Mt. Beadnell and although takes a long climb is likely the most hassle free approach to Rodger's Ridge. Ask at the Lodge about current trail conditions.

One of the fastest access routes is from Sihun Creek. To reach this side of the mountain drive west on Highway 28 from Campbell River toward Gold River and turn left (south) off the highway at the Quinsam Coal Mine road. Take the Argonaut Main to your right and drive it around the south shore of Quinsam Lake. Take Granite Main to the left which climbs high up into the Sihun Creek valley. Spurs off Granite Main run close to Beadnell Lake, Rodger's Ridge and Lupin Mountain.

Alexandra Peak and Mt. Adrian are also reached from Oyster River logging roads which is found off Cranberry Road on the Island Island Highway 19. Some prior arrangement with the logging company is bound to be needed to use any of these roads.

Turns

Good ski descents can be found on Alexandra Peak's north side. Look in the basin south-west of the summit of Mt. Adrian and also on the opposing bowl to the north-east. On Rodger's Ridge there are lines down to the east and north-east in the bowls on those sides of the mountain. Also some good terrain is found on the west flank of the ridge.

Tours

A decent and uncommiting ski tour can be done by climbing up the logging road off the Buttle Lake Parkway to the pass between Mt. Adrian and Jack's Fell. Head northward over Mt. Adrian, Rodger's Ridge and on to Lupin Mountain. There is one tricky gully to negotiate through a cliff band between Adrian and Rodger's Ridge which may be capped by a cornice and require a rope to pass safely. At the north end descend logging roads off the north end of Lupin Mountain to a pass at the head of Hawkins Creek, then drop off to the west down to Buttle Narrows and retreive your vehicle.

Additional Info: Island Alpine 1st Edition p.178-181

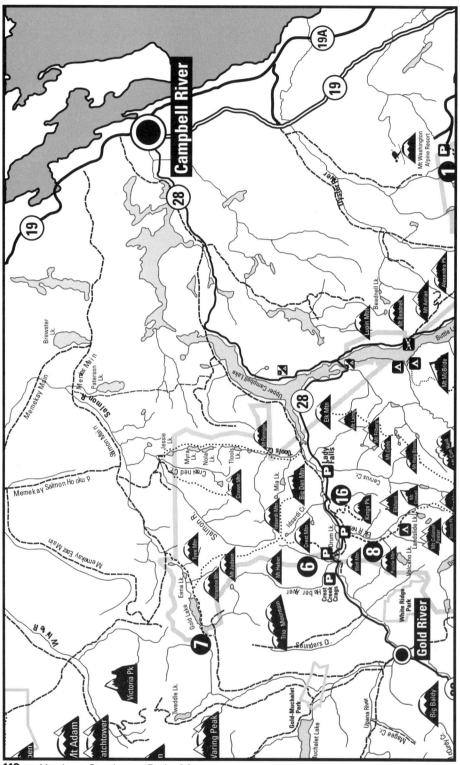

Northern Strathcona Park

The topography of northern Strathcona Park is characterized by long, interconnecting sub-alpine ridges dividing deep river valleys and a few craggy summits most notably Crown Mountain, Big Den Mountain and Mt. Judson. There are only a couple of tiny remnant glaciers and year round snowfields and the region isn't an obvious area to plan a ski tour into. However the relatively benign terrain and long ridge systems do in fact provide good touring terrain and can be a smart choice for beginners or for any party during poor weather.

Highest Point: Summit of Crown Mountain 6,057 ft. / 1,846 m.

Most Vertical Descent Possible: ~600m

Map Sheets: 92 F/13 Upper Campbell Lake

Access:

Highway 28: This road runs 90 km between Campbell River and Gold River providing the main access to the northern region of Strathcona Park including the Crest Mountain Trail, Big Den and Mt. Heber.

Elk River Timber Co. Road: An important complement to the highway access is the Elk River Timber Company Road which follows the west shore of Upper Campbell Lake as far as Tlools Creek. The ERT Road used to cut right through Strathcona Park to Gold River but is now gated and deactivated adding to the hike approaching Big Den Mountain.

East Main: From Gold River the East Main off Nimpkish Road (Woss-Gold River) East Main provides gravel road access to Gold Lake and the north-west corner of Strathcona.

Menzies Main: From 14 km north of Campbell River on the Island Highway 19 the Menzies Main and North and South Forks of the Salmon River Main give access to the north boundary of the park and the east side of Gold Lake. Between them these logging roads almost completely encircle North Strathcona.

Cabins: Mt. Flannigan

Turns

A quick look at the topo maps will reveal that there are few long descents possible in northern Strathcona and the region's forté is certainly touring over turns. However a few gems are hidden away here including a long 1,800 ft. descent off the north side of Crown Mountain down the Crowned Glacier and into the gully below. If snow conditions are good this run might be skiable all the way down to Winnifred Lake. From the summit of Crown Mountain a beautiful airy line takes the east ridge for a 1,500 ft vertical drop onto a timbered shoulder and skiing this line is a good reason to elect to undertake the Crown Mountain Horseshoe in an anti-clockwise direction.

On Idsardi Mountain a 1,000 to 1,500 ft ski is possible down the arcing south ridge depending on snow conditions and your appetite for climbing back up the ridge. There is tree skiing all along the south flank of Idsardi Mountain with short gentle runs entering the trees.

Tours

Certainly a better reason to look to northern Strathcona than the descent terrain is the touring terrain. Very high logging roads on Mt. Flannigan make this sub-alpine mountain an attractive daytrip destination and worth it for the outstanding perspective on the peaks surrounding the Elk and Cervus valleys. A decaying three-floor cabin next to the old TV antennae makes a good lunch stop but an overnight stay on Flannigan might be testing its interest.

The Crown Mountain Horseshoe looks like it would make an excellent circuit in winter with the bonus of a climb on an infrequented summit and the descent terrain down the north cirque. From Highway 28 the haul up the Crest Mountain trail is a good choice for beginners or foul weather with plenty of good touring terrain on the high plateau and the option of heading further around the Idsardi Creek headwaters over Idsardi Mountain to Big Den Mountain.

Grise Creek

River

Jessie
Lake

Salmon

Mt. Evelyn

Tyee
Mountain

Myra
Lake

Crowned Creek

S t r a t h c o n a
P r o v i n c i a l   P a r k

Nora
Lake

Winnifred
Lake

Mt. Judson

Crown
Mountain

Ranald Creek

Mt. Flannigan

Idsardi
Mountain

Tlools Creek

Big Den
Mountain

Mt. Heber

Upper Campbell Lake

Idsardi Creek

Crest Creek

28

Crest
Mountain

Elk River

N

0km   1km   2km   3km

6

Drum Lakes 8

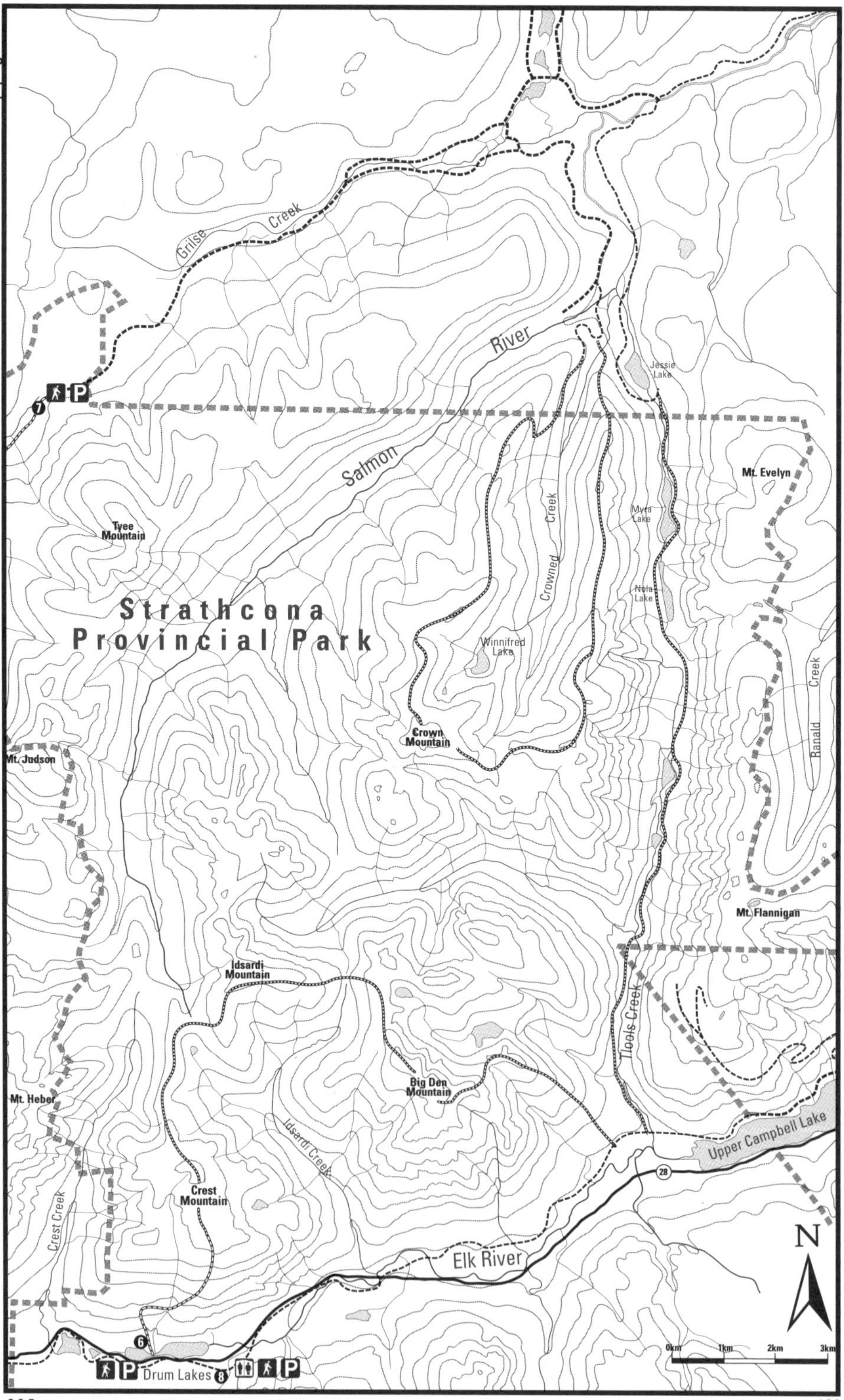

▼ see map page128

Crown Mountain Horseshoe

Crown Mountain east aspect from Cortes Island, May.

Crown Mountain Horseshoe

Crown Mountain has enjoyed relative obscurity tucked away in the centre of the Big Den Conservancy area but its close proximity to Campbell River, superlative views of central Strathcona Park, the strikingly beautiful alpine approach ridges and easy climbing terrain contrive to make Crown Mountain a desirable winter destination and one of this author's most highly recommended moderate peaks in any season.

Highest Point: Summit of Crown Mountain 6,057 ft. / 1,846 m

Most Vertical Descent Possible: ~600m

Difficulty/Duration: B3 / 2-5 days

Map Sheets: 92 F/13 Upper Campbell Lake

Access: Drive north on Island Highway 19 from Campbell River for 14.5 km to the Menzies Bay Main. Turn left (west) on Menzies Bay Main and follow it to just past 36 km where a there is a lefthand junction on to South Fork Main. Take this road to SF 900 and drive as far as you can up SF 900 and park here.

Route Description: From your vehicle continue on foot or ski up SF 900. As the road rounds the toe of the ridge and enters the Crowned Creek valley it has been debuilt and a path along the old road bed continues until ending in a clearcut. From this point head uphill to reach the old growth and pick up a flagged route on to the crest of the north ridge. Continue on the height of land watching the map and keeping an eye on the compass to avoid any one of a number of 'sucker spurs' that might entice you off the main ridge. Eventually, near Peak 5412, the trees open up giving a clear view of the mountain ahead. There are lots of good camp sites all along the ridge with numerous lakes and ponds.

Head up and over Peak 5412 and then choose a safe line to traverse down and leftward into the glacial cirque between the twin summits. Both Crown Mt. and Ellison Peak may be climbed directly from the col between them although both lines are fairly steep. Alternatively continue your traverse underneath the north ridge of Crown to join the east ridge of the mountain and ascend it easily to the summit.

To continue around the horseshoe route, descend the east ridge to a forested col and then swing north-eastward toward Peak 5016. The height of land on Peak 5016 arcs north-west and then to the north so watch the route finding in poor visibility. Otherwise the line is straightforward along the ridge top until it tapers down into the main Salmon South Fork valley and out of the Strathcona Park boundary and back into the world of clearcuts and logging roads. Hike the logging roads back to your vehicle. If the snow level is low and an easy, safe crossing can be found over Crowned Creek it might be possible to take a shortcut back to SF 900 by striking straight across the valley floor.

Additional Info: Island Alpine 1st Edition p.197-198, IB 1992 p.10

Crown Mountain east aspect from Quadra Island, April.

Ski touring in terrain typical of Crest Mountain.

Crest Mountain-Big Den

Big Den Mountain south-east from Mt. Flannigan, April.

Crest Mountain-Big Den Mountain

Crest Mountain's gentle summit plateau and the adjacent ridges onto Idsardi Mountain are a perfect destination for a moderate weekend tour. There is little significant descent terrain but as a consequence there is also little objective hazard, making it a safe choice for beginners, poor weather/avalanche conditions and especially appropriate for snowshoeing.

Highest Point: Summit of Big Den Mountain 5,827 ft. / 1,776 m.

Most Vertical Descent Possible: 1,500 ft off south ridge of Idsardi Mountain

Best Time to Visit: December to May

Difficulty/Duration: B2 / 2-4 days

Map Sheets: 92 F/13 Upper Campbell Lake

Access: To reach the Crest Mountain trailhead drive west on the Gold River Highway 28, 60km past Campbell River, note the Elk River trailhead on your left (south) and then just around the bend on Drum Lakes is the clearly signposted Crest Mountain Trail. Follow the trail up switchbacks to the alpine.

Turns

Don't get too excited about the descent terrain on these rounded ridges but if conditions allow a couple of places to look are off the north-west flank of Crest Mountain through the trees to the little lake in the Idsardi Creek head and also down the elegant south ridge of Idsardi Mountain on which you might squeeze a 1,500ft descent.

Tours

A complete horseshoe traverse is possible from Crest Mountain around the headwaters of Idsardi Creek to Big Den Mountain although since the Elk River Timber Co. Road was decommissioned the exit at Big Den requires a bit of old road travel to reach Highway 28. The travel is straightforward but some care in navigation is needed passing through the complicated three watershed pass at the head of the Salmon, Idsardi and Crest valleys to gain or descend the south ridge of Idsardi Mountain. Further along this route there will need to be some care negotiating a short steep gully off Big Den Mountain's east ridge on to the east shoulder. Strong skiers may just ski the gully but others may prefer to boot down it or even use a rope and rappel.

A horseshoe route may also be completed to the west from Crest Mountain to Mt. Heber around the headwaters of Crest Creek.

Additional Info: Island Alpine 1st Edition p.189-193

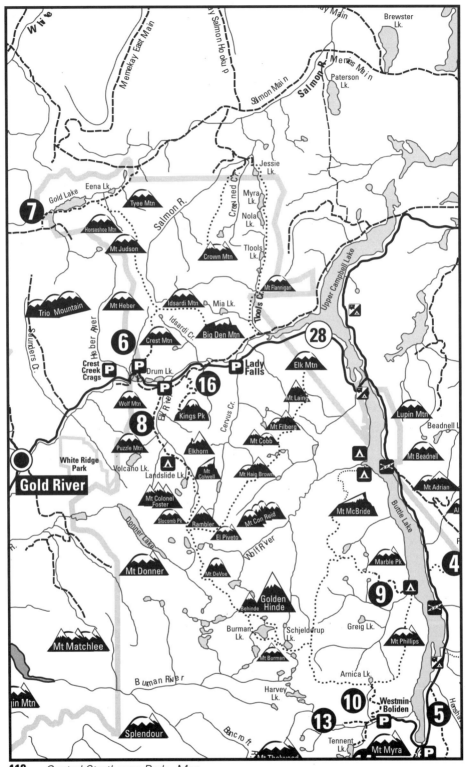

Central Strathcona Park

Central Strathcona Park

The wilderness heart of Vancouver Island lies within the bounds of the central Strathcona Park region. This area is defined as the land south of Highway 28, west of Buttle Lake, north of Myra Creek and delineated by the park boudary to the west. Along with extensive tracts of wilderness forest and a maze of sub-alpine and alpine lakes central Strathcona is home to many of Vancouver Island's highest summits including: the Golden Hinde (1), Elkhorn (2), Mt. Colonel Foster (4), Rambler Peak (5), Mt. McBride (7), King's Peak (8), Mt. Filberg (10) and Mt. Cobb (12). Not surprisingly then many fine ski turns and tours can be found here including one of the Island's best ski tours (Elk River to Phillips Ridge) and some of the longest descents (Golden Hinde south-east couloir, Mt. Colonel Foster south-east glacier and Mt. McBride glacier).

The mini-interior of the sub-alpine Ucona-Burman valleys keeps temperatures a little cooler than other regions of the Island alpine and relative to other areas of similar elevation the winter snow seem to linger in central Strathcona a little later in the summer.

Highest Point: Summit of the Golden Hinde 7,219 ft. / 2,200 m.

Most Vertical Descent Possible: ~1000m

Map Sheets: 92 F/13 Upper Campbell Lake, 92 F/12 Buttle Lake

General Access: Access into central Strathcona Park is made from the north off Highway 28, from the east by crossing Buttle Lake by boat from the Buttle Lake Parkway and from the Myra Falls mine site at the south end of Buttle Lake. Access to the west side of the park is only by air or water from Gold River or Tofino.

Highway 28: The Gold River Highway 28 between the communities of Campbell River and Gold River provides vehicle access to the north end of central Strathcona. The King's Peak trail and the Elk River trailhead are found around 60 km west of Campbell River and several other routes leave from the roadside or from logging roads near to the highway including Volcano Lake and Matchleee Mountain.

Buttle Lake Parkway: 45 km west of Campbell River on Highway 28 the highway cuts across a bridge over the short stretch of river linking Upper Campbell Lake to Buttle Lake and on to Gold River. Heading straight southward down the lake system from Buttle Narrows is the Buttle Lake Parkway which provides access to the many trails found along its route and services the mine at Myra Falls.

To reach much of the terrain in central Strathcona including the Marble Meadows trail, Wolf River and the Phillips Ridge traverse from Buttle Lake a boat crossing of the lake is required from the Parkway. The Augerpoint Day Area is suitable for a canoe crossing to Phillips Creek but for a power boat or just general convenience launch at the Karst Creek boat ramp a little further south.

The terminus of the Buttle Lake Parkway, at the south end of Buttle Lake, is at the Myra Falls mine site where parking is available for the Phillips Ridge trail (and the Mt. Myra and Upper Myra Falls trails into southern Strathcona).

Cabins: Wheaton Hut, Marble Meadows

Turns

The highest peaks and most dramatic alpine terrain on Vancouver Island are found in central Strathcona Park. The jagged character of these mountains lends itself more to alpine climbing than to ski descents but nevertheless some of the longest descents on the island are secreted on their flanks. Look for great descent terrain on King's Peak, Mt. Colonel Foster, Mt. Colwell, Mt. De Voe, the Golden Hinde and Mt. McBride.

Tours

Central Strathcona is the most remote and wild region of the park and some of the Island's best backcountry ski tours are found here including: the Elk River-Phillips Ridge traverse, Phillips Ridge Watershed traverse and Marble Meadows to Mt. McBride.

The south end of Volcano Lake and the encircling ridge, Mt. Colonel Foster beehind, May.

Volcano Lake

Volcano Peak (L) and Elkhorn (R) from ridge above Volcano Lake, May.

Volcano Lake

Volcano Lake is perched on a high ridge on the west divide of the Elk River just south of Puzzle Mountain. It is an infrequently visited area but the high granite ridges that rim the dramaticly situated lake make great ski touring terrain with stunning surroundings. Elkhorn, Mt. Colonel Foster and Matchlee Mountain dominate the views from Volcano Lake and the adjacent Puzzle Mountain, Wolf Mountain and Volcano Peak are within easy reach of a camp near the lake.

Highest Point: Summit of Puzzle Mountain 5,997 ft. /1,828 m.

Most Vertical Descent Possible: ~400m

Difficulty/Duration: B1-B2 / 1-2 days

Map Sheets: 92 F/13 Upper Campbell Lake

Access: Volcano Lake is most easily reached by approaching from old (and perhaps new) logging roads in Camel Creek, the valley west of Camel Ridge. Leave Highway 28 a few kilometres past Saunders Creek heading south on a rough gravel road. Take Br 80 south across the Heber River and up the floor of the Camel Creek valley. Locate the highest open spur road or head for any remaining old growth and climb the hillside eastward to gain the crest of the rim around Volcano Lake, south of Puzzle Mountain.

Turns

There is a surprising amount of vertical relief from the summit of Puzzle Mountain down to Volcano Lake, as much as 1,800 ft! At a point due south of the lake a prominent bowl offers 900ft right off the ridge top (see photo to left) and there a number of short steep lines around the ridge down to the lake. From the summit of Puzzle Mountain the exposed north-east bowl offers a 1,000 ft run but be cautious here as the run out is horrendous dropping several thousand feet off into the Elk River.

The open bowl on the north-west aspect of Puzzle Mountain might provide a very long run down to the Camel Creek valley and if snow stability is right offers a very fast way out of the alpine back to

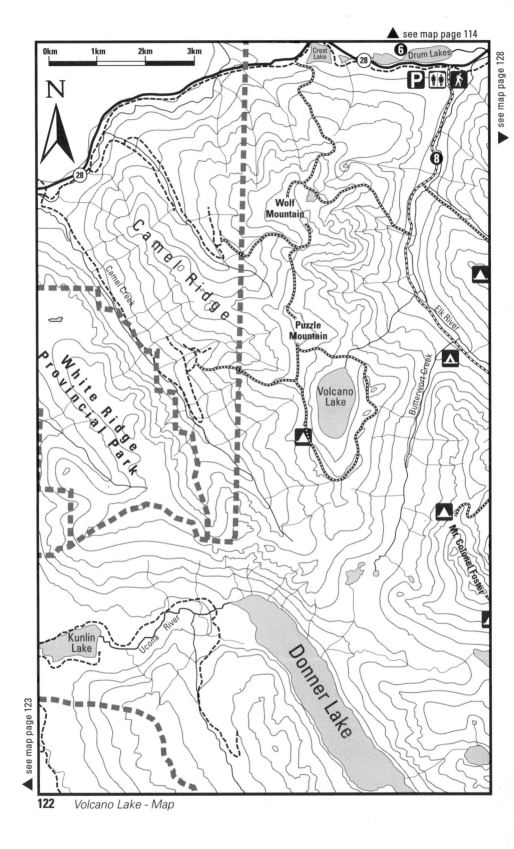

see map page 114

see map page 128

see map page 123

0km 1km 2km 3km

N

Crest Lake

28

6 Drum Lakes

P

28

8

Wolf Mountain

Camel Ridge

Camel Creek

White Ridge Provincial Park

Puzzle Mountain

Elk River

Butterwort Creek

Volcano Lake

Mt. Colonel Foster

Kunlin Lake

Ucona River

Donner Lake

Puzzle Mountain south aspect from south of Volcano Lake, June.

Highway 28. Similarly the bowl to the west of Puzzle's summit is a fast route in and out of the area but might be complicated by a long trudge down the logging roads in the valley between the White Ridge and Camel Ridge back to Highway 28.

Tours

A tour can be done from Highway 28 at Crest Lake taking the very steep route from Crest Lake gaining the alpine on the north-east ridge of Wolf Mountain. From here follow the height of land right over the summit of Wolf Mountain continuing generally southward over the summit of Puzzle Mountain and down to the end of the ridge south of Volcano Lake. It may be feasible to make a complete circuit around the rim of Volcano Lake.

Additional Info: Island Alpine 1st Edition p. 210-213

Phil Stone & Roy Cutler snowshoeing up Wolf Mountain from ERT, February.   photo: Corrie Wright

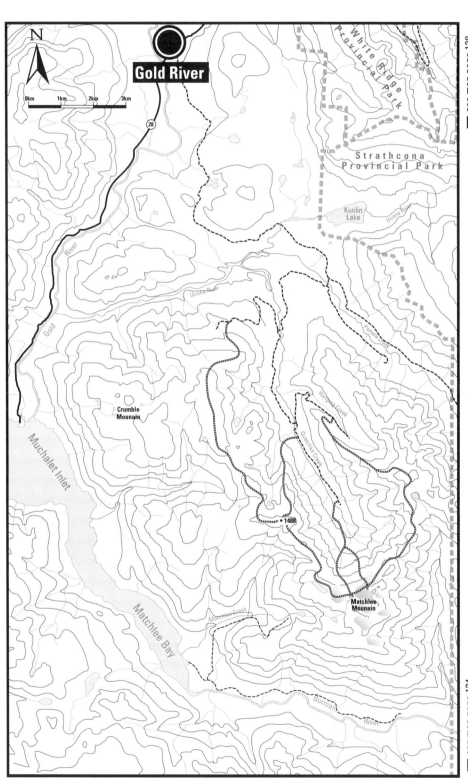

N

Gold River

0km 1km 2km 3km

28

White Ridge Provincial Park

Strathcona
Provincial Park

Kunlin
Lake

Ucona River

Gold River

Ucona River

Pamela Creek

Crumble
Mounain

Hanney Creek

Quatchka Creek

Muchalet Inlet

•1488

Matchlee
Mounain

Matchlee Bay

Matchlee Creek

Burman River

Matchlee Mountain

Matchlee Mountain east aspect from Mt. Colonel Foster, May.

Matchlee Mountain

Matchlee Mountain is found on the Ucona-Burman River divide, south of the community of Gold River, at the head of Quatchka Creek. Its glaciated summit plateau is surrounded by steep rock buttresses that provide some fine alpine climbing. Through the 1980s, then Gold River residents, John & Fred Put built excellent access trails and established some fine climbs on Matchleee. The peak and surrounding area was studied for inclusion within Strathcona Park during the late 1990s but wasn't designatred parkland afterall. The name is a derivative of 'Muchalet' the name of the nearby inlet and means 'fish on top of water' referring to the historical salmon runs of the area.

Highest Point: Summit of Matchlee Mountain 5,925 ft. / 1,806 m.

Most Vertical Descent Possible: ~600 m.

Difficulty/Duration: B3 / 1-3 days

Map Sheet: 92 F/12 Buttle Lake - GR 8501

Access: From Gold River, head south on the Ucona Road and follow it into the Quatchka Creek valley. Near the end of the road look for a rough path leading down into a small stand of old-growth around the creek. In this stand pick up the overgrown Matchlee trail and follow it through thick bush into an avalanche basin below the mountain. Two options lead up to the glacier. To the left a long wide snow/scree gully and to the right a narrow trail which winds up an exposed rock rib and steep forest to the glacier above.

Turns

Matchlee Mountain is a mountain of diverse character. Known for its alpine climbing routes on steep buttresses running off the summit Matchlee also has some of the longer ski descent lines on Vancouver Island in the right conditions. From the summit glacier the whole north side of the mountain encircles the head of the Quatchka Creek valley in a huge horseshoe with several long skiable gully lines linking the upper glacier shelf to the valley below..

Tours

As described Matchlee Mountain forms a large horseshoe around Quatchka Creek, the arms of which particularly on the west side offer good touring terrain both as a possible route to the mountain and as a complete horseshoe traverse from the confluence of Hanging Creek and Quatchka Creek.

Additional Info: Island Alpine 1st Edition p. 318-321

126   *Windswept Mountain Hemlock on the lower north-west ridge of King's Peak*

Elk River

Elkhorn (L), Rambler (C) and Mt. Colonel Foster (R) north aspect from King's Peak, January.

Elk River

The greatest concentration of high peaks is found in the Elk River area with eight of the top twenty highest summits on Vancouver Island found on the ridges surrounding the Elk River valley and adjacent Cervus Creek. The jagged nature of these peaks brings images of great climbing to mind more readily than ski touring and indeed the terrain lends itself at first glance to long descents rather than any notable tours. However for the determined and experienced some commiting traverses and long descents are possible amongst these most impressive of Island peaks.

Highest Point: Summit of Elkhorn Mountain 7,106 ft. / 2,166 m

Most Vertical Descent Possible: ~400m

Difficulty/Duration: B3 / 1-3 days

Map Sheets: 92 F/13 Upper Campbell Lake, 92 F/12 Buttle Lake

Access: Access into the Elk River area mountains is dominated by the importance of the aptly named Elk River Trail. The 'ERT' runs from Highway 28, 10 km up to Landslide Lake below Mt. Colonel Foster. Spur routes branch up off on two approaches to Elkhorn and higher up the Elk River valley to Elk Pass and Rambler Peak. The north-west approach route on to Elkhorn is a steep but well travelled route and the best for a direct approach to the peak and the surrounding ski terrain. The south-west approach route strikes up from just south of the gravel flats camp site on the ERT and is a good line to reach the open slopes of Mt. Colwell's west side and as an alternative route up or down from Elkhorn. For complete details see Island Alpine.

Beyond Elk Pass two major backcountry routes continue: 1) southward past the Golden Hinde to Phillips Ridge, and 2) north-east around the head of Cervus Creek along the Cervus-Wolf divide to Elk Mountain. Both of these routes are serious expeditions in remote and challenging terrain.

The King's Peak trail provides speedy access to that peak and is the fastest and most direct route in Strathcona Park to high alpine terrain. There are two possible starts to the trail one from the old Elk River Timber Co. Road whose future is doubtful as other sections of this road have already been decommissioned, and secondly with a 4x4 a higher trailhead can be reached along the rough road that runs underneath the twin powerlines just west of where they cross Highway 28.

see map page 114

see map page 122

see map page 130

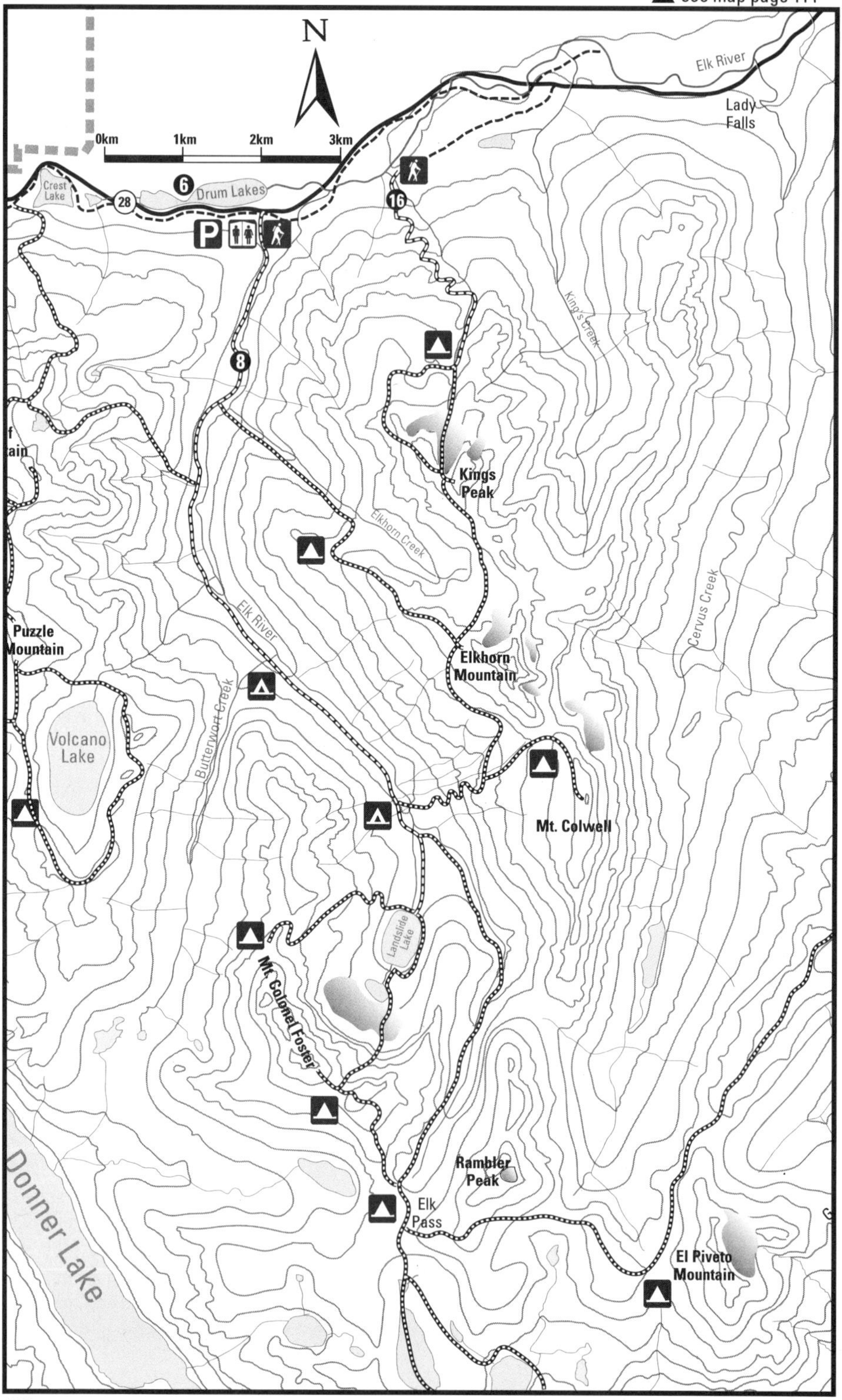
N
0km
1km
2km
3km
Elk River
Lady Falls
Crest Lake
6
Drum Lakes
28
16
8
King's Creek
Kings Peak
Elkhorn Creek
Elk River
Cervus Creek
Elkhorn Mountain
Puzzle Mountain
Butterwort Creek
Volcano Lake
Mt. Colwell
Landslide Lake
Mt. Colonel Foster
Rambler Peak
Elk Pass
El Piveto Mountain
Donner Lake

see map page 134

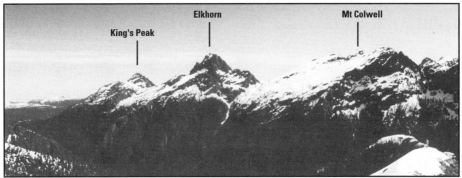

King's Peak (L), Elkhorn (C) & Mt. Colwell (R) south-west aspect from Mt. Colonel Foster, June.

Turns

King's Peak is one of the more popular alpine peaks in Strathcona Park, it has quick access from Highway 28 up a well maintained trail and an excellent ski/snowboarding line from the summit down onto the North Glacier and from there down to the lower meadows and further down as conditions dictate.

It would be a lot of work to pack skis up the Elkhorn north-west approach but once above treeline there are some cool lines down onto the Elkhorn Glacier or even just down the West Basin which could be awesome on a sunny spring afternoon with stable snow. Just to the south of Elkhorn, the wide open west slope of Mt. Colwell is the most obvious destination for a backcountry visit to the Elk River. A high camp near the Elkhorn-Colwell col at the foot of Elkhorn's south ridge would be ideal for dropping the 1,500 ft. of vertical on Colwell's west aspect.

Across the valley looms Mt. Colonel Foster with its unique relief. The wide snowfield that scoops down from the South Col to Foster Lake has been skied several times and gives close to 3,000 ft of vertical right down to Landslide Lake.

At the head of the Elk River around Elk Pass and Rambler Peak is some less commiting descent terrain but it's a long way back here and you'd want to be planning a more ambitious trip to bother taking advantage of these slopes. Plan on a few turns here if en route to Rambler Peak or while passing through on the Elk River-Phillips Ridge Traverse.

Last but not least at the north end of the Cervus Creek-Wolf River divide are the twin bowls on Elk Mountain which together with terrain on the south and east sides of Elk Mountain and the outstanding logging road access from Highway 28 make Elk Mountain a great ski destination.

Tours

As stated the mountain terrain found around the Elk River-Cervus Creek valleys is pretty serious and travelling in the high country here is suggested for experienced parties only. A less serious trip option, but not without its hazards is to follow the Elk River trail up to Landslide Lake. This is a good trip to use snowshoes on or choose the right snow conditions for skiing.

Elk Mountain north aspect from Mt. Flannigan, April.

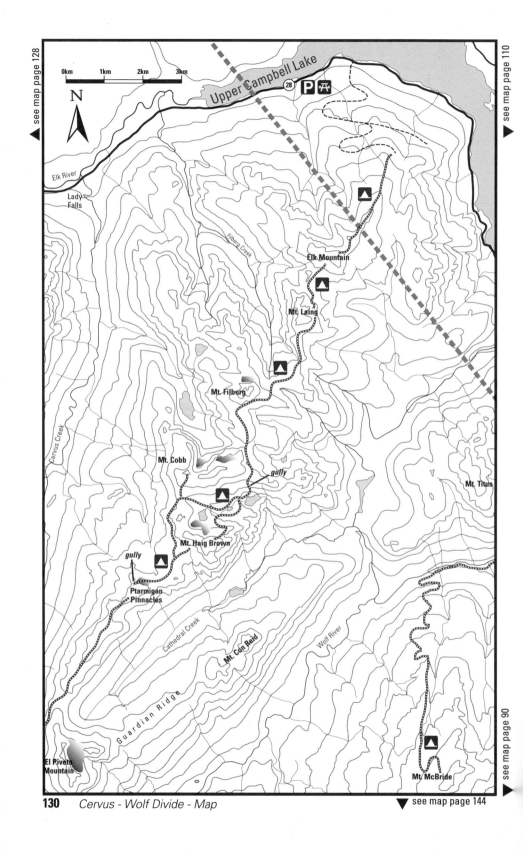

see map page 128

see map page 110

0km 1km 2km 3km

N

Upper Campbell Lake

28 P 🏕

Elk River

Lady
Falls

Filberg Creek

Elk Mountain

Mt. Laing

Mt. Filberg

Cervus Creek

Mt. Cobb

gully

Mt. Titus

Mt. Haig Brown

gully

Ptarmigan
Pinnacles

Cathedral Creek

Mt. Con Reid

Wolf River

Guardian Ridge

see map page 90

El Piveto
Mountain

Mt. McBride

see map page 144

King's Peak and North Glacier from Highway 28

A serious ski tour might be undertaken from King's Peak approaching up the trail from Highway 28 to the summit and from here descending into the basin between King's Peak and Elkhorn. To reach King's Peak follow the King's Peak trail description as far as the lower meadow then choose between the following two options as prevailing conditions dictate:

1) The creek that the trail line follows continues up a gully on the left (east) side of the meadow through a cliff band directly to the north glacier. This gully is very seductive because of the quick line it provides when full of snow but it is exposed to avalanches through winter and spring and the snow breaks up by June forming hazardous moats. Nevertheless in good conditions it is a fast line to the King's-Queen col.

2) Alternatively, take the hikers' route right (west) across the lower meadow and into a smaller upper meadow. Find an obvious well travelled gully through the trees to the crest of Queen's Ridge, at the same elevation as the toe of the glacier. Follow the ridge crest with some exposure in places to the King's-Queen's col.

To continue south to Elkhorn make a long angled descent from the King's-Queen col down into the huge basin between the two peaks and then up onto the Elkhorn Glacier. A steep climb out of the Elkhorn Glacier up an obvious gully puts you on the lower north-west ridge from where you can continue through the west basin and traverse under the west face of Elkhorn and onto Mt. Colwell. After taking in the summit of Colwell and some turns down its west face, descend to the Elk River trail on the Elkhorn south-west route.

Another major route through serious terrain would be to complete the Cervus-Wolf divide from El Piveto to Elk Mountain. by approaching Elk Pass on the Elk River trail and following the detailed summer route description found in Island Alpine as prevailing conditions allow.

Additional Info: Island Alpine 1st Edition p.214-259

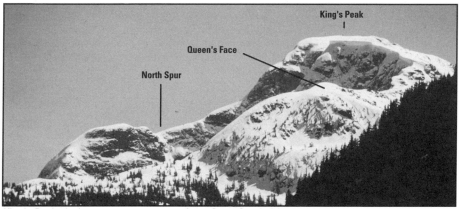

King's Peak north-west aspect as seen from Crest Creek, May.

132 *Ryan Stuart and Cameron Powell at Elk Pass en route to winter ascent of Rambler Peak.*

Elk River-Phillips Ridge

Golden Hinde   Behinde   Mt De Voe

Elk Pass

Looking south from Mt. Colonel Foster across Elk Pass to the Golden Hinde, May.

Elk River - Phillips Ridge Traverse

This route is a journey through the wilderness heart of Strathcona Park between the Gold River Highway 28 in the Elk River valley and the mine site below Phillips Ridge in the Myra Creek valley at the south end of Buttle Lake. The route can be traversed in either direction and offers additional variations to undertake longer tours including exiting or entering the route from Marble Meadows (see page143) or continuing south from Schjelderup and Carter lakes into the north fork of the Myra Creek valley and from there either out along the Myra-Thelwood divide to Tennent Lake and the Mt. Myra trail or extending the route further into the Thelwood Creek valley and the Jim Mitchell Lake Road. The furthest extension of tour would be to travel as far as the Drinkwater or Ash valleys all the way to Port Alberni.

The character of the terrain encountered along the Elk River - Phillips Ridge traverse differs from that found on the high ridge traverse in eastern Strathcona on the Comox-Buttle divide. Here the landscape is not as high in elevation on average and there is more forested sub-alpine terrain and no significant glaciers en route. The traverse can be completed in either direction and is described here from north to south ie: Elk River to Phillips Ridge.

Highest Point: Summit of Golden Hinde 7,218 ft. / 2,200 m

Most Vertical Descent Possible: ~800m

Difficulty/Duration: C3 / 5-8 days

Map Sheets: 92 F/13 Upper Campbell Lake, 92 F/12 Buttle Lake

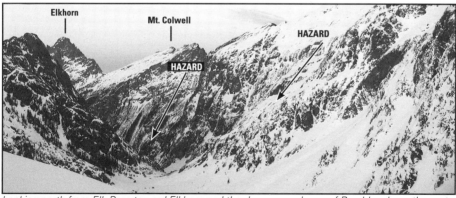

Elkhorn   Mt. Colwell   HAZARD   HAZARD

Looking north from Elk Pass toward Elkhorn and the dangerous slopes of Rambler above the route.

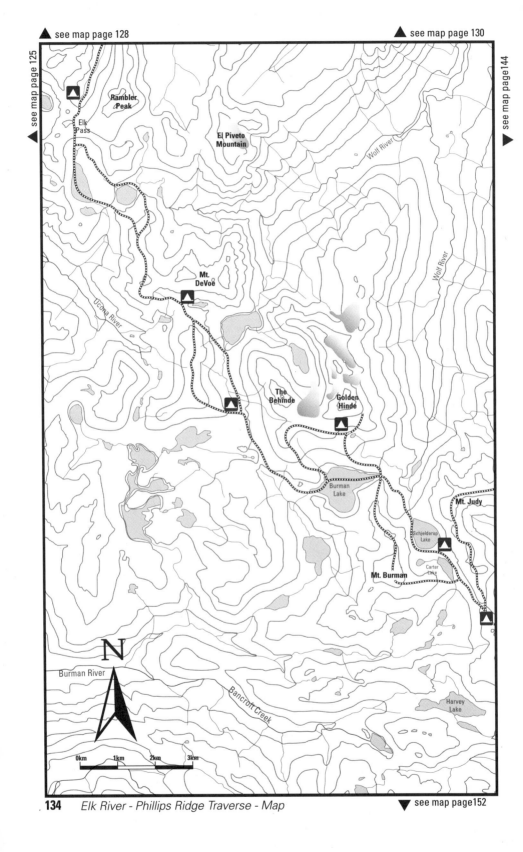

Rambler Peak

Elk Pass

El Piveto Mountain

Wolf River

Ucona River

Mt. DeVoe

The Behinde

Golden Hinde

Wolf River

Burman Lake

Mt. Judy

Schjelderup Lake

Mt. Burman

Carter Lake

N

Burman River

Bancroft Creek

Harvey Lake

0km 1km 2km 3km

Looking south from Elk Pass along the Burman-Ucona divide (L), January.

Access: The Elk River - Phillips Ridge traverse may be started at either the north end on the Elk River trail or from the south end up the Phillips Ridge trail. The Elk River trailhead is on Highway 28 60 km west of Campbell River. The Phillips Ridge trail starts from the mine site in Myra Creek at the end of the Buttle Lake Parkway. For complete details on the trail routes read the trail descriptions on page 77-78.

Golden Hinde south aspect from Phillips-Burman col, February.

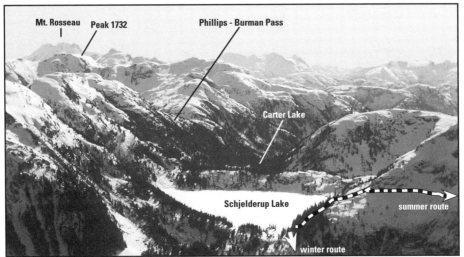

Looking south from the Golden Hinde across Schjelderup Lake to Phillips Ridge, February.

Route Description: From the Elk River trailhead, on the Gold River Highway 28, head south along the route of the Elk River Trail through the gorgeous old-growth forest. The trail keeps to the west bank of the Elk River under the flanks of Wolf Mountain, Puzzle Mountain and Volcano Peak. During the winter and particularly during spring thaw be aware that massive avalanches can run down the open gullies and slide paths that cross the trail. Don't linger on these features especially on warm days.

Pass the Gravel Flats campsite then cross Landslide Creek on the footbridge and head up the open rock slab scoured by the 1946 landslide toward Landslide Lake. Just a couple of hundred metres past the bridge flagging and a faded sign point left (south) to the route in to the upper Elk River valley. Leave Landslide Creek and follow the main Elk River into the old-growth. The route weaves up through the forest and then drops down to the Elk River at the base of several huge slide paths off the west face of Mt. Colwell. Again exercise extreme caution around these slide paths as the devestation here demonstrates an avalanche here would make short work of a few skiers.

Between two of these avalanche paths is a pocket of large old-growth Western Hemlock trees. This grove is the last good camp before Elk Pass and thus a popular place to spend a night. From the hemlock grove keep to the regular summer route climbing steadily and traversing along the lower reaches of Rambler Peak high above the east bank of the Elk River. This is another area to be aware of the extreme danger posed by avalanches coming off the high north ridge of Rambler Peak. The slopes several thousand feet above can rip over a cliff pouring into the creek bed. Once your route joins the creek, cross to the west side of the creek giving the runout of these avalanches as wide a berth as possible. Eventually the valley widens giving plenty of room to keep out of harm's way and the route continues directly up the floor of the valley to make a short steep climb into Elk Pass.

From Elk Pass descend southward to the north end of the large alpine lake below the pass. Travel through this part of the traverse is decidedly easier in winter/spring conditions when the sub-alpine bush is covered with snow and the lakes are frozen and can be crossed. The most direct route is to cross the lake to the far south shore and then follow the outlet creek for a few hundred metres before leaving the creek continuing south-eastward ascending the ridge at GR 9609 to its crest just north-west of Mt. De Voe. Follow this ridge southward and choose a safe line past the west peak of Mt. DeVoe and drop into the col on the west side of the summit of Mt. DeVoe. There are a few good ski lines around the triple summits of Mt. De Voe and it may be worth camping in the high pass just south of the peak to take advantage of them. The summit of De Voe is the central of the three peaks and is easily climbed up the west ridge.

Descend south into high pass previously mentioned at GR 9707. Take a gentle climb onto an isolated section of alpine ridge. Ski down the crest of this ridge and at the south end of the ridge descend south-east to the Wolf-Burman-Ucona Pass at GR 9904.

Looking up to Mt. Burman's north bowl from winter route in Wolf River meadows, February.

From this three watershed divide the safest low elevation winter route crosses Burman Lake to reach the toe of the north ridge of Mt. Burman. For parties interested in climbing either the Behinde or Golden Hinde ascend the long ridge that sweeps off the south side of the Behinde from the outlet of Burman Lake on the lake's west shore. The ridge leads on to a shoulder below the south face of the Behinde and makes a good if exposed camp. From this shoulder the Golden Hinde may be climbed by any of a number of routes and the Behinde tackled up the standard south ridge route. Descend the standard summer route from the tarn below the Golden Hinde's south face to the toe of Mt. Burman's north ridge. To avoid avalanche exposure in Mt. Burman's north bowl (see photo above) the winter route descends 150m or so into a small sub-alpine meadow in the upper reaches of the Wolf River just north of Schjelderup Lake.

Climb up to Schjelderup Lake keeping to the right (west) of the Wolf River flowing out of the lake. Cross Schjelderup Lake directly or follow the west shore in thaw. If snow stability is good then the usual summer route can be taken up the north ridge of Mt. Burman to a prominent and exposed bench that cuts across the north cirque of the mountain and offers a line down to Schjelderup Lake from there.

From the south shore of Schjelderup Lake head up over the low pass onto Carter Lake and cross that lake too. Make a gradually ascending traverse up the timbered slope to the left (east) and gain Phillips Ridge at the Phillips-Burman Pass (see photo page 136). From here keep to the height of land on Phillips Ridge past Peak 1732 and onto Arnica Lake (see Phillips Ridge Horseshoe traverse details).

Additional Info: Island Alpine 1st Edition p. 241-248, 267-277

Looking across Buttle Lake to Phillips Ridge east aspect from Rees Ridge, May.

Chris Barner finishing the last steps on to the Golden Hinde summit, Phillips Ridge behind.

Phillips Ridge Horseshoe

Looking across from Phillips Ridge to Grieg Ridge and the Golden Hinde, February.

Phillips Ridge Horseshoe

The Phillips Ridge Horseshoe is a classic Strathcona traverse following the height of land around the Phillips Creek watershed. It takes in some of the most beautiful country found in the park including passing through the exquisite Marble Meadows, the full length of Phillips Ridge with its awesome travelling, views of the Golden Hinde and Wolf River valley, and the summits of Mt. Phillips overlooking Buttle Lake. The ridge system around the Phillips watershed is best described as an 'E' shape with Mt. McBride terminating the end of the north branch, Greig Ridge forming the middle arm and Mt. Phillips at the south end.

Highest Point: Summit of Mt. Phillips 5,652 ft. / 1.723 m

Most Vertical Descent Possible: ~300

Difficulty/Duration: B3 / 5-8 days

Map Sheets: 92 F/12 Buttle Lake

Access: The Phillips Ridge Horseshoe is classically started from Buttle Lake on the Marble Meadows Trail and the route traversed anti-clockwise from the meadows around the watershed to Mt. Phillips descending off Mt. Phillips north peak back down to Buttle Lake. Undertaking the route this way takes in all the best the traverse has to offer including the infamous ascent and descent from and back to Buttle Lake.

Looking west from Rees Ridge across Phillips Ridge to the Golden Hinde, May.

To reach the Marble Meadows trail, cross Buttle Lake from the Buttle Lake Parkway from either the Augerpoint Day Area or Karst Creek Boat Ramp, to the north bank of Phillips Creek at the outlet of the creek into Buttle Lake. The trailhead is easily located in the timber and followed up a long series of switchbacks into the alpine. Take care in winter conditions on the last 200m of the route as it takes an open, exposed route to the plateau. Look for safer lines among the sparse trees to the left (south) of the summertime trail.

Alternatively, and without the logistical complication of a boat crossing of Buttle Lake, the traverse may be begun and finished on the Phillips Ridge trail from the Myra Falls mine. Lastly and most strenuously the majority of the route can be done by approaching along the Elk River following the Elk River-Phillips Ridge traverse as far as the Phillips-Burman col. Instead of exiting south to the Phillips Ridge trail head north along Phillips Ridge to Marble Meadows and descend the Marble Meadows trail to the outlet of Phillips Creek, cross the creek and ascend the ridge back up to the alpine on Mt. Phillips and exit on the Phillips Ridge trail to the mine, an Island epci!

Route Description: As stated the classic way to complete the tour is starting up the Marble Meadows trail from Buttle Lake. Follow the details of the Marble Meadows Trail (page 78) and head across the meadows past the Wheaton Hut to gain the northern end of Phillips Ridge on either side of Morrison Spire and head south into Rainbow Pass. Climb slightly up onto the plateau-topped Limestone Cap and the first of the best views of the Golden Hinde.

A narrow section of ridge continues southward to the high top of Tibetan Mountain at 1,800m (GR0603). Descend off Tibetan Mountain south into the Wolf-Phillips Pass a.k.a. Gallstone Col which makes a

good camp and a point from which to explore Greig Ridge. Continuing the traverse climb up onto Crystal Mountain which is the high point at the junction of Greig Ridge and Phillips Ridge. If time allows Greig Ridge is worthy of a trip along to the end and the possibility of a ski descent down to Greig Lake, or swing west from the top of Crystal Mountain to continue along the route to Mt. Judy at GR 0401.

The views of the Golden Hinde, lying immediately across the Wolf River valley, are breathtaking from this part of the route. The ridge returns to its north-south orientation from Mt. Judy. Follow it south over several high points and through a low point in the Phillips-Burman Pass. From this pass the route to the Golden Hinde and Elk River heads west down to Carter and/or Schjelderup lakes. Climb up out of the pass south over several more knolls avoiding difficulties on the crest by taking the open bowls on the east flank of the ridge. Follow the height of land as the ridge gradually swings to the east at Peak 1732. Peak 1732 can be skirted along its south flank and a long gradual descent made down to the sub-alpine forest around Arnica Lake where the Phillips Ridge trail descends to the mine.

Continue east past Arnica Lake and over a large open knoll and then down to a col overlooking Buttle Lake from where the ridge changes direction to the north up on to Mt. Phillips. From the summit of Mt. Phillips continue north along the high ridge with a small descent before making the last climb on to the north summit of Mt. Phillips. From here make a long descent into the timber keeping slightly east of north on the gentler angled ridge that leads down to the outlet of Phillips Creek. Cross the creek to your boat and cross Buttle Lake back to the road.

Additional Info: Island Alpine 1st Edition p.262-269

Looking west from Marble Meadows to Greig Ridge and Phillips Ridge across Phillips Creek, February.

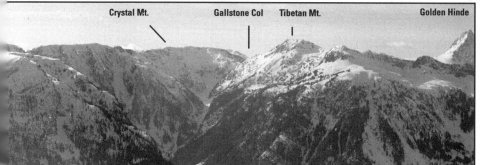

Marcus Kellerhals above Buttle Lake, Marble Meadows.

Golden Hinde

Limestone Cap

Morrison Spire

Marble Meadows

Mt McBride north aspect from King's Peak, January.

Marble Meadows

Perched high above the west shore of Buttle Lake, Mt. McBride is an unmistakable landmark from the Buttle Lake Parkway with a distinctive uplifted, Rocky Mountain look. Mt. McBride is the highest point of a network of alpine peaks, ridges and meadows that includes Phillips Ridge and the sublime Marble Meadows. The 'Meadows' are found on a high limestone plateau west of Buttle Lake and to the south of Mt. McBride. It is an exquisite environment in any season and winter is no exception. The open, benign terrain is perfect for exploration on skis. Small ridges separate and link a multitude of lakes dotted across the plateau. In later spring as the winter snow retreats outcrops of grey limestone are revealed along with karst pavements and carpets of wildflowers by high summer.

The effort of access to Marble Meadows in the winter warrants at least 3-5 nights stay (it may take one night just to cross Buttle Lake and hike/skin up to the meadows!). In spring however Mt. McBride is a feasible if strenuous day trip from Buttle Lake. A trip to the Marble Meadows area gives options to ascend Mt. McBride, one of the highest skiable peaks on the Island, and lengthy tours out to the Myra Falls mine site along Phillips Ridge or north to Highway 28 via the Golden Hinde and Elk River Trail. The Wheaton Hut north of Marble Peak makes a superb base from which to explore Marble Meadows. If you aren't familiar with the hut's location make sure you bring avalanche probes to help find it!

Highest Point: Summit of Mt. McBride 2081m

Most Vertical Descent Possible: ~400m

Difficulty/Duration: C2 / 3-7 days

Marble Meadows and Mt McBride south aspect from Marble Peak

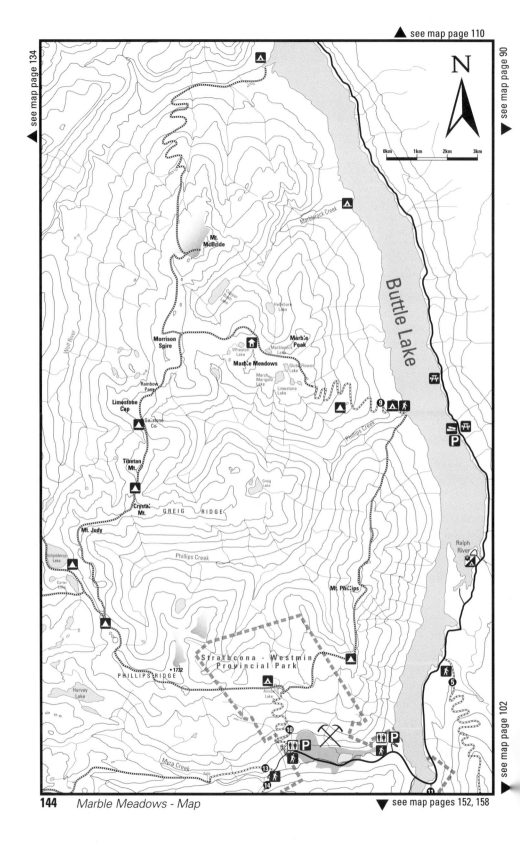

N

0km 1km 2km 3km

Buttle Lake

Marblerock Creek

Mt. McBride

Copper Gulch Lake

Hellebore Lake

Morrison Spire

Wheaton Lake

Marble Peak

Marblejack Lake

Marble Meadows

Globe Flower Lake

Marsh Marigold Lake

Limestone Lake

Rainbow Pass

Wolf River

Limestone Cap

Ganstone Col

9

Phillips Creek

Tibetan Mt.

P

Crystal Mt.

GREIG RIDGE

Greig Lake

Mt. Judy

Phillips Creek

Schjelderup Lake

Carter Lake

Mt. Phillips

Ralph River

Strathcona - Westmin Provincial Park

PHILLIPS RIDGE

•1732

Harvey Lake

Arnica Lake

5

10

P

P

Myra Creek

Falls

13

14

Looking southward across Marble Meadows from Mt. McBride, June.

Map Sheet: 92 F/12 Buttle Lake

Access: To reach Marble Meadows, the best route is via the Marble Meadows trail on the west shore of Buttle Lake (see page 77). Cross the lake from either the Augerpoint Day Area or the Karst Creek Boat Ramp to the north bank of Phillips Creek at its outlet into the lake. The trail climbs up steep switchbacks and is one of the longer such trail ascents in the Park, reaching the plateau finally at 1,400 m. Hike north-west across the meadows to a col at the toe of Marble Peak's south-east ridge overlooking Marblerock Lake. Continue around the lake and to the Wheaton Hut at GR106077. The Wheaton hut makes an obvious location for a winter base camp and is well situated to explore Marble Meadows or head further afield to Mt. McBride, Morrison Spire and points beyond.

Turns

Not surprisingly there isn't much significant vertical on the Marble Meadows plateau itself but a few long lines lead down off the plateau to some of the lower elevation lakes. There looks to be an awesome 500m run off the north-east end of Wheaton Ridge down to Copper Bush Lake. And off the south side of Wheaton Ridge a 200m line leads down to Wheaton Lake with options heading further down that drainage to the large lake at GR0906.

For some wide open terrain better to pack a day pack and head over to the slopes off the south flank of the ridge between Morisson Spire and Mt. McBride (see photo below). The south slopes of Morrison Spire down to Rainbow Pass give a 240m drop.

Mt.McBride itself has a huge wide open north-west facing slope and glacier which skied from the summit to the treeline gives over 600m of vertical and is one of the best ski/snowboard destinations on the Island. To really take advantage of the vertical on McBride it makes more sense to approach the mountain directly from Buttle Lake by bushwhacking up the Wolf River. This is a full on Island ski touring classic with incredible forest, bush, rivers and big ski terrain.

Golden Hinde and Morrison Spire east aspect from Wheaton Ridge, February.

Marcus Kellerhals skiing out of Marble Meadows down to Buttle Lake.   photo: Chris Lawrence

Tours

Exploring Marble Meadows on skis or snowshoes can offer several days of easy touring with exquisite lakes, lightly treed meadows and awesome vistas off the edge of the Marble Meadows plateau overlooking Buttle Lake, the Phillips Creek watershed and the more mountainous country toward Mt. McBride. Marble Peak is a worthy climb taking a line up the west ridge, there's some exposed scrambling near the top. The summit ridge may be corniced and there a few gaps in the ridge to be wary of but any high point on the peak is going to improve the view so just go as far as conditions allow.

Mt. McBride is the major tour destination from the Meadows and one of the main attractions to visiting the area. To reach Mt. McBride from the hut hike up to the top of Wheaton Ridge from where a clear view can be had of Mt. McBride and the route ahead. Head west across a wide pass between Phillips Creek to the south and Marblerock Creek to the north. Skin up a slope to the crest of the ridge between Mt. McBride and Morrison Spire. Continue north to a col at the foot of the south ridge of Mt. McBride. Make an exposed traverse northwestward from the col at the base of the ridge around a prominent basin to gain the west side of the mountain and the McBride Glacier above. Skin right up the wide open slope to the summit ridge crest. Be wary of the snow stability and the huge exposure (not steep but a big ride!) take particular care of cornices overhanging the south face.

Some long runs can be had on the remnant glacier on McBride's huge north east slope overlooking the Wolf River. If time allows the snowfield can be run right down to the treeline well past the point the route from Marble Meadows joins it. This requires an ascent for the return trip though. To take the most advantage of the terrain on this aspect of McBride, consider moving camp to the col at the foot of the south ridge or best of all approach Mt. McBride from Buttle Lake right up the Wolf River to a base camp at a small tarn at the foot of the north-west face of the mountain.

Marble Meadows & Golden Hinde east aspect from Mt. Albert Edward, March.

Marble Peak, Marble Meadows and the Golden Hinde east aspect from Mt. Washington February.

Two longer tours can be started or finished at Marble Meadows as well. The Phillips Ridge Horseshoe traverse which takes a circular route from the mouth of Phillips Creek on Buttle Lake or from the Phillip's Ridge trail from the mine. The route may be undertaken in either direction around the 'E' shaped ridge system that encircles the Phillip's Creek valley system.

A second more ambitious tour links the Elk River - Phillips Ridge traverse to Marble Meadows. This route may also be completed travelling in either direction with the deciding factor likely to be the logisitics of crossing Buttle Lake to or from the Marble Meadows trailhead. A boat or canoe drop-off on Buttle Lake is likely the more certain option to try with a competent solo boater/canoeist/driver making the return trip back to the Karst Creek boat ramp after dropping your party off at the Marble Meadows trailhead.

Follow the earlier described details and ascend the trail up to Marble Meadows, past the Wheaton Hut and gain the main Phillip's Ridge system near Morrison Spire. From Morisson Spire head south along the ridge over Limestone Cap and Tibetan Mountain, through Gallstone Col and on to Crystal Mountain. From this high point Greig Ridge branches off to the east and makes an awesome side trip exploring the gentle ridge and possible ski lines down to Grieg Lake.

Continuing down Phillip's Ridge from Crystal Mountain head west and then make a descent southward into either of two cols immediately east of Schjelderup Lake. Descend a safe line to Schjelderup Lake and from here pick up the route description for the Elk River-Phillip's Ridge traverse heading north past the Golden Hinde to the Elk River exiting on to Highway 28 down the Elk River trail. Follow these trail descriptions for more info.

Additional Info: Island Alpine 1st Edition p. 248, 262-272, IB 1997 p.22, WIM #21 p.18

Marble Peak south-west aspect, February.

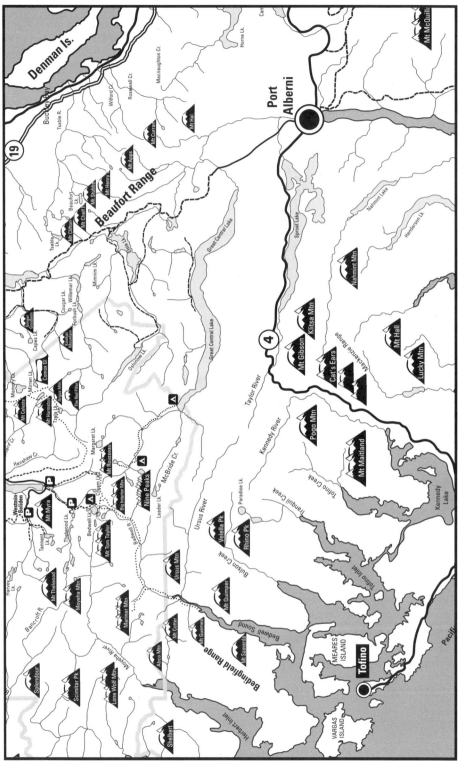

Southern Strathcona Park

Southern Strathcona Park

When moisture laden air rolls onto Vancouver Island from the open Pacific Ocean it is the west coast and the mountains overlooking the coastal sounds and inlets that catch the brunt of the weather and receive the greatest amounts of precipitation. The peaks of southern Strathcona Park bear witness to this phenomenon and illustrate it with their glaciers and heavy winter snowfalls.

Highest Point: Summit of Mt. Rosseau 6,437 ft. / 1,962 m

Most Vertical Descent Possible: ~600m

Map Sheets: 92 F/12 Buttle Lake, 92 F/5 Bedwell River,

Access: Access into southern Strathcona Park is made from the centre of the park off the Buttle Lake Parkway, from Port Alberni via Great Central Lake and the Della Falls Trail or from the south-west by air or water from Tofino into Bedwell Sound.

Buttle Lake Parkway: Drive from Campbell River up Highway 28 to Buttle Narrows. Pass the junction to Gold River leaving Highway 28 and continue south on the Buttle Lake Parkway along the shore of Buttle Lake. The road runs all the way down the lake shore to the south end where it crosses Thelwood Creek and climbs into the Myra Creek valley and terminates at the mine site.

Jim Mitchell Lake Road: At the south end of Buttle Lake on the Buttle Lake Parkway cross the bridge over Thelwood Creek and immediately turn left onto Jim Mitchell Lake Rd., a gravel road at the base of the hill which leads up to the Myra Falls mine. This road services the hydro electric facility in Thelwood Creek which provides power to the mine and follows the creek up to Jim Mitchell Lake. Access to this road can be limited in winter as it is only plowed by the mining company as they require, as they have an underground tunnel to the lake this is rare. Drive up the road for 6 km to the clearly signposted Bedwell Lake trailhead or continue up the last few steep switchbacks to Jim Mitchell Lake where there is also parking for routes into the Thelwood valley.

Clayoquot Sound: Approaching the mountains from the ocean is a unique facet of coastal mountaineering and leaving Tofino for the peaks above Bedwell Sound is a classic Island alpine experience. Sea kayak or water taxi are two options to reach the mouth of the Bedwell River and the Onimitis trail.

Cabins: None but some of the mine facilities can offer some shelter eg: tunnel at Jim Mitchell Lake.

Turns

Southern Strathcona is one of the best regions on Vancouver Island to look for great backcountry ski/snowboard descents. Although the peaks are as much as a thousand feet lower than some of their more illustrious cousins to the north, the terrain is more suited to skiing. Part of the reason for this difference in topography is due to the granite that forms these peaks resisting the scouring action of the glaciers during past ice ages. The result are more rounded mountain shapes ideal for ski touring with many convex slopes offering commiting ski descent lines. Look for ski lines on Mt. Myra, Moyeha Mountain, Big Interior Mountain and Mt. Septimus/Rosseau.

Tours

Similarly high quality to the descents are the ski tours found in southern Strathcona Park. Long sections of high ridges, wide open glaciers and sub-alpine valleys dotted with frozen lakes make travel through this area a joy and in some instances far more enjoyable than during the summer months when the notorious bush of the valleys makes for some trying bushwhacking.

Some of the better ski tours include: the Onimitis high traverse from Bedwell Lake over Mt. Tom Taylor to Mariner Mountain and Bedwell Sound, a circumnavigation of the Mt. Septimus/Rosseau massif which takes in a number of small glaciers and gives the option of some great descents off the peak and around Mt. Myra and along the Myra-Thelwood divide there are a number of tour options amongst some fairly benign but magical terrain.

Curtis Lyon ducking the rain for lunchtime on a spring run up the Tennent Lake Trail

Mt. Myra

Sandbag Lake

Tennent Lake

A foreshortened view of Mt. Myra's north-west aspect from Phillips Ridge, February.

Mt. Myra

Mt. Myra overlooks the south-west corner of Buttle Lake above the mine site in the lower Myra Creek valley. The mine's activities are concentrated both underground beneath Mt. Myra and above ground on its north and west flanks. Mt. Myra and some of the surrounds are within an entirely separate park created to accommodate the mining activity, Westmin-Strathcona. Myra is an excellent winter destination with a slightly shortened approach as the parking lot at the mine is just above 300m. Myra is a good all-weather destination as much of the lower terrain is free from avalanche hazard and can be navigated in poor visibility with little trouble as far as Tennent Lake and the surrounding meadows.

The Mt. Myra trail also offers access to the Thelwood-Myra divide which runs west from Mt. Myra and is a superb touring route toward Mt. Thelwood and Moyeha Mountain. The terrain around Mt. Myra makes an excellent ski touring destination and there are even a few waterfalls in the vicinity which freeze up in winter for some rare island waterice climbing.

Highest Point: Summit of Mt. Myra 5,938 ft. / 1,810 m

Most Vertical Descent Possible: 800+m

Difficulty/Duration: B2-B3 / 1-3 days

Map Sheet: 92 F/12 Buttle Lake

Mt. Myra north-east aspect from Buttle Lake, June.

see map page 102

see map page 134

see map page 158

Buttle Lake
Strathcona - Westmin Provincial Park
Price Creek
Andrew Lake
Big Jim Lake
Bedwell Lake
Baby Bedwell Lake
Jim Mitchell Lake
Mt. Myra
Tennent Lake
McNish Lake
Thelwood Lake
Carwithen Lake
Greenview Lake
Upper Thelwood
Falls
Harvey Lake
Bancroft Peak
Mt. Thelwood
Moyeha Mountain
Moyeha River
0km
1km
2km
3km
N
5
10
11
12
13
14

see map page 162

see map page 162

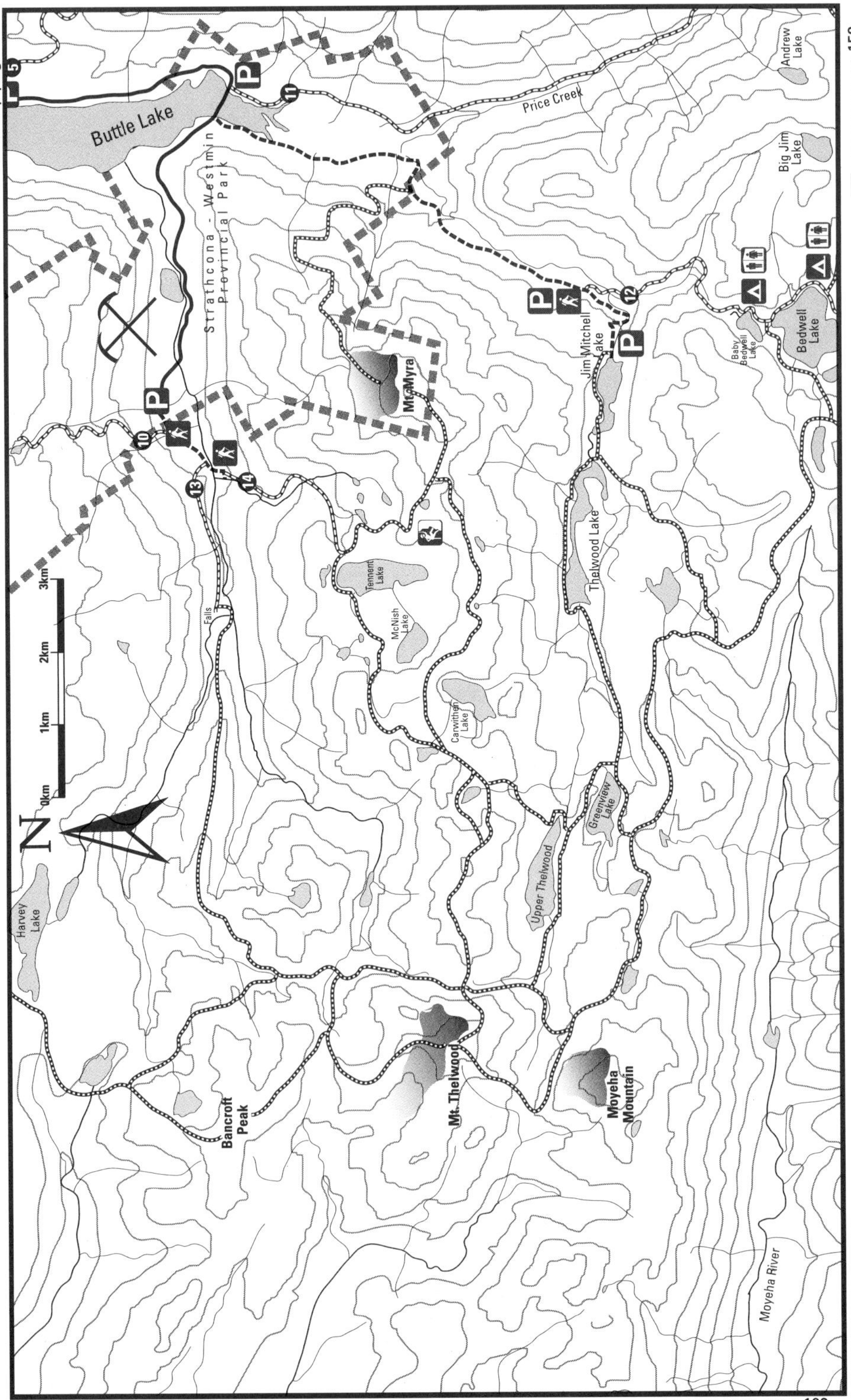

Mt. Myra north-east aspect from Mt. Albert Edward, March. Note Mariner Mountain in background (R).

Access: Best reached by the Mt. Myra Trail from the Myra Falls mine via Tennent Lake. Park at the signposted lot at the west end of the mine facility. Walk down the gravel road to the bridge over Myra Creek and locate the trailhead before the noisy powerhouse at the end of the road. The trail takes an old cat track steeply up the hillside to the dam at Tennent Lake which feeds the hydro electric powerhouse below. The route from the dam becomes less distinct (than a cat road!) and swings south-east to cross open meadows then climbs up a steep gully past Sandbag Lake and onto the south-west ridge of Mt. Myra. Follow the ridge keeping to its south side over a knoll and then down into a col below the final summit dome.

Myra may also be reached from the old road to the mine's ventilation shaft on the north-east flank of the mountain. The road leaves Jim Mitchell Lake Rd. just above the Thelwood Creek Powerhouse.

Turns

The great descent terrain and relatively good access are the big attractions of Mt. Myra. If conditions are right, descents close to 1,000m are possible and there are ski lines all around the mountain suitable for a variety of snow and weather conditions. The Mt. Myra trail and much of the most easily reached terrain is north facing and prone to heavy snowfalls fed from moist air coming in off the Pacific and up Herbert Inlet and the Moyeha River valley. Deep snowfalls with difficult trailbreaking can make the steep climb up the Mt. Myra trail an arduous task. Once at Tennent Lake though the terrain opens up and a wide choice of possibilities present themselves.

Some short treed lines may be found by following the summer route past Tennent Lake to the meadows below the cliff band below Sandbag Lake. Continue traversing past the gully that makes the steep climb to Sandbag Lake and past the base of the waterfall draining that lake (the Happy Warrior goes at WI 4+ if it's formed up) and into an open meadow which makes a good sheltered camp location. The short descent lines are found among the trees ringing this meadow and on the way out it is possible just to drop right off the edge of this meadow and join the Myra trail lower down.

For the very best ski terrain you'll need to head higher up along the summer route toward the summit. In spring conditions the summer route can be skied back down, to well below Sandbag Lake, but in fresher snow it may take a bit of poling to get all the way down the ridge. From the two cols immediately to the south-west of the summit a pair of huge gullies lead down on the north-west side over 800m straight down to the Mt Myra trail. Watch for the cornices at the top of these gullies and rocks and cliffs halfway down but otherwise the lines go. A great run to end your tour on!

The longest lines on Myra are off the north side of the peak down the north-west ridge into the trees and also down the remnant glacier, continuing right down the main drainage that leads directly to the mine site.

Getting on to the summit in winter to reach the north-west ridge and north glacier has its challenges but an alternative approach up the north-east ridge might be considered. This ridge can be started

Mt. Myra north-west aspect from Tennent Lake meadows, April.

off the Jim Mitchell Lake Road which also serves the Bedwell Lake trailhead between the turn off and the old mine road that breaks off to the right at the top of the first big switchback on the road. Much of the slope up onto the road was burned by prospectors and the silver, weathered snags sticking out of the snow make an interesting landscape to ski through. Continue up onto the crest of the north-east ridge and follow it to below the subsidary north peak of Mt. Myra and pick a safe traverse line into the basin between the two peaks. Carry on as the terrain, exposure and snow cover dictate to the Myra Glacier which can be skinned right up to the summit.

Tours

Possible tours around Mt. Myra include an up and over trip in either direction between Tennent Lake and the north-east ridge over the summit. A less commiting route may be taken from Tennent Lake heading west along the first part of the route to Mt. Thelwood. Gain the main Myra-Thelwood Ridge north-west of McNish Lake then swing south-eastward heading along the ridge between McNish and Carwithen Lakes and eventually east toward Mt. Myra. Continue right up to the summit of Mt. Myra if conditions allow and descend either the summer route via Sandbag Lake to Tennent Lake or drop down one of the longer runs described on the north side of the mountain back to the Mt. Myra trail.

Additional Info: Island Alpine 1st Edition p.285-286

Mt. Myra north-east aspect from Buttle Lake, May.

Mt. Thelwood - Moyeha

Mariner Mountain, Moyeha Mountain and Mt. Thelwood north aspect from Phillips Ridge, February.

Mt. Thelwood-Moyeha Mountain

The isolated summits of Mt. Thelwood and Moyeha Mountain are found west of Mt. Myra and the south end of Buttle Lake at the headwaters of the Moyeha River, Thelwood and Myra Creeks, and Bancroft Creek. The character of these mountains is rounded, glaciated granite massifs surrounded by sub-alpine valleys ideal for ski touring and a few classic descents.

Highest Point: Summit of Moyeha Mountain 5,918 ft. / 1,804 m.

Most Vertical Descent Possible: 600m off north face of Moyeha Mountain

Difficulty/Duration: B2-B3 / 2-5 days

Map Sheet: 92 F/12 Buttle Lake

Access: There are three main routes into the Thelwood-Moyeha area. Most commonly used is the Mt. Myra trail from which there are two main points of deperature, one west from Tennent Lake and one higher up on Sandbag Knoll. Both join the Myra-Thelwood divide which runs west to join Mt. Thelwood's south-east ridge. Secondly is a route from the Upper Myra Falls trail along a prominent ridge that separates the two main forks of Myra Creeek. The ridge offers a gradual ascent into a cirque on Mt. Thelwood's north-east flank and links well with the Myra-Thelwood divide for a circuit.

Moyeha Mountain east aspect from Flower Ridge, May.

Moyeha Mountain (L) and Myra-Thelwood divide (R) above Jim Mitchell Lake, January.

Lastly and of most interest in late winter/spring is the approach from the end of the Jim Mitchell Lake Road at the mine's hydro-dam facility. The road is steep beyond the Bedwell Lake trailhead so if in doubt park there. From the end of the road near the water intake house either cross Jim Mitchell Lake to the far south-west shore taking advantage of the cat track which becomes exposed at low water levels or take a steep sidehill traverse around the north shore to Thelwood Lake. Plan this trip for later season with ample snow cover as Jim Mitchell Lake is better to cross than to negotiate the talus and boulder fields around its shores. The lake level varies as water is drawn out for power generation and this can affect the stability of the ice cover. More open terrain continues up the valley across or alongside the lake chain due west to the eastern side of Moyeha Mountain.

Turns

One of the Island's most awesome looking ski descents runs down the north glacier and ridge of Moyeha Mountain (right skyline in photo page 155). This 600+m run sweeps from right off the airy summit of the peak down to the col between Moyeha Mountain and Mt. Thelwood. The convex roll of the glacier is cause for extra care in assessing this line's stability but also adds to its exposure and huge atmosphere. This line would make a superb day trip from a camp anywhere just east of the mountain.

Another cool looking line drops down through Mt. Thelwood's north-west bowl into the Bancroft Creek valley. This valley is very alluring and a ski down the glacial cirque overlooking it is bound to have a true wilderness feel to it. Other than these few gems the Mt. Thelwood-Moyeha Mountain area really excels as a touring destination with its rolling ridges and numerous frozen lakes.

Tours

There are a number of possible ski tours that can be pieced together around Mt. Thelwood, Moyeha Mountain and Bancroft Peak. In fact winter may very well be the preferred seaon to experience this area as the extensive sub-alpine forest in the valleys has notoriously thick bush that makes summer time travel particularly arduous. The numerous large sub-alpine lakes around these peaks are far faster to ski across with a blanket of winter snow than to thrash around the shore in summertime.

Some of the touring possibilities include: heading west up the Thelwood Creek valley from the end of the Jim Mitchell Lake Road across Jim Mitchell and Thelwood lakes to Greenview and Upper Thelwood lakes. From here Moyeha Mountain may be ascended and a touring route continued up onto the Myra-Thelwood divide and either back from Mt. Thelwood toward Tennent Lake or even Mt. Myra, or northward past Mt. Thelwood to Bancroft Peak exiting down the Myra Creek valley. From Thelwood Lake a circuit may be completed southward to Bedwell Lake exiting on the Bedwell trail.

Mt. Thelwood can be reached quite directly from Tennent Lake by following the Myra-Thelwood divide westward to Crystal Pass and then up the south-east ridge. An alternative approach or exit to form a circuit with the Tennent Lake route is up the ridge between the two forks of Myra Creek. This ridge can be found by leaving the mine powerhouse road on the Upper Myra Falls trail and watching for the signpost pointing to a crossing of the north fork of the creek just below the falls. Because of the lower elevation of this route choose a time with a low snowline.

Additional Info: Island Alpine 1st Edition p.287-291

Big Interior - Nine Peaks

Big Interior Mountain north aspect from Baby Bedwell Lake, March.

Big Interior Mountain - Nine Peaks

Big Interior Mountain and Nine Peaks have some of the best descent terrain of the southern Strathcona Mountains combined with quick access via the Bedwell trail. As a result these peaks are some of the more popular ski touring destinations on the Island.

Highest Point: Summit of Big Interior Mountain 6,109 ft. / 1,862 m

Most Vertical Descent Possible: 600m

Difficulty/Duration: B2-B3 / 2-5 days

Map Sheets: 92 F/5 Bedwell River

Access: The best way to reach Big Interior and Nine Peaks is from Buttle Lake via the Bedwell Trail off the Jim Mitchell Lake Rd. Access to the trailhead in winter varies with snow cover, whether or not the road is plowed or snow free and the gate being open.

Turns

There are several wide open cirques on the north and west aspects of Big Interior Mountain giving descent lines up to 600 m of vertical. Check out the possibilities right off the main summit straight down the glacier to the north, or take a skier's rightward traverse following the usual ascent route to the base of the north-east cirque. With deep snow cover the drainage out of the north-east cirque can be skied out down to the meadows to Bedwell Lake, no need to follow the standard summer line.

The cirque between the Big Interior summit and Marjorie's Load looks very promising right down to the small tarn at its base. And heading toward Nine Peaks the ridge past Marjorie's Load down to You Pass will go quickly on skis. Take care to avoid exposure on the slopes above Della Lake, there is a steep cliff below the bench on the east side of the ridge dropping into the cirque.

On Nine Peaks the glacier can be skied right off the summit 700+m down to Beauty Lake. Keep to the north side of the glacier trending to skiers left, or just head more northward and drop right back down to You Pass and on down to Della Lake.

Big Interior Mountain and Nine Peaks (R) north-west aspect from Bedwell-Moyeha divide, June.

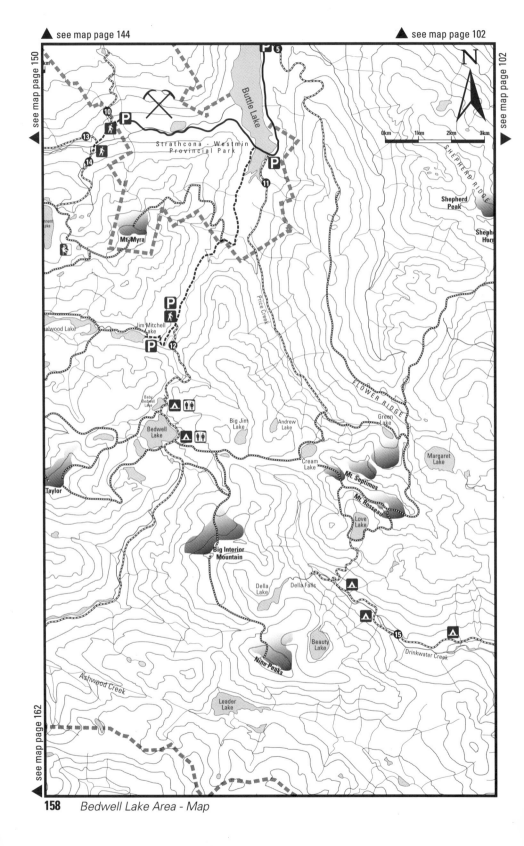

N

0km   1km   2km   3km

Buttle Lake

Strathcona - Westmin Provincial Park

SHEPHERD RIDGE

Shepherd Peak

Sheph Horn

Mt. Myra

Price Creek

P 5

P

11

P

12

Jim Mitchell Lake

elwood Lake

FLOWER RIDGE

Baby Bedwell Lake

Bedwell Lake

Big Jim Lake

Andrew Lake

Green Lake

Margaret Lake

Cream Lake

Mt. Septimus

Mt. Rosseau

Love Lake

Taylor

Big Interior Mountain

Della Lake

Della Falls

Beauty Lake

Nine Peaks

Drinkwater Creek

15

Ashwood Creek

Leader Lake

East aspect of Big Interior Mountain from near Cream Lake

Tours

Skiing from the Bedwell trailhead out and back to Nine Peaks over Big Interior is a classic Island tour and passes through some great ski terrain. Start up the Bedwell Trail to the campsite at Bedwell Lake. From here either take the route to Cream Lake south-eastward up to the Bedwell-Drinkwater Pass and traverse across the summer route into the base of the main north cirque, or try a more direct approach by leaving the Cream Lake route much lower than the pass and traverse into a meadow below Big Interior's north-east cirque. Follow the creek draining the cirque right up to a headwall where it takes a steep sided gully through the wall. If conditions are right the gully may be ascended directly otherwise look on either side of the headwall for a safe line into the cirque base. However you reach it the base of this cirque makes an excellent campsite.

To get higher on the peak and to continue on to Nine Peaks head directly up the snout of the glacier heading south toward the summit, traverse under the north side of the North-East Summit to less exposed ground on the south-east side of the ridge. The ridge up to the summit becomes gradually more exposed but in good conditions you can ski right to and off the summit.The approach up the Bedwell trail to Bedwell Lake and on to the Drinkwater-Bedwell Pass is essentially hazard free and if conditions aren't favourable for your planned destination there's always the consolation of continuing over to Cream Lake, keeping on more moderate ground.

Additional Info: Island Alpine p. 292-295

Nine Peaks from Cream Lake, June. Note outflow of Della Falls at bottom left.

Mt. Septimus-Rosseau

Mt. Rosseau north-east aspect from Green Lake, May.

Mt. Septimus-Rosseau

The Mt. Septimus-Rosseau massif is a sprawling complex of serrated summit towers, steep gullies and several remnant glaciers. Access to the peak is good and it is a perennial favourite destination with Island climbers. Despite its jagged appearance from afar the terrain around and on the massif lends itself well to ski touring with some dramatic descent lines between the spires.

Highest Point: Summit of Mt. Rosseau 6,437 ft. / 1,962 m

Most Vertical Descent Possible: 600m

Difficulty/Duration: B3 / 2-4 days

Map Sheets: 92 F/5 Bedwell River, 92 F/6 Great Central Lake

Access: Mt. Rosseau may be reached from several approach options: the Bedwell Trail, Price Creek Trail, Flower Ridge Trail and even the Della Falls Trail. For a simple in and out trip to Cream Lake and the Septimus Glacier the Bedwell Trail is the safest and fastest route. From Bedwell Lake follow the signposted route to Cream Lake up a gentle ridge and into the Drinkwater-Bedwell col. A traverse line past Little Jim Lake and across a bench system leads straight to Cream Lake from where the route onto the Septimus Glacier and the west shoulder is clear.

The north side of Mt. Rosseau may be approached from either the Price Creek to Green Lake or Flower Ridge Trail to Price Pass. With so many approach options the trip possibilities around the massif are diverse.

Turns

Overlooking Cream Lake is one of the longer and more mellow of the descent possibilities down the Septimus Glacier from the west shoulder. The south aspect of the massif overlooking Love Lake has some shorter lines but strong skiers may find longer lines right down to Love Lake. The Pocket Glacier under Margaret Peak offers some gentler terrain with more of the dramatic surroundings typical of the massif. Around to the north side of the mountain there looks to be a long 700m line possible down to Margaret Lake from the east end of the summit ridge. Above Green Lake on the impressive north face are several wild ski lines. Checkout the Misthorn Glacier down to Price Pass, the main central gully between the Misthorns and Mt. Rosseau and lines of the wide North Glacier of Mt. Septimus crossing the face back down to Green Lake.

Mt. Septimus above Cream Lake, north-west aspect, June.

Tours

The touring terrain around Septimus-Rosseau is worthy of a trip but comes with the caveat that it is more exposed than most of the recommended tours in this guide. The route around the mountain is exposed at a number of places to any avalanche activity off the steep terrain above and in addition there are a couple of places notably above Love Lake and Margaret Lake where traverses are necessary above steep cliffs with serious consequences in event of a slide. So choose conditions to visit Septimus-Rosseau carefully. When conditions are right a circumnavigation of the massif takes in the finest terrain on the montain reaching all the good descent lines and is easily executed from the Bedwell or old Price Creek trails or even Flower Ridge.

There is no single best way to start the route around Septimus-Rosseau, each approach has its advantages and disadvantages. The Bedwell Trail offers a direct route to Cream Lake and the Septimus Glacier but once around the mountain at Green Lake a long climb will be required on the Price Creek trail back up to Cream Lake to exit on the Bedwell trail. Price Creek trail is no longer maintained by BC Parks and as it is a lower elevation route it may require packing skis in and/or out especially in late season. In addition (and this applies to either route option including this section of the Price Creek trail) the upper part of the Price Creek trail approaching Cream Lake crosses a large avalanche path and then continues up a hundred metres or so of terrain exposed to slides off a huge slope off Mt. Septimus.

Lastly is the Flower Ridge trail, although this offers by far the longest approach and involves a steep climb into the alpine right at the start along with dealing with the upper part of the Price Creek trail which is common to all the options these are the only notable disadvantages. On the plus side the Flower Ridge route provides fairly fast alpine access into mellow touring terrain along the ridge, great views of Septimus-Rosseau and the Cliffe Glacier peaks and high level access in and out of the massif traverse through Price Pass. Of course either of these three options can be combined with another but the vehicle logistics will need to be addressed. The Price Creek and Flower Ridge trailheads are close enough to walk between or hitch a ride from the mine traffic.

Additional Info: Island Alpine p. 296-301

The back of the Shepherd-Flower Ridge Horseshoe & Septimus-Rosseau from Rees Ridge, May.

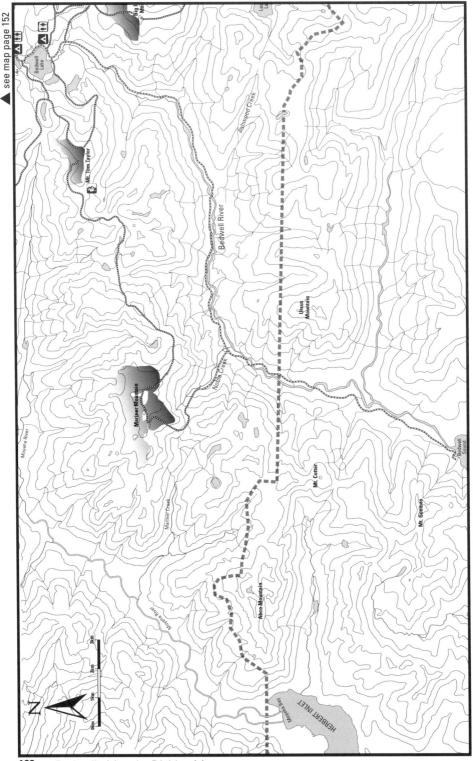

▲ see map page 152

▲ see map page158

Bedwell Lake

Big Mo

Leac
Lake

Ashwood Creek

Mt. Tom Taylor

Bedwell River

Ursus Mountain

Moyeha River

Mariner Mountain

Noble Creek

Bedwell Sound

Mariner Creek

Mt. Cotter

Mt. Gienes

Moyeha River

Abco Mountain

N

6cm 11cm 2km 3km

Herbert Bay

HERBERT INLET

Moyeha Bay

Bedwell - Moyeha Divide

Mt. Tom Taylor north aspect from Phillips Ridge, February.

Bedwell-Moyeha Divide

Vancouver Island's largest glaciers are found along the Bedwell-Moyeha divide, draped over the sprawling massifs of Mariner Mountain and Mt. Tom Taylor. No surprise then that the traverse from Bedwell Lake up to the summit ridge crest of Mt. Tom Taylor and from there westward along the height of land to Mariner Mountain is a fine Island ski tour.

The position of these peaks close to the Pacific Ocean is not only responsible for the heavy snowfalls and large glaciers remaining on the mountains but also adds a unique dimension to the approach options offering the possibility of a true ocean to alpine expedition.

Highest Point: Summit of Mt. Tom Taylor 5,833 ft. / 1,788 m

Most Vertical Descent Possible: ~300m

Difficulty/Duration: C3 / 3-5 days

Map Sheets: 92 F/5 Bedwell River

Access: The Bedwell-Moyeha traverse may be tackled from either direction starting at either Bedwell Lake or Bedwell Sound.

To start from the Bedwell Lake end, approach Mt. Tom Taylor along the Bedwell Trail from Jim Mitchell Lake Road off the Buttle Lake Parkway. From the Buttle Lake Parkway turn off to the left (south) after crossing the Thelwood Creek Bridge at the south end of Buttle Lake and drive 6 km up the gravel road to the Bedwell trailhead and park in the lot. See Bedwell Trail description (page 78) for more details.

Mt. Tom Taylor south-east aspect from Baby Bedwell Lake, May.

Mt. Tom Taylor north-east aspect from Mt. Albert Edward, March.

From the west end of the ridge Mariner Mountain may be reached from the Bedwell River valley via an old miners trail in Noble Creek. From Bedwell Sound, which may be reached from Tofino by air or sea, hike up the Oinimitis trail which runs initially up the north side of Bedwell River. After 9 km locate the Noble Creek trail. Noble Creek may also be reached from Buttle Lake via the Bedwell Lake Trail 15 km down river from Bedwell Lake.

Hike up Noble Creek northward through forest then into a deep moraine covered cirque. Continue hiking up the scree to the Mariner-Noble col at GR 9980. From here depending on the season either snow or open rock slabs lead up to the south glacier. Ascend the glacier to a col between the two main peaks.

The Bedwell-Moyeha traverse may be extended at the west end as far as Abco Mountain. Abco Mountain can be best approached or exited from Herbet Inlet via a long ridge parallel to Cotter Creek.

Route Description: Logistically the easiest way to undertake the Bedwell-Moyeha traverse is from east to west, approaching Bedwell Lake up the Bedwell trail and starting up Mt. Tom Taylor. The route heads west from Tom Taylor to Mariner Mountain, descending the old miners' trail down Noble Creek to the Oinimitis trail which can be taken back to Bedwell Lake and the trailhead.

Hike or ski up the Bedwell trail route to Baby Bedwell Lake. If the lake is frozen, cross the lake to its outlet or follow the trail route to Bedwell Lake. Again cross Bedwell Lake to the far west shore or follow the trail route around the east and south shore to the outlet and cross the outlet and locate a good route around to the creek entering Bedwell Lake at the west side.

Ski south-westward passing two lakes through some beautiful open meadows and gain the toe of Mt. Tom Taylor's south ridge. After an initially steep climb the south ridge opens out and sweeps elegantly up to gain the summit ridge of Mt. Tom Taylor at about the middle. There is one short route finding problem about halfway up the ridge which is best solved by keeping to climber's right (east) of the crest.

Once on the summit ridge pop on to the Taylor Glacier and descend a little to the west down into a prominent col at the toe of the east ridge of the summit tower. From the col descend north down a scoop feature in the Taylor Glacier, Keep to skiers left and exit the scoop onto a wide shoulder on the glacier below the main summit tower. In winter/sping the summit of Mt. Tom Taylor can be climbed directly up the north side from the glacier.

Mariner Mountain north-east aspect from Mt. Albert Edward, March.

Mariner Mountain north-east aspect from Flower Ridge, May.

Ski west across the wide open Taylor Glacier below the summit towers to the crest of the west ridge. The ridge crest swings southward over a small knoll and down to a prominent col at GR065828. Descend the small valley directly west of the col to a small lake and then follow the drainage down to a deep pass between two tributary creeks of the main Bedwell and Moyeha rivers. Travel through this pass is going to be far better with snow cover than during summer as it is choked with thick slide alder and hundreds of huge boulders. So with a smug smile ski across the pass westward and into the base of a long, prominent gully that leads steeply up on to the ridge above with some exposure.

Turn to the south-west following the ridge crest down to a col overlooking the massive (by Island standards) east cirque of Mariner Mountain. There are some ski lines to be had in this cirque and a camp down at the lake in its base is a good place to reach them. But this is remote, serious terrain so choose your lines with care.

To gain the Mariner glaciers ski west along the main ridge ascending the south-east ridge of the mountain until a safe line can be seen to hop onto the wide open glacial shelf to your right (north). Although it is tempting, there is no route around to the left on the south face above Noble Creek. Cross the glacier northward or weave in between several of the rocky summit towers to eventaully reach the south glacier overlooking Bedwell Sound. An awesome 500m+ ski descent south-westward down this glacier leads into a deep col between Noble Creek and Mariner Creek. If the snow level is still fairly low another 600m ski descent leads down the huge talus slopes into Noble Creek. Enter the timber on the right (west) side of the creek and pick up the miners' trail down to the floor of the Bedwell River valley and the Oinimitis trail. Take the trail east back to Bedwell Lake and the trailhead or continue south-west to a pre-arranged pickup at Bedwell Sound.

Additional Info: Island Alpine p. 302-307, 309.

Mariner Mountain east aspect from Bedwell-Moyeha divide, June

Rugged Mountain and the Rugged Glacier, Haihte Range.

Northern Vancouver Island

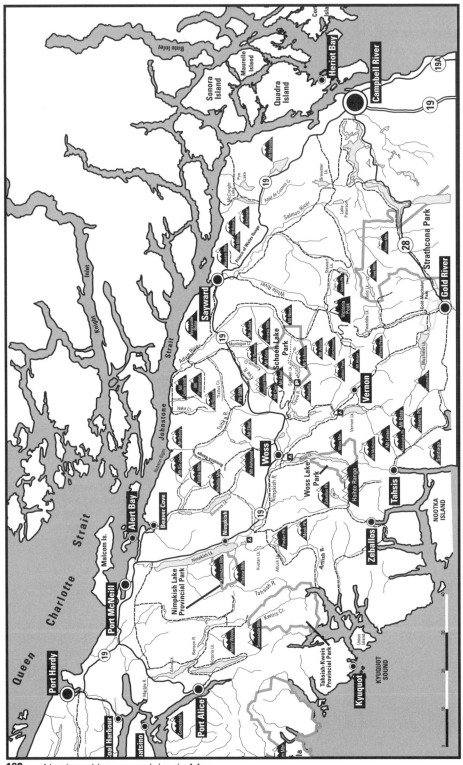

Northern Vancouver Island

Northern Vancouver Island offers the winter backcountry traveller a variety of excellent destinations but as to be expected access presents compounded difficulties in the months of low elevation snow cover. Fortunately the presence of a superb rustic lift area at Mt. Cain provides a backup option on weekends and holidays and adds greatly to the attraction and charm of skiing and snowboarding on the North Island.

Most of the area is Crown land under tree farm licenses to private logging companies. There are several smaller Provincial Parks and numerous Forest Service recreation sites scattered throughout the area. Parks in the northern island region of interest to the backcountry skier include Schoen Lake and Woss Lake Provincial Parks and Mt. Cain Regional Park.

The mountains have a very distinct character. Unlike the topography to the south in Strathcona Park the mountains in the northern Island are more rugged and for the most part separated from one another by deep passes and valleys, with few stretches of high continuous ridgelines. So the peaks and massifs become individual destinations rather than part of longer traverses. The Tlupana and Haihte ranges are possible exceptions to this.

Access:

Island Highway 19: Provides paved road access along the eastern side of the Sutton Range between the communities of Sayward and Woss and then continues on to the tip of the Island at Port Hardy. Logging road mainlines branch off from the Island Highway into the White River, Adam River, Eve River and Davie River valleys among many others and all can be used to approach the mountains.

White River Main: Leave the Island Highway at the Sayward Junction, 64 km north of Campbell River. Turn left and keep straight at the sudden right fork. Cross the White River to the gas station and turn right. Turn right yet again at a junction and after 200 m turn left uphill on the newly designated White River Main. Halfway up the valley a sharp right leads down to the White River and a bridge. White River Main crosses the bridge and continues upriver on the west side (on the east side is Victoria Main, a good 2WD road). About 30 km from the highway is a T-junction with Stewart Main. For Victoria Peak and Warden turn right, whence you will soon cross Consort Creek and then the White River.

Upper Adam Main: Heads south 10 km north of Sayward off the Island Highway into the east side of Schoen Lake Park. Joins Moakwa Main through Gerald Creek & links on to the White River Main.

Nimpkish Road: A public gravel road running along the west side of the Sutton Range between Gold River and Woss. This road has several spurs which provide access into the Sutton Range including: East and West Mains, Lower Alston Road, Murlock Road, Stuart Road, Fiona Road the Mt. Cain access road and Davie Main into the west side of Schoen Lake Provincial Park.

To reach the south end of Nimpkish Road drive to Gold River on Highway 28, 90 km west of Campbell River. To reach the north end of Nimpkish Road drive north on the Island Highway from Campbell River to the Schoen Lake-Mt. Cain junction 119 km north of Campbell River and 21 km south of Woss.

Turns

Northern Vancouver Island is home to some great backcountry ski terrain and some of the longer possible runs. Highlights in the region include: Victoria Peak & glacier, Sutton Peak, the dramatic Haihte Range and the gem of it all Mt. Cain and the surrounding backcountry.

Tours

While the northern part of the Island lacks the interconnecting ridge systems found in Strathcona Park there are a number of excellent tour destinations including some possible classics yet to be completed. Day tours from Mt. Cain are excellent along with the possibility of trips up to several nights in the upper Abel Creek. The Prince of Wales is a gem, the Haihte Range a prime attraction worth a visit up to a week in duration to make the arduous access worth the effort. For the pioneer look to the Tlupana Range and the Kaipit Ridge out to Zeballos Peak for some little known exploration.

Additional Info: Island Alpine 1st Edition p. 333-436

Members of the Strathcona Nordics Ski Club on Newcastle Ridge. photo: Pal Horvath

Lorraine & Lyle Fast nearing the summit of Mt. Hkusam. photo: Paul Kendrick

Prince of Wales Range

Hkusam Mtn

Stowe Creek col

Main ridgeline
to Big Tree Creek

Aerial view of Hkusam Mountain west aspect.   *photo:John Caswell*

Prince of Wales Range

The Prince of Wales Range is one of the most accessible but most overlooked alpine areas on the Island but there are many reasons to put it on your next trip plan. The range runs pretty much west east from Sayward village to Amor de Cosmos Creek and McCreight Lake. The main ridge system from Hkusam Mountain to Mt. Kitchener is around 20 km in length and offers stunning views over Johnstone Strait, the northern Discovery Islands and into the Coast Range mountains on the mainland. In fact the Prince of Wales Range has the best views on Vancouver Island of the Coast Range particularly of the Waddington and Whitemantle ranges which are just across Johnstone Strait.

The Prince of Wales Range is a very good candidate for a chain of huts. There is highway access, the ability to easily shuttle vehicles or hitch-hike and the land is neither park nor private. Three huts, one at the Sayward end near the Stowe Creek col, one at the Mt. Milner-High Rigger col and one in the Big Tree Peak-Mt. Roberts col would make a charming asset to Vancouver Island's alpine recreation options.

Highest Point: Summit of Mt. Hkusam 5,481 ft. / 1,670 m

Most Vertical Descent Possible: 600m

Difficulty/Duration: B3 / 2-4 days

Map Sheets: 92 K/5 Sayward

Access: The Island Highway 19 runs along the whole length of the south-west foot of the Prince of Wales Range. The proximity of the highway does nothing to detract from the experience high up on the ridge but does add greatly to the security and logistical ease of undertaking a trip in this range. Logging roads from the highway into the valleys on the south-west aspect provide the principle access into the mountains. Big Tree Main leaves the highway 46.5 km north of Campbell River and gives access to Mt. Roberts and Mt. Kitchener. Elsewhere as second-growth harvesting picks up new roads and re-opened old roads will certainly proliferate.

Dyers Main leaves the Island Highway 19 close to Sayward on the north side of the Stowe Creek bridge 62 km north of Campbell River off Timber Road. Take the road out of the logging company yard up the Stowe Creek valley to the trails on the east and north sides of Hkusam Mountain.

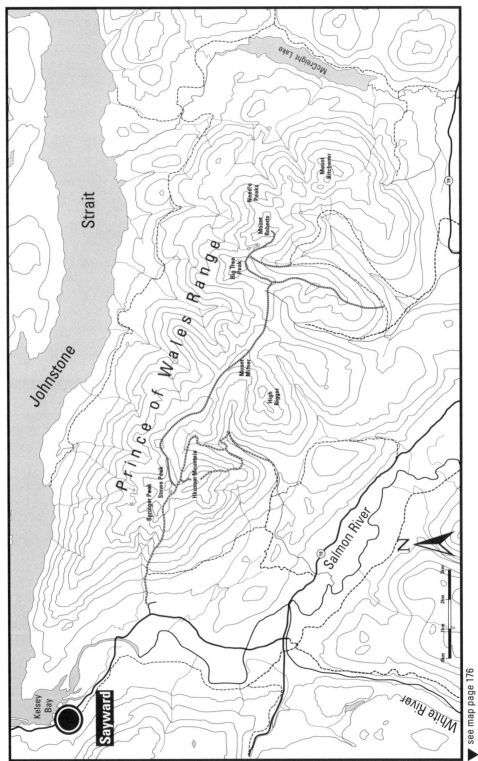

Johnstone Strait

McCreight Lake

Prince of Wales Range

Mount Kitchener

Needle Peak

Mount Roberts

Big Tree Peak

Mount Milner

High Rigger

Springer Peak

Stowe Peak

Hkusam Mountain

Kelsey Bay

Sayward

Salmon River

White River

N

0km 1km 2km 3km

▶ see map page 176

Mt. Roberts west aspect, June.

Turns

The easiest accessed and longest ski terrain is found on the west and south-west aspects of Mt. Hkusam. This area is best reached from the Stowe Creek approaches up Lyle's Trail. Shorter, steeper terrain graces the east and north-east sides of Hkusam but there are more cliffs here and the terrain much more committing than that found on the west side.

There are possible lines off the main Prince of Wales Range east of Hkusam Mt. back into Stowe Creek. This area was burned by a huge forest fire and has left wide areas of silvery snags that in the right conditions might offer some pretty surreal tree skiing. On the north-east side of the main ridge in this same vicinity are several bowls which overlook Johnstone Strait. They secret some fine ski terrain but reaching them unless on a tour of the main ridge is a lot of work and some of the gullies that must be negotiated to get down into the main bowls are steep and committing. New logging roads will certainly improve access on the north-east side of the range in coming years.

At the east end of the range both Mt. Roberts and Mt. Kitchener have some decent descents and are accessible in a long day trip in good conditions. On Mt. Roberts check out the short slopes in the col between Roberts and Big Tree Peak (Peak 4660). The east aspect of Mt. Roberts has a nice bowl feature overlooking Big Tree Creek and the ridge to the north-east down toward Needle Peaks may offer some good skiing. Some of the best and safest lines on Roberts are down the west face a 300m descent may be had off the steep ground from the summit into the narrow valley with the small lake chain that leads into the Mt. Roberts-Big Tree Peak col. After poling through the col to the north a further 220m drop leads down the drainage overlooking Johnstone Strait.

On Mt. Kitchener the open terrain on the south-west flank of the mountain down into the expansive clearcuts below the peak offer fine skiing.

Tours

Day trips or single overnighters to Hkusam Mountain or Mt. Roberts hit the best of the range on limited time but where the Prince shines is in completeing a traverse right down the spine between Sayward and Big Tree Creek. As Highway 19 parallels the range along its south base a two vehicle approach, dropping one off at Big Tree Main or the Big Tree Creek Highway Rest Area en route to a start at Sayward works well or simply hitch a ride on the highway back to your starting point with a single vehicle. The route works well travesing it in either direction. It is described west to east.

Begin up either Bill's Trail from the road next to the Coral Reef pub in Sayward to the Stowe Creek col or take the Stowe Creek trail up (low elevation snow may rule out a close vehicle approach). Hkusam Mountain is best taken in as a side trip or ignored when underway on a traverse down the range as hoofing a multi-day pack over the peak is unnecessary unless desperate for exercise. From the Stowe Creek col a careful route should be chosen from just below the col's east side (Stowe Creek side) up short, steep gullies to gain the ridge crest.

Additional Info: Island Alpine 1st Edition p. 397-403 **Note**: a completly revised and updated chapter on the Prince of Wales Range is available as a downloadable Acrobat pdf file at: www.wildisle.ca/islandalpine.

Adjacent Areas of Interest: Newcastle Ridge

John Roberts returning through the logging slash at the end of a Sutton Range ski trip.

Victoria Peak

Victoria Peak and glacier from White River valley floor

Victoria Peak

Victoria Peak and its companion Warden Peak are distinctive landmarks from the Campbell River-Discovery Islands area with their fang like profile dominating the north-west skyline. What is not apparent from this angle is the full scale of the huge vertical relief from the summit of Victoria Peak down to the White River at it's base which is generally considered to be the greatest and certainly some of the most dramatic on Vancouver Island. Some of this huge vertical offers superb descent terrain with the atmosphere of one of the Island's most impressive peaks.

Highest Point: 1,800 m at the Warden-Victoria col.

Most Vertical Descent Possible: 650 m

Difficulty/Duration: B2-B3 / 1-3 days

Map Sheets: 92 L/1 Schoen Lake

Access: Victoria Peak can be reached either from Sayward along the White River Main logging road or from Gold River near Twaddle Lake on the East or West Main. Logging roads (branch WR500) climb to around 3,500 ft from the White River side and from the Gold River side to 4,000 ft on branch W-79 of West Road. Access on these roads will vary with seasonal snow cover and logging activity. From either WR500 or W-79, a short steep hike through the remaining forest reaches the crest of Victoria Peak's south ridge. The south ridge is a beautiful hike in its own right with small alpine lakes and incredible views of Strathcona Park, Nootka Sound and back toward Campbell River.

To reach the Victoria Glacier and Warden Peak, the fastest access is now from branch WR380 which is currently at an elevation of around 2,100 ft. A flagged route from the end of the road leads across a long traverse to the small lake and knoll at GR0649 and then on to the Victoria Glacier.

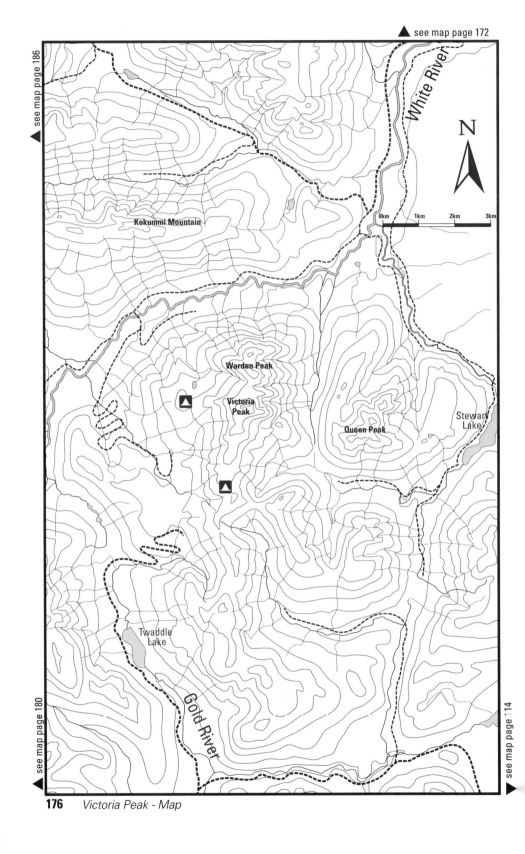

see map page 172

see map page 186

see map page 180

see map page 14

White River

N

0km 1km 2km 3km

Kokummi Mountain

Warden Peak

Victoria Peak

Queen Peak

Stewart Lake

Twaddle Lake

Gold River

Elbow Creek - Consort Creek
Divide

South aspect of Victoria Peak from King's Peak, January.

the old route off WR381 is steeper but new roads may eventually go higher on this flank of the mountain. More logging acitivity around Victoria is inevitable changing the access with road construction. New logging roads in Consort Creek now open this original but previously difficult route to the mountain to quick access.

As almost all the low elevation timber has been logged out of the White Gold river valleys it is foreseeable that winter/spring logging from year to year may keep some of the high road access open.

Curtis Lyon and Corrie Wright scoping lines on the Victoria Glacier.

Spring view of Victoria Peak's North-west aspect. Long descents over 2,000 ft. are possible down this large snowfield to the treeline. Logging roads from the white River give access to around 3500 ft on this side of the mountain.

Turns

The are some very long runs to be had on Victoria Peak if conditions are right, in fact some of the longest ski descents on the Island are found on the greater Victoria-Warden massif. From the White River side look for the obvious lines down the Victoria Glacier and the West Basin. The high knoll at GR0548 makes a great basecamp location for runs on the Victoria Glacier and the west basin. For a more sheltered camp, stay at the small lake just to the north of that knoll at GR0649. The runs in the west basin can be dropped into right off the south ridge by strong skiers and riders or for the more cautious or if cornices cap the ridge just climb up a good skin track to a safe high point. In the right conditions runs close to 3,000ft can be descended into the timbered (and clearcut) meadows below. and even the south face. On the opposing side of the south ridge from a high point right under the south face of Victoria Peak the longest potential ski run on the Island drops down a huge slide path into the timber in a tributary of the north fork of Consort Creek. You'll want a helicopter or a vehicle shuttle on the Consort Creek logging roads to make this one work. Note that on some maps Consort Creek is called 'Stewart Creek' like the nearby lake.

Tours

Following the standard hiking approach route along the south ridge of Victoria Peak makes a fine ski tour especially if combined with a climb of the peak or some turns down the west basin. Approach the south ridge from either the White River or Gold River logging roads as conditions allow and gain the ridge crest with a short steep climb through the remaining sub-alpine timber. Follow the ridge northward toward Victoria Peak or check out the route to the south to the small peak just above and to the east of Twaddle Lake.

A tour might work out of Consort Creek climbing up onto the divide betwen Consort Creek and Elbow Creek and following that divide west joining the south ridge of Victoria Peak. This might be one way to get the long south face descent in without too much logistical difficulty or expense, by doing a round trip from a vehicle parked in Consort Creek.

Additional Info: Island Alpine 1st Edition p.346-352

Sutton Range

South aspect of Sutton Peak from King's Peak, January.

Sutton Range

The Sutton Range is bounded to the west by the upper Nimpkish River valley with Schoen Creek and the White River draining its eastern side. The range proper includes from south to north: Waring Peak Mt. Alston, Sutton Peak and Maquilla Peak. It is these last two massifs, Sutton and Maquilla peaks, that are of most interest for backcountry skiing. The proximity of these peaks to Mt. Cain should help lift them higher on the radar of backcountry skiers than the relatively low level of interest they currently have.

Highest Point: 6,000ft approximately on the summit of Sutton Peak

Most Vertical Descent Possible: 2,000ft

Difficulty/Duration: B2-B3 / 1-4 days

Map Sheets: 92 L/1 Schoen Lake

Access: The best approach to Sutton Peak is from the logging roads in Maquilla Creek that rise onto the mountain's west flank. If drivable these roads provide outstanding access with only a 30 minute hike to the alpine. From the Island Highway, 55 km north of Sayward and 15 km south of Woss, turn off at the Mt. Cain - Schoen Lake Park junction. Take the first right onto the public gravel road to Gold River, the Nimpkish Road. Drive 30 km then turn left onto Stuart Road. Continue along Stuart Rd. and then turn right on Fiona Road. Turn onto a spur road which climbs high on the hillside due west of the summit.

On the crest of an obvious ridge park and hike through the clearcut to reach old growth which can be followed up to treeline and a series of satellite peaks west of the summit. Ski along the height of land over another broad sub peak and on to the north-west ridge of the summit tower.

Turns

Peak by peak look for possible ski descents on: Mt. Alston down the bowl immediately west of the summit or down the south-west ridge back to logging roads in the drainage west of the peak. Off Alston Fin the prominent spire north-west of the summit there looks to be a great line down the subtle main ridge to the lake at GR9745, there's over 1,800ft of vertical down to the lake so could be worth the effort of getting out of there but its skiability is unconfirmed.

Sutton Peak has the most high alpine terrain of any of the mountains in the range and likely has the best ski descents. The mountain is comprised of a system of high ridges each with nicely angled slopes dropping off in a variety of aspects. Of particular note is the very steep 800ft line right off the summit tower to the west. If a safe line can be found right down to the deep basin and lake north of

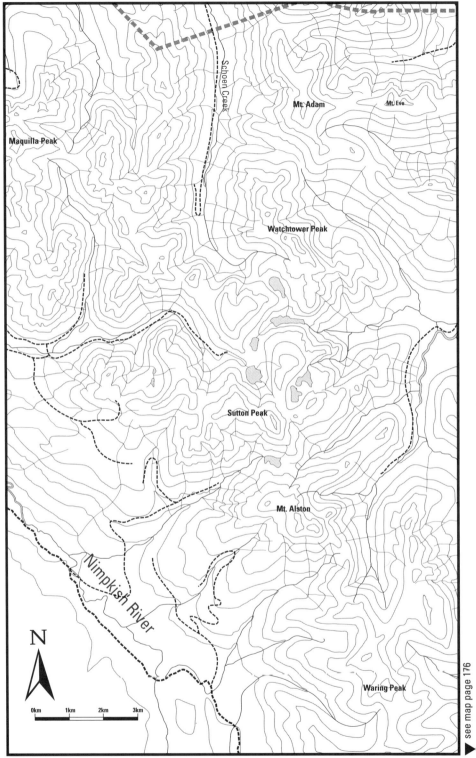

▲ see map page 186

Schoen Creek

Mt. Adam

Mt. Eve

Maquilla Peak

Watchtower Peak

Sutton Peak

Mt. Alston

Nimpkish River

N

0km   1km   2km   3km

Waring Peak

see map page 176 ▶

Sutton and Victoria Peaks north-west aspect from Rugged Mountain, March.

the summit it clocks in at 2,500ft of vertical. The large south facing cirque west of the summit tower has some wide open terrain with about 1,200ft down to the treeline. Down the huge north facing cirque off the ridge immediately west north-west of the summit there may be a line all the way to the base of the cirque. If so it has just over 2,000 ft of vertical. There are numerous other shorter bowls in the 500ft vertical range and combined with the great touring terrain on the ridge tops and a fine summit with unique views of Victoria Peak and surrounds, Sutton Peak is one to put on your to-do list.

Maquilla Peak is perhaps the easiest of the three main peaks in the Sutton Range to reach in winter and has some good ski terrain particularly on the west flanks of the mountain.

Tours

Sutton Peak is probably the best massif to explore on skis. Regardless of the condition of the descent lines Sutton offers a maze of ridge systems and a great summit to climb. It may be possible to traverse the whole Sutton Range on skis from Mt. Alston to Maquilla Peak. This would be a pretty serious ski mountaineering tour but with the attraction of great terrain between the difficulties.

Additional Info: Island Alpine p. 353-358

One of the many bowls and ridges that form the Sutton Peak massif, June.

Shea Wilson skiing off Mt. Abel's south bowl.

Schoen Lake Park Area

Mt. Abraham north aspect from meadows in Abel Creek headwaters, March.

Schoen Lake Park Area

The high elevation access provided by the Mt. Cain ski area road can be exploited to reach some of the other alpine terrain in the 'Genesis Range'. From the Abel Main logging road, part way up the drive to the Cain parking lot, the south face of Mt. Abel can be reached along with the valley between Mt. Abel and Mt. Sarai and most impressive of all, the upper Abel Creek valley underneath the north face of Mt. Abraham which is within Schoen Lake Provincial Park.

Highest Point: Summit of Mt. Schoen 6,109 ft. / 1,862 m

Most Vertical Descent Possible: ~300m

Difficulty/Duration: A1-B3 / 1-3 days

Map Sheets: 92 L/1 Schoen Lake

Access: The Abel Main logging road breaks off the Mt. Cain ski area road at the base of the long side cut hill on the first major switchback. The junction is hard to miss on your right as you head up the hill. In winter there is often a deep snowplow berm blocking the junction and regardless the road is unused and therefore unplowed. So park in the plowed pullout well out of the way of the skihill traffic and begin skiing or hiking up the road. If you are very lucky and snow conditions allow particularly in late season/spring drive up Abel Main.

To reach Mt. Abel keep left at the first major junction and to head toward Mt. Sarai, Mt. Abraham and the upper Abel Creek take the right fork. Both roads eventually lead into a massive clearcut on the lower south flanks of Mt. Abel giving a clear view of all the routes ahead.

For Mt. Abel continue along the logging road as it switchbacks up Abel's south flank right to the very end of the road. From here continue up your choice of line through the cutblock and enter the remaining timber from the cutblock's upper right corner. Follow the left side of a creek into the base of Abel's south bowl.

To reach Mt. Sarai, the valley between Sarai and Mt. Abel (Abel Creek north fork) and the Upper Abel Creek and Mt. Abraham, follow the right fork on Abel Main as mentioned, this branch also reaches

Camp in Nisnak Meadows, Schoen Lake Park, April.

the huge clearcut on Mt. Abel. The road forks again on a flat shoulder. The left branch heads up the south flank of Abel and toward the valley between Abel and Sarai. Keep to the left of the creek entering the valley on a short, steep sidehill traverse.

The right branch drops down a long cut into the Abel Creek valley and should be followed right to the end to reach the Schoen Lake Provincial Park boundary and the gorgeous meadows below Mt. Abraham. From near the end of the road start a steady climbing traverse to enter the timber high above the left back of the creek and continue traversing back into the valley until a natural line brings you to the creek's edge. Criss-cross the creek taking a natural line back into the valley and the maze of lakes and meadows.

Turns & Tours

Just outside the Schoen Lake Park boundary Mt. Abel is the next most obvious peak to look for good ski terrain adjacent to Mt. Cain. Mt. Abel can be reached by touring out from the Mt. Cain base area across Cain Creek or from Abel Main. Climb up the ridge on the right (east) side of the wide south bowl to the summit of Mt. Abel. Great ski terrain can be found throughout this bowl.

Less inviting but still worth a visit is the valley between Mt. Abel and Mt. Sarai. Routes lead up out of the upper part of this valley onto the flanks of both peaks with one or two notable gully lines descending back down into the valley floor.

View from summit of Mt. Cain south toward Mt. Schoen, January.

The most attractive destination and a long overlooked Island classic is the upper Abel Creek meadows below the north face of Mt. Abraham. This stunning area of high alpine lakes lies within Schoen Lake Provincial Park and is a highly recommended tour. Follow the access details along the logging roads and into the upper part of the valley. The meadows are worth a night or two's visit and have the bonus of being a suitable destination in any weather/avalanche condition as the terrain on the valley floor is mellow and more serious terrain may be entered by choice as conditions allow.

Look for breathtaking ski lines down the imposing gullies on Mt. Abraham's north face (see photo page 183). Sweet lines may be found throughout the meadows or climb up through the trees on Mt. Sarai's south side and look for ski lines back down into the valley. Just exploring this exquiste valley is worth the trip, the complexity of the terrain, magical lakes and a stunning view from the back of the valley overlooking Schoen Lake all combine to make this one of the very best Island weekend tours.

In the heart of Schoen Lake Park the Nisnak Meadows has excellent touring cross country-style, terrain. A circuit can be done from the Adam River Road through the meadows, to Schoen Lake and exiting to the roads in Compton Creek. There's plenty of higher ground on Mt. Schoen and Genesis Mountain.

Additional Info: Island Alpine p.365-367

Mt. Abel south aspect from the Upper Adam Main, March.

Below: west end of Schoen Lake Park and the Sutton Range north aspect from Mt. Abel, January.

Maquilla Peak

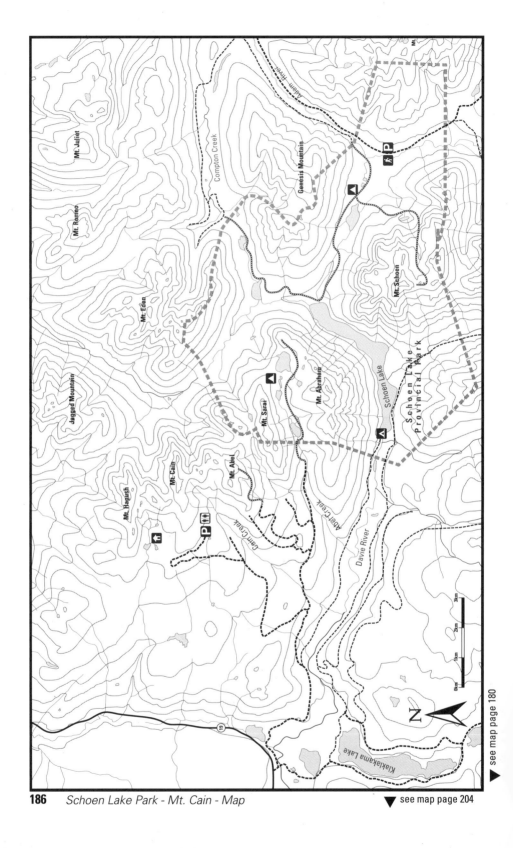

▲ see map page 180

▼ see map page 204

Mt. Cain

East Bowl of Mt Cain from lift area boundary

Mt. Cain

You can pull out all the superlatives in the book to describe Mt. Cain. For starters there's the little ski area which is open weekends and holidays through the winter. The ski area is run as a non-profit society with assistance from the Mt. Waddington Regional District and various local sponsers. Regulars at the 'Little Area That Rocks' will tell you it is the community atmosphere, friendly faces, bottomless powder and access to great backcountry terrain that brings them back time after time. If you have even a passing interest in backcountry descents on Vancouver Island then Mt. Cain should be top of your list of places to visit.

The road servicing the ski area offers vehicle access to the alpine in winter which is in very short supply on the Island. The lift area has two T-bars which are stacked one above the other and get you to the top of 1,500 vertical feet of open runs, glades and some of the finest tree skiing anywhere. On either flank of the ski area are wide open bowls (the 'West Bowl' and 'East Bowl') both of which can be dropped right out of the ski area boundary and have good traverse lines which return you to the bottom of the lifts.

Because of the access the lift area provides, these mountains see a high number of people leaving the boundary and going "out of bounds" often poorly prepared and during various levels of avalanche hazard. It is worth remembering that the ski patrol are at Mt. Cain for the safety of the people using the lift area and should not be expected to respond to an incident out of bounds. Nor should the presence of the patrol be used as a factor in deciding to leave the lift area. This is serious terrain and each party should be as prepared for skiing the bowls as if they were on any backcountry tour. Experienced backcountry skiers can share their knowledge here with novices (or the plainly ill-prepared) by drawing attention to hazards and keeping kids inbounds especially on bad weather days of which Mt. Cain sees plenty. It's one thing to need a rescue on a blue sky day but when the wind is howling and the visibility down to a hundred metres the stakes get way higher for everyone.

Highest Point: 5700 ft on the West Ridge.

Most Vertical Descent Possible: ~500m

Difficulty/Duration: A1-B3 / as long as you can stay!

Map Sheets: 92 L/1 Schoen Lake

Nick Lawrence huck'n it big at Mt. Cain.

Looking west across the West (Tsitika) Bowl of Mt. Cain toward Hapush, January.

Access: From the Island Highway, 55 km north of Sayward and 11 km south of Woss, turn off at the Mt. Cain - Schoen Lake Park junction. Follow the clearly posted signs for Mt. Cain to the base of the ski lift area, taking about 40 minutes from the highway depending on seasonal road conditions.

Turns

The ski area of Mt. Cain offers 1,500 vertical feet (450m) of terrain with 18 runs of vaying difficulty With a fresh dump of powder or stormy weather the T-bars can offer all you need in a day of skiing or snowboarding. But when conditions are right and you decide to duck the ropes and look for some out-of-bounds turns The West (Tsitika) and East Bowls are the two best places to look. Both bowls can be reached by literally riding right under the ski area boundary rope.

Before you do, though, be sure to read and note the disclaimer at the beginning of this book and look for and read the posted notices around Mt. Cain describing the society's policy on people leaving the area's boundaries. Note also that their policy may change at anytime and it is your responsibility to be apprised of it.

As it is the interface of a ski area and the backcountry where many accidents happen each winter it is worth stressing here that all parties travelling in the backcountry are obliged to carry self-rescue equipment and be trained and practiced in its use. As well, parties should have obtained a current avalanche forecast and are well-advised to be capable of conducting their own snow stability test before entering avalanche terrain.

Looking east across the East Bowl of Mt. Cain toward the Dream Chute & Mt. Abel, January.

Mt. Abel north-west aspect from top T-bar Mt. Cain, January.

That all said, access into the the West Bowl can be found at two main locations along the upper part of the Ridge Run at a hundred metres and at two hundred fifty metres down the run from the top of the top T-bar. Large cornices often form at the lip of the bowl so choose a spot to jump in well away from these. One of the best entry point into the West Bowl is found by hoofing up the hill behind the lift shack at the top of the top T-bar and heading a short way along the ridge crest above to a notch overlooking both bowls. The first drop here is pretty steep and at an angle that sees its fair share of avalanche acitivity so treat this drop-in with care. From this notch a better fall line can be taken to the bottom of the bowl.

The West Bowl is characterized by the shape of a well curved, wide open cirque. There is a convex bench that breaks the bowl in half from the ski area side to a deep and wide gully in the middle of the bowl. Further across the bowl are some beautiful treelines separated by steep narrow slide paths these can be reached by making a long traverse as high up in the bowl as you can with prevailing snow conditions. Take care with the convex roll in the bench mentioned. Visibility is limited below the apex of the curve and there are a few cliffs and rocks to be avoided. First timers should stick to the big central gully and get a good look around before venturing onto any of the more commiting lines.

The exit out of the West Bowl takes a gentle line across the floor of the bowl trending leftward (south-east) and then up through the trees on a short climb back onto the ridge. Continue through

Base Area

Top T-Bar

the trees toward the lift area to eventually pop out on the lower part of the Ridge Run takes about 10-15 minutes. Often there is a well packed trail showing the way but don't count on it! If you think you've missed the point to climb back up to the Ridge Run then just carry on out the floor of the bowl keeping left close to the base of the slope of trees until you reach the lift area road.

Smilarly the East Bowl can be reached by skiing or riding directly from the lift area boundary. From the top of the top T-bar head skier's left (east) keeping as high as possible. The boundary rope is just a hundred metres or so from the lift shack and puts you right at the top of a sweet open snowslope at the top of the East Bowl. A few turns can be had down this slope with time to traverse back in-bounds or continue down the fall line into the funnel-like gully that forms the best line down the East Bowl. It is well worth the 10 minute slog up onto the ridge behind the lift shack for the extra turns at the head of the bowl. There are a number of variations possible to start the East Bowl descent all from various points along Mt. Cain's West Ridge right up to the Cain Couloir which is the most prominent gully feature on Cain's west summit as viewed from in-bounds.

Once in the gully just keep to it until the gully begins to open up above the clearcut and at a point where a couple of other gullies converge including the Dream Chute. Some aging, faded flagging to skier's right signals the start of the traverse line which keeps a constant elevation across the treed slope perpendicular to the line you've just descended back to the bottom of the ski area. There are some signs you are on the right route, lots of stumps and fallen logs that were felled to open up the line and sporadic flagging. Take care crossing the deep creek gorge at about half way. This creek comes out of the east meadows in the ski area boundary above and in fact can be snowboarded (or skied if you have to) with a deep powder dump from the boundary down to the traverse. The line is called 'the Full Pipe'. The remainder of the route back is straightforward right into the parking lot. If you do miss the traverse line just make it uphill as best you can, there's no significant obstacles anywhere in the forest except the creek which you have to cross regardless.

On the opposite side of the west ridge to the East Bowl is the North Bowl (strictly speaking the 'East Bowl' is the South Bowl of the mountain proper, it gets its name from being to the east of the ski area). The North Bowl is also a huge feature and a section of the top can be descended with a traverse to skier's left of a jutting rock tower to a prominent col between the North Bowl and West Bowl. From here a drop down the West Bowl finishes the tour. The North Bowl has been skied but be warned it's a lot of work skinning or boot-packing out of its bottom.

The line that catches everyone's eye to the east is the 'Dream Chute'. Watching the plumes of powder catching the late-afternoon light as a group descends this line is a Mt. Cain tradition. The top of the chute is reached by making a wide traverse from the top T-bar through the east boundary rope and across the wide slope at the base of Mt. Cain's south face. Take particular care in choosing to head across this face as not only is there a lot of mountain face above you but the consequences of being swept down the south face are pretty serious.

Mt. Cain south east aspect from the top of the Dream Chute, note base area at left, April.

192   *Tim Stanton catching a last evening ride above the top T-bar, Mt. Cain.*

Once at the col between Mt. Cain and Mt. Abel take the safest line, switchbacking up the steep ridge crest heading southward. The Dream Chute is easily located higher up the ridge. After riding the chute join the traverse line back to the base area from the bottom of the East Bowl.

Tours

Most of the backcountry terrain around Mt. Cain requires some amount of touring to reach or exit so pack your skins and alpine skiers and snowboarders should carry alpine trekkers and snowshoes respectively, unless positive that the routes back to the Mt. Cain base area are boot-packable.

For an easy tour just to have a look around, follow the sporadic cross country route signs off the Lower Ridge Run into the base of the West Bowl. Skiing at Mt. Cain has its roots in this bowl and if you look carefully you'll see a few run lines cut out of the trees where the original rope tow ran. The decaying A-Frame was constructed with the remains of a more elaborate cabin that served as the first lodge at Mt. Cain in the 1970s. Continuing across the base of the bowl eventually leads to a drainage which comes down off Mt. Hapush. There a few small lakes in the col at the head of this creek which are quite pretty and worth a look if you're up for a short steep climb. There are often snowmobile tracks in the West Bowl which can help in getting around, but don't be lured off route by them, remember they can cover a lot of ground while just cruising aimlessly.

The base of the West Bowl can also be reached by skinning up a short spur road that heads uphill off the main Mt. Cain Road about 1 km downhill of the parking lot. There is a pullout and snowmobile tracks can point the way.

The south face of Mt. Abel has some great descent terrain and can be reached by touring from Mt. Cain in a very strenuous day trip. Choose good travelling conditions before setting out on this one. From the parking lot head south-east across the meadows and descend the treed slope into the clearcut Cain Creek valley. Cross the valley and head up the small open snow slope clearly visible from Mt. Cain to the shoulder on Mt. Abel's south-west ridge. There is a huge clearcut on the south side of Mt. Abel and a long traverse heading right finally leads to the edge of the remaining timber. A short pull through the trees brings you into the base of an open bowl. Either continue right up the bowl or take the gentle arcing ridge to your right and follow it to the summit. There are lots of good lines to ski down this face, enough to make it worth a single overnight stay.

Additional Info: Island Alpine 1st Edition p. 359-365, 368-369

Adjacent Areas of Interest: Jagged Mountain.

Paul LePerrier sliding down the Dream Chute, April.

Tlupana Range

Mt. Stevens and Mt. Bate north-east aspect from Mt. Cain, February.

Tlupana Range

The Tlupana Range is one of the least visited mountain areas on Vancouver Island yet by estimation it probably is home to the single largest breadth of high alpine terrain on the island. While summer exploration is in its infancy winter knowledge of this area is positively nascent. There have been a few recorded trips into Mt. Stevens and Woss Mountain but the interior part of this range is relatively unknown especially in winter.

This could change soon as the attractions of the long high ridge traverses become better known and entice backcountry skiers to test themselves in this rugged wilderness area. A complete traverse of the main Tlupana ridge from Mt. Stevens to Mt. McKelvie begs completion with possible extension of this route as far as Woss Mountain.

Highest Point: Summit of Mt. Bate 5,511 ft. / 1,680 m

Most Vertical Descent Possible:~300m

Difficulty/Duration: B3-C4 / 2-6 days

Map Sheets: 92 L/2 Woss Lake, 92 E/16 Gold River, 92 E/15 Zeballos

Mt. Bate south-east aspect from Muchalet Lake, June.

Access: The Tlupana Range may be reached from spur logging roads off the gravel Woss-Gold River Road or from spurs off the Tahsis-Head Bay Forest Service Road. Specifically from the Woss-Gold River Road checkout branches into the Sebalhal, McIvor and Youkwa valleys and from the Tahsis Road the best options are found in the Conuma, Canton and Perry valleys. There is also a flagged route right from Tahsis up the long ridge onto Mt. McKelvie.

Turns

One of the most impressive snowfields in the Tlupana Range is found on the south-east face of Mt. Bate. This permanent snowfield is one of the few such south facing features and in winter/spring is of considerable size.

Tours

Some of the suggested ski tours in the Tlupana Range include: Mt. Stevens from Canton Creek, Peter Lake and the surrounding peaks Mt. Alava, Mt. Bate and the are around the Shangri-La valley and the main Tlupana Range ridge system.

Additional Info: Island Alpine 1st Edition p.379-391

Mt. Leiner and Mt. McKelvie north-east from Mt. Cain, February.

196 *Sitter hucking some post-storm air off Viking Dome.*

Haihte Range

North-east aspect of the Haihte Range from Mt Cain, January.

Haihte Range

Outside of Strathcona Park the Haihte Range is arguably the most impressive group of mountains on Vancouver Island and one of the very best destinations for ski touring. The jagged skyline of the range and the foreshortened view from Mt. Cain is enticing and impressive but also belies the variety of terrain to be discovered here. The Haihte Range has a rich if recent history of exploration by ski and snowboard with activity during the early 1990s occasionally seeing several parties visiting the range at once, an almost unheard of Island experience, particularly during the winter.

The Haihte Range is now part of Woss Lake Provincial Park whose boundary runs along the height of land over the mountain tops. As a result land to the south in the Nomash River valley lies outside of the park and may offer suitable helicopter landing sites, the use of which here has some, albeit debatable, precedents.

Highest Point: 5,400 ft. on the East Ridge of Rugged Mountain.

Most Vertical Descent Possible: ~400m

Difficulty/Duration: B3-C3 / 3-6 days

Map Sheets: 92 L/2 Woss Lake

Aerial view of Rugged Mountain north-east aspect above Woss Lake, March.

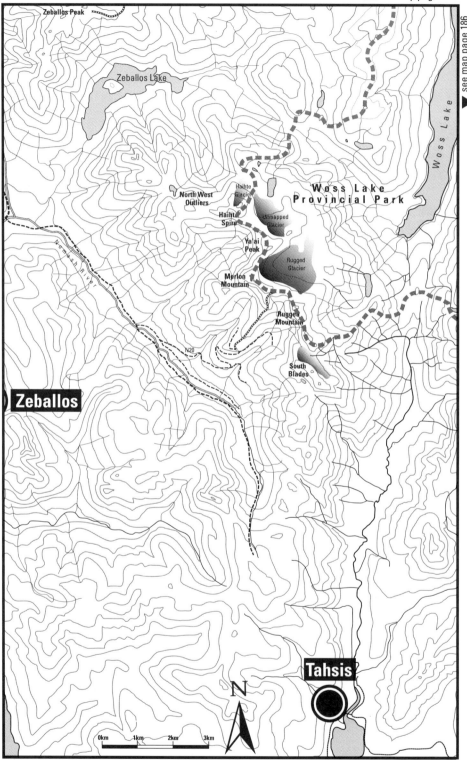

▲ see map page 204

see map page 186 ▲

Zeballos Peak

Zeballos Lake

North West
Outliers

Haihte
Glacier

Woss Lake
Provincial Park

Woss Lake

Haihte
Spire

Unmapped
Glacier

Ya ai
Peak

Rugged
Glacier

Merlon
Mountain

Nomash River

Rugged
Mountain

N20

South
Blades

Zeballos

Tahsis

N

0km   1km   2km   3km

198 *Haihte Range - Map*

Looking up from the base of the Rugged Glacier to the spires ringing the cirque.

Access: Originally the Haihte Range was approached by boat from Woss Lake. While that route is still possible and remains an excellent way to experience the unique coastal experience of approaching a mountain by water it has fallen out of favour in preference for the extensive logging road networks in the Nomash River and Zeballos River valleys.

Nomash Main: From the Island Highway, 151 km north of Campbell River and 21 km north of Woss, turn south on the Zeballos Forest Service Road (Atluck Main becomes Pinder then Zeballos Main). The Zeballos Road is a well maintained gravel road. It is one of the few 'mountain roads' on the Island cutting through narrow valleys along the flanks of Pinder and Zeballos Peaks. 33 km south of the Island Highway and a few kilometres north of the town of Zeballos turn left (east) on to Nomash Main. 7.3 km up the valley turn left onto N20 which winds high up below the south-west face of Rugged Mountain. This spur is not driveable and is becoming overgrown in its upper parts although there has been recent clearing work done by the Heathens. Drive then hike up this spur to locate the flagged, established route into Nathan Creek col.

Heroin Run

St. Paddy's Chute

Aerial view of the Unmapped Glacier and Ya'ai Peak north aspect, March.

Snowboarders rippin' the Heroin Run, Unmapped Glacier.

Turns

The Haihte Range can lay claim to the greatest concentration of good ski descent terrain on the Island. The length of the runs are fair but the variety of lines is the great attraction here. The cirque surrounding the Rugged Glacier has numerous possibilities most of which have been skied or ridden. Of note is the spectacular line off the east shoulder of Rugged Mountain proper. From the west shoulder of Ya'ai Peak the open expanse of the Unmapped Glacier offers an awesome descent of moderate angle while tucked in beside a bulging rock cliff "St. Paddy's' takes a more challenging and commiting line (see photo page 199).

The Haihte Glacier which droops down the north-west side of Haihte Spire looks like a great line making a graceful arc off a high shoulder on the spire back down to Haihte Lake. If you can get around the east ridge of Rugged Mountain there may be some commiting descents had down the Blades Glacier.

Aerial view of Haihte Spire north-east aspect, March.

Tours

The superb descents found in the Haihte Range are matched by the quality of the touring terrain. The range is characterized by a series of large glaciated cirques which are all connected by short gaps or gullies through the separating ridges. Travel between Rugged Glacier west across the Unmapped Glacier, Haihte Lake and onto the Haihte Glacier is particularly straightforward. The two best routes are 1) A steep gully system directly from the Rugged Glacier up the east flank of Ya'ai Peak on to a shoulder at the toe of Ya'ai Peak's north-east ridge which is right at the top of the Unmapped Glacier or 2) from the toe of Rugged Glacier a sweet alleyway leads between two rock features right to the toe of the Unmapped Glacier.

Travel from the Unmapped Glacier to the Haihte Glacier is best when Haihte Lake is frozen otherwise a wide swing has to be made along the rocky ridge that bounds the lake's outlet. The least explored terrain in the range is at the west end amongst the North-West Outliers (below). Careful route finding on bench systems lead from Haihte Glacier in to this group, good touring but few if any descents.

An exposed drop off the East Ridge of Rugged Mountain may offer a line eastward onto the enticing glacier below the Blades but the route is not confirmed and the terrain looks steep and exposed.

Additional Info: Island Alpine 1st Edition p.421-435

Haihte Spire and the North-West Outliers north-east aspect from Mt. Abel, April.

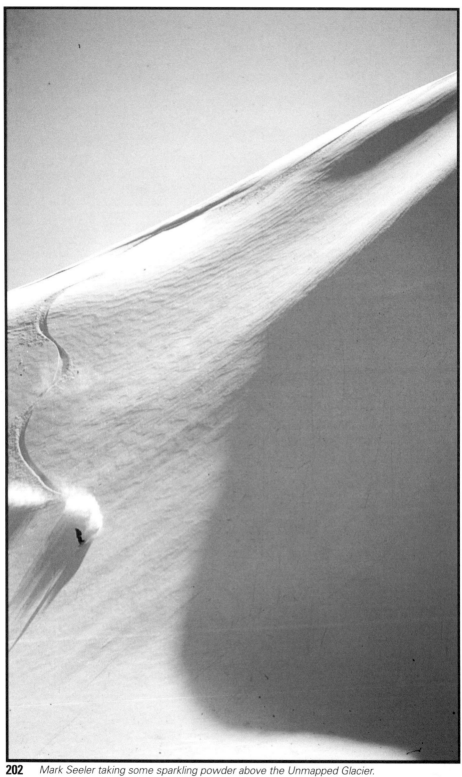

Mark Seeler taking some sparkling powder above the Unmapped Glacier.

Kaipit Ridge - Zeballos Peak

Zeballos Peak, north-east aspect from Mt. Abel, April.

Kaipit Ridge - Zeballos Peak

Zeballos Peak is an isolated, steep sided peak located between the south end of Woss Lake to the east and the Zeballos River valley to the west. Approaches to the mountain are difficult, due to the steep cliffs that surround it, with the notable exception of the long high alpine ridge that joins Zeballos Peak from the north-east over Kaipit Peak from the west shore of Woss Lake. There are a few short ski descents to be found along the Kaipit Ridge and some steeper lines on the peak itself but the true attraction of the area is the wonderful long ski tour following Kaipit Ridge onto the Zeballos Peak massif.

The route along Kaipit Ridge is dominated by superb views over the surrounding lake country and into the Haihte Range. The terrain is characterized by numerous meadows and sub-alpine lakes

Highest Point: Summit of Zeballos Peak 5,170 ft. / 1,576 m

Most Vertical Descent Possible: ~300m

Difficulty/Duration: B3 / 2-5 days

Map Sheets: 92 L/2 Woss Lake

Access Details: Leave the Island Highway at Woss and head through town toward Woss Lake. Turn left (south) on West Woss Main Road which runs down the west shore of Woss Lake. From either spurs in Clint Creek or Fiddle Creek (Budlite Rd).

The Kaipit Lake area can also be reached from Kaipit Main, a spur that heads due south off Nimpkish Road. Leave the Island Highway at the Zeballos turn off and just after crossing the high bridge over the Nimpkish River turn left (south) onto Nimpkish Road. About 8 km south of the junction the road crosses a bridge over Kaipit Creek. Either take Canon Creek Main on the west side of Kaipit Creek and use the Kaipit Hookup to join Kaipit Main which may also be found 1.5 km east of the Kaipit Creek bridge. Drive down Kaipit main to the Kaipit Lake trailhead.

Route Description: The elevation of the snowline and the current condition of the logging roads used to reach the north-east end of the ridge will determine where the ridge crest can be gained. The first high point on the ridge at GR6757 just west of Woss Lake is the likely candidate to aim for in winter/spring right from spurs off the main line down Woss Lakes west shore.

The ridge top is wide to start but quickly narrows into a sharp ridge heading south-west on to peaks 4473 and 4536. More gentle terrain leads to a slight descent in to a col from where some turns might be had depending on the snow to the south-east down a basin toward a lake at GR6554. From the col the route swings more westward and the ridge narrows again up to the top of Peak 4484.

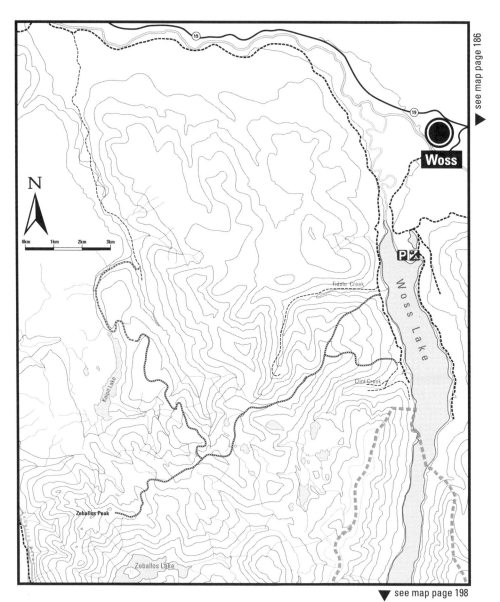

see map page 186

N

0km 1km 2km 3km

Fiddle Creek

Kaipit Lake

Woss Lake

Clint Creek

Zeballos Peak

Zeballos Lake

Woss

see map page 198

Zeballos Peak south-east aspect from Haihte Glacier, March.

From Peak 4484 the route enters more open terrain and in poor visibility some care should be exercised with route finding. From the top of Peak 4484 head due south through a col and over two small humps on the ridge. There is a steep step onto the first hump which if problematic should be avoided by dropping down to the right (west) and making a traverse through the bowl above a lake at GR6454 to regain the ridge crest in a wide pass just to the south. This area has a number of camp site options.

Continue south-west over Peak 4748. The terrain around Peak 4748 offers some great ski descents in almost every direction with up to 1,500ft of vertical and is situated among a myriad of lakes and meadows inviting exploration on skis. A camp near this peak is highly recommended.

After leaving Peak 4748 descend its south-west ridge into a col and then over a small knoll and a further descent south-westward to the low point of the route a pass at 3,200ft between tributaries draining into Kaipit and Zeballos lakes to the north and south respectively. For its low elevation and shelter this pass might offer a good choice for a final approach camp from which to make a day trip return to Zeballos Peak

From this low pass begin a steady ascent up onto Zeballos Peak heading first south up a prominent ridge then changing to the west at the 3,800ft mark. Follow the ridge to the east summit and on to the main summit choosing a safe line as prevailing conditions dictate. In fair weather a high camp may be had at the tiny tarn at the base of the cirque between the main and east summit towers.

Return along the same route back to Woss Lake or desend the valley north of the peak which wraps around the mountain from its north-east flank westward to join the Zeballos River if you've planned ahead and have a shuttle vehicle or other suitable arrangements.

Another possibility is to enter or leave the ridge system from the Kaipit Lake Trail off Kaipit Main. Take the trail to the lake then gain the ridge on the east shore of the lake and follow the height of land to join the route from Woss Lake near Peak 4748.

Additional Info: Island Alpine 1st Edition p.436

Zeballos Peak (L) and Kaipit Peak (R) north-east aspect from Mt. Abel, April.

Fred Michaud touring up the lower north slopes of Mt. McBride.

Appendices and Index

Island Peaks over 6,000 ft.

Jan Neuspiel and Robin Sutmoller on Rees Ridge.

1. Golden Hinde	2,200	7,218
2. Elkhorn Mountain	2,166	7,106
3. Victoria Peak	2,163	7,096
4. Mount Colonel Foster	2,135	7,005
5. Rambler Peak	2,105	6,906
6. Mount Albert Edward	2,093	6,867
7. Mount McBride	2,081	6,827
8. Kings Peak	2,065	6,775
9. Mount Celeste*	2,045	6,709
10. Mount Filberg	2,035	6,676
11. The Red Pillar	2,034	6,673
12. Mount Cobb	2,030	6,660
13. The Behinde	2,018	6,621
14. Mount Harmston	2,009	6,591
15. Argus Mountain	1,994	6,542
16. Mount Colwell*	1,989	6,526
17. Iceberg Peak	1,987	6,519

18. Alexandra Peak	1,983	6,506
19. El Piveto Mountain	1,980	6,496
20. Mount Regan	1,975	6,480
21. Warden Peak	1,969	6,460
22. Comox Glacier	1,963	6,440
23. Mount Rosseau	1,958	6,424
24. Mount Haig Brown	1,948	6,391
25. Mount Frink	1,948	6,391
26. Shepherd's Peak*	1,945	6,381
27. Mount Septimus	1,941	6,368
28. Peak 1,931 (0 .5 km south of Mount George V)	1,931	6,335
29. Misthorns	1,917	6,289
30. Peak 1,917 'Shepherd's Horn'	1,917	6,289
31. Peak 1,909	1,909	6,263
32. Mount George V	1,884	6,181
33. Tzela Mountain*	1,884	6,181
34. Margaret Peak*	1,870	6,135
35. Mount Adrian	1,869	6,132
36. Mount Schoen	1,862	6,109
37. Sutton Peak	1,862	6,109
38. Rugged Mountain	1,861	6,106
39. Siokum Mountain*	1,860	6,102
40. Big Interior Mountain	1,857	6,092
41. Syd Watts Peak*	1,856	6,089
42. Sid Williams Peak*	1,849	6,066
43. Nine Peaks	1,847	6,060
44. Crown Mountain	1,846	6,056
45. Mount Mitchell	1,842	6.043
46. Slocomb Peak*	1,840	6,037
47. Augerpoint Mountain	1,839	6,033
48. Morrison Spire*	1,830	6,004
49. Maquilla Peak	1,829	6,001

List compiled by Lindsay Elms from 1:20,000 trim maps
* Unofficial name.

Glossary

alpine: technically speaking 'alpine' is an abbreviated form of 'alpine tundra zone' however, colloquially it refers to both the mountain hemlock (subalpine) zone and the alpine tundra zone.

alpine tundra zone: describes the bio-geoclimatic zone found above 5,000 ft where no trees grow.

arete: a narrow fin or edge of rock or snow found at the crest of a ridge, often formed by glaciation.

aspect: a direction from which a feature is viewed. The north aspect means looking from the north southward to the north side.

belay: a word of wide meaning in climbing rope techniques referring to the securing of climbers by rope and other climbing hardware to a rock, snow or ice surface. A belay station or fixed belay is a place where anchors and a rope paid out to a leading climber create essential security in a roped system. A running belay is a point where a piece of hardware such as a piton, stopper, camming unit or ice screw has a lead climber's rope running through it and provides essential secondary security on a roped climb. The act of paying out or reeling in rope to a climber through a braking device that may arrest a fall is called 'belaying'.

bergschrund: A gaping crack in snow or ice. Often formed at the base of mountain faces when the lower snow/ice settles, breaking away from that securely anchored to the steeper ground above.

cairn: pile of rocks used to mark the way to travel.

chockstone: a large boulder that has become wedged in a chimney, couloir or gully forming an obstruction that is often difficult to surmount.

cirque: a curved bowl-shaped formation carved by a glacier against a mountainside. May vary widely in size from a few hundred feet high to many thousands of feet on larger mountains.

clearcut: an area cleared of old-growth trees by commercial tree harvesting.

col: a low point or pass between two mountains or between smaller mountain features such as summits or pinnacles.

cornice: an overhanging lip of snow created as wind pushes snow over a ridge crest, often cap gullies, prone to collapse and should be avoided.

couloir: a steep gorge, ravine or gully running vertically up a mountain face. Often snow-filled and suitable for snow/ice climbing or skiing.

crevasse: a large crack in a glacier formed by stress in the ice as the glacier moves. Presents a serious mountaineering hazard requiring skilled navigation and specialized rope techniques to negotiate safely.

cwm: (koom) Welsh word for a cirque

gendarme: From the french word for policeman, a pinnacle of rock usually sticking out of a ridge.

glacier: a river of ice which as it slowly flows downhill, carves many common mountain features.

hanging valley: a geological feature formed by a glacier at higher elevation being intersected at roughly 90° by a second deeper glacier. As the ice retreats the higher valley is left with a steep drop off into the larger one giving rise to the term 'hanging'.

horn: a pinnacle of rock usually sticking out of a ridge.

massif: a self-contained portion of a mountain range. For example Mt. Albert Edward, Mt. Regan, Mt. Frink and Castlecrag could be though of as part of the same massif.

moat: A similar formation to a bergschrund formed during the annual thaw when snow and ice melts away from rock faces leaving a deep fissure between the two. Typically a later season phenomena.

mountain hemlock zone: describes the bio-geoclimatic zone between 3,000 and 5,000 feet where the predominate trees are mountain hemlock and yellow cedar.

nevé: a type of mature snow with a solid plasticine consistency formed by repeated freeze-thaw cycles, ideal for climbing.

old-growth: a forest which has not been logged and so is comprised of a wide variety of tree species at a range of ages. This is the native forest sometimes refered to as 'pristine'.

pfd: stands for personal floatation device. A vest of buoyant material secured to the torso during watersport activities for safety. Wearing one is now mandatory for boating in Canada.

pitch: the distance climbed between two fixed belays. Therefore a length no greater than the length of climbing rope employed (typically 50 m / 145 ft.). In practice a pitch may vary in length from a few feet to a hundred metres or more depending on the rope length and climbing undertaken.

rappel: to descend a climbing rope which is secured to a fixed belay anchor, with a retrievable system, by means of a friction device through which the rope passes under control.

rime: a thick coating of frost.

route: an unmarked and unimproved line of backcountry travel requiring skill and experience to navigate.

saddle: a low point between two high points (typically mountains) forming a saddle-shaped feature, akin to a pass or col.

satellite summit: a small adjacent summit to a larger peak. For example the Behinde is a satellite of the Golden Hinde.

scree: a field of frost or glacier created boulders or gravel usually found under a steep rock face or in gullies.

serac: the exposed end of a glacier separated from the rest of the glacier by a crevasse. Often seracs are jumbled piles of ice blocks which pose a serious risk to climbers below if they should break off.

slide alder: a tough relative to our common Red Alder tree which frequents the subalpine zone in avalanche paths and other steep areas where heavy snowfalls accumulate. Difficult to travel through in summer conditions.

snag: a dead standing tree.

subalpine: the zone found between 3,500 ft. and 5,000 ft which is the highest regions in which trees and many other alpine plants can grow.

strustugi: a peculiar type of wind effected snow with a cake-like consistency, can often be sculpted in isolated shapes across a hard packed surface, difficult to ski or ride through.

switchback: a zig-zag up or down a slope. Many island trails follow a path of switchbacks as they zig-zag up the hillside to reduce the effort and rate of ascent.

talus: an area of frost or glacier created boulders found under steep rock faces.

tarn: a small mountain lake.

transceiver: an electronic device that can emit and receive a steady radio signal as a series of beeps. A trained operator can use a transceiver to locate a buried victim in an avalanche who is wearing a transmitting unit.

verglass: thin ice which can coat rock and vegetation during and after freezing rain falls. Can make travel and climbing particularly treacherous.

One of the Island's more major avalanche chutes on the west face Mt. Colwell upper Elk River.

Index

John 'J.D.'Waibel touring up the Jim Mitchell Lake Rd.

Big Country! Robin Slieker in the Waddington Range.

Mt. Abel 183,193
Mt. Abraham 183
Mt. Adrian 109,111
Mt. Albert Edward 81,91,97
Mt. Alston 179
Mt. Apps 64,68,69
Mt. Arrowsmith 17,49,51
Mt. Bate 195
Mt. Beadnell 109
Mt. Becher 17,34,81,85
Mt. Benson 47
Mt. Brenton 45
Mt. Brooks 87
Mt. Burman 137
Mt. Buttle 45
Mt. Cain 187–193
Mt. Celeste 98
Mt. Chief Frank 61,65,67
Mt. Clifton 68
Mt. Cokely 49,51
Mt. Colonel Foster 17,129
Mt. Colwell 129
Mt. De Voe 136
Mt. Elma 87
Mt. Flannigan 113
Mt. Frink 91
Mt. George V 97
Mt. Gibson 53,56
Mt. Hal 65
Mt. Harmston 104
Mt. Henry Spencer 69
Mt. Joan 61
Mt. Kitchener 171
Mt. Klitsa 53,55
Mt. Landale 45
Mt. Maitland 57
Mt. McBride 139,143
Mt. McKelvie 194
Mt. Moriarty 47,49
Mt. Myra 79,149,151–154
Mt. Phillips 141
Mt. Roberts 171
Mt. Septimus-Rosseau 149,160–162
Mt. Service 45
Mt. Stevens 194
Mt. Stubbs 65
Mt. Thelwood 151,155–156
Mt. Tom Taylor 163,164
Mt. Whymper 45
Mt Joan 65
Munday, Don 35
Munday, Phyllis 35

N

Nahmint Mountain 55
Nanaimo Lakes 47
Nimpkish Road 169
Nine Peaks 157–159
Nisnak Meadows 185
Nomenclature 18
No Trace 31

O

Oyster River Main 82

P

Paradise Meadows 87
Paradise Meadows to Comox Glacier
    95–100,101
Paradise Meadows to Flower Ridge 105
Peak 1909 97
Peak 1920 97
Phillip's Ridge 147
Phillips Ridge 133,137,139
Phillips Ridge Horseshoe 139–141
Photographs 19
Plateau Road 74,82
Pogo Mountain 57
Prince of Wales Range 171–173
Puzzle Mountain 121

Q

Quatchka Creek 125

R

Ralph Ridge 97
Rambler Peak 129,136
Red Pillar 104
Rees Ridge 98,103
Rescue 13
Rescue Coordination Centre 17
Resources
    Internet 30
    Maps 29
    Publications 29
River Crossing 21,23
Rodger's Ridge 109–111
Rossiter, Len 35
Routes 21
Rugged Glacier 201
Rugged Mountain 197
Ruth Masters Lake 93

The last word - the late Pat Baker comin' off Bucky's Bench in epic Mt. Cain powder!

S

San Juan Ridge 42
Schjelderup Lake 135,136,137
Schoen Lake Park 183–186
Scotty's Pond 51
Shepherd Peak 106
Shepherd Ridge 107
Shepherd Ridge - Flower Ridge Horseshoe
    106–108
Siokum Mountain 97,98
Skis
    randoneé 7
    ski mountaineering 7
    telemark 7
Sleds 7
Snow
    Conditions 15
    Layers 12
    Stability 12
Snowmobiles 14
Snowshoeing 7
Splitboard 7
Spring 6
Steamboat Peak 57
Strathcona Park 71–165
Strathcona Parkway 74,82
Sutton Peak 179–181
Sutton Range 179

T

Tangle Mountain Meadows 47
Tennent Lake 17,153
Tents 7
Terrain 6,11,15
Ticks 22
Tit Mountain 57
Tlupana Range 194–195
Toboggans 7
Top Tens 9
    Day Trips 9
    Descents 9
    Ski Tour Expeditions 9
Trails
    Augerpoint Trail 77.See also Jack's Trail
    Becher Trail 76
    Bedwell Trail 78,160,163
    Bill's Trail 173
    Brigade Lake Trail 53
    Century Sam Lake Trail 79
    CPR Trail 51
    Crest Mountain Trail 77

Della Falls Trail 79,160
Elk River Trail 77,127,136
Flower Ridge 77
Flower Ridge Trail 160
Gem Lake Trail 79
Glacier Trail 76,96
Gold Lake Trail 77
Jack's Trail 77,92
Kaipit Lake Trail 205
King's Peak Trail 79,127
Lyle's Trail 173
Marble Meadows Trail 78
Mt. Myra Trail 78,153
Paradise Meadows Trail 76
Phillips Ridge Trail 78
Price Creek Trail 78,160
Strathcona Park Trails 75
Upper Myra Falls Trail 78
Transceivers 13
Trip Ratings 19
Tsable Lake 69
Tsable Mt. 65
Tzela Lake 104,105

U

Using This Guide 18

V

Valley Connector 74,82,101.
    See also Comox Lake Main
Vancouver Island Marmot 47
Vegetation 22
Victoria Peak 175–178
Volcano Lake 121–123

W

Weather 16
Wepsala, Gertie 33
White River Main 169
Wildlife 21
Wolf Mountain 123
Wood, Clinton 33,34
Woss Mountain 194

Y

Yurts 7

Z

Zeballos Peak 203–205